SOUTH MOUNTAIN ROAD

◆

A DAUGHTER'S JOURNEY
OF DISCOVERY

HESPER ANDERSON

SIMON & SCHUSTER

NEW YORK • LONDON • SYDNEY • SINGAPORE

SIMON & SCHUSTER
Rockefeller Center
1230 Avenue of the Americas
New York, NY 10020

SIMON & SCHUSTER and design are trademarks of Macmillan Library Research USA
Inc. under license by Simon & Schuster, the publisher of this work.

Designed by Ellen R. Sasahara
Manufactured in the United States of America

10 9 8 7 6 5 4 3 2 1

Library of Congress Cataloging-In-Publication Data

ISBN 0-7432-4246-7

For information regarding the special discounts for bulk purchases, please contact Simon
& Schuster Special Sales at 1-800-456-6798 or business@simonandschuster.com

For my children
Cathy, John and Kenneth

SOUTH MOUNTAIN ROAD

CHAPTER ONE

M Y MOTHER killed herself on the first day of spring. Her crocuses must have been coming up, small green shoots between patches of old snow, as she crossed the driveway for the last time. No other green would have been visible yet. That would come later, in April and May, all the shoots and then flowers of the hyacinths, daffodils and tulips that she'd planted and tended. The forsythia, lilacs and dogwoods that bordered the driveway wouldn't have stirred yet, and her roses around the fishpond would've still been covered in burlap.

I don't know just what it looked like on that last night, because I wasn't there. I don't know if it was raining or if the moon was new or clouded when my mother, in a negligee and mink coat, walked out the glass door, across the flagstones, across the pebbled drive and entered the garage, determined to die this time. It was her eighth try and couldn't be construed as a cry for help because she'd made sure that everyone was away and that she'd have the necessary time. But even though I don't know what the night was like, how dark or how cold, I know what her gardens must have looked like. I'd lived in those seasons all my life and knew, without thinking, when the willows first turned a pale green, when the dogwoods were white and when the berries were red, when the lily of the valley appeared in the woods and when the hazelnuts were ripe.

When my brother called me in North Carolina, I knew that the crocuses would just be coming up at home—it was that time. I was in my second year of college and doing well, even though my parents had separated the past fall and I'd been the one to save my mother on a couple of those seven earlier tries. I thought it would be my mother calling, as I ran down the dormitory stairs to the phones on the first floor. I was starring in a play, and she was supposed to drive down the next week to see me. I was excited; she and I were making up. We were starting to be friends. I ran into the little room off the hallway where the phones were, happily picked up the receiver and then heard my brother Alan's voice.

"Hep?" he said, using my nickname as he always did, because he was the one who'd given it to me.

"Alan!" I said, surprised. I loved my brother dearly, but he didn't usually call me at college.

"Hep," he said slowly, "your mother died last night, or this morning—I'm not sure. Lenya found her this morning, in the garage. You have to come home."

"But—but the play," I said, the shock just beginning to set in.

"I know, honey, I'm sorry. You have to come home. Daddy'll meet you."

"Where's Daddy?"

"He's flying back. He'll meet you."

That's all I remember of the phone call, but I can vividly see the little room in which I was standing, the glass of the phone booth opposite me, the shadows and giggles of the girls in the hallway. The shock was moving all through me in those minutes, numbing parts of me that wouldn't thaw for years.

The next day my father picked me up at La Guardia Airport. There was a crowd around our car—reporters and flashbulbs—that unnerved me. I was used to my father being famous, but, as a playwright, his was an anonymous kind of fame. His name was known, but not his face, and my father always avoided publicity, so we were relieved as Lester, our chauffeur-handyman, maneuvered the station wagon away from the curb and photographers and into traffic. I kissed my father then and took his hand. And even though he smiled, I had the sense that all of him was sagging—his eyes, his jowls, his chin, his arms—sagging with more despair than he'd ever carried before.

I sat back on the leather seat and picked up the *New York Daily News* that he'd tossed there. The date was March 24, 1953, and my mother's picture was on the front page of the paper. The headline read, MRS. MAXWELL ANDERSON A SUICIDE. As I stared at the picture I understood the reporters and flashbulbs; we'd never been front-page news before. I stared at my mother's face, grainy black-and-white newsprint, a pretty, fixed smile, and wondered why I always knew when a smiling face in a newspaper was alive or dead. There was something about the dead faces, smiling straight out—I could always tell. And I knew in that second, looking at my mother's dazzling smile, that she really was dead.

Lester drove in silence, his cap pulled low, making himself scarce, as we made our way to the West Side Highway, across the George Washington Bridge, the Hudson below filled with whitecaps, and, finally, entered the woods and fields of Rockland County. I knew that I wasn't supposed to be happy on this day, but I was happy to see them, always happy to see those familiar fields and signposts. We were almost home.

I held my father's hand all the way, loving the feel of his warm, stubby fingers, but we said only a few words. I asked about his life in Los Angeles, about Gilda, the woman that he was living with, and he asked about college. We'd written every week and talked on the phone often since he'd left, so we didn't have much catching up to do. Silence was comfortable between us, and we let it be. I gazed out the window, savoring the oaks and birches and underbrush, the little towns—Congers, Tappan, New City—everything that said that we were coming closer and closer to South Mountain Road.

On Route 202, I sat straighter, peering ahead, waiting for

With my mother in New York, the fall of 1945

the first trees of Conklin's orchards. And then there they were, acres of fruit trees, the weathered barn and the sign at the roadside, CONKLIN'S FARMS. I leaned forward, squeezing my father's hand, my heart lifting as it always did as we reached the huge elm and turned right onto South Mountain Road. If we'd gone straight for about a mile we would've come to the tiny town of Mount Ivy, where Burgess Meredith lived in a converted barn and Alan Jay Lerner lived in the restored, whitewashed brick house that had been Mad Anthony Wayne's headquarters during the Revolution. Lerner had written *Brigadoon* in that house, and he was a friend. Burgess had starred in a couple of my father's plays, and he was a friend as well. They'll be at the house, I thought. They'll all be there.

My thoughts came back to the road; it was always called "the road," as if there were no other. I looked above the trees and fields to the low ridge of mountains and found High Tor and the beacon that meant that we were really home. During my childhood the airplane beacon on the granite ridge, the highest point of South Mountain, had been my North Star. Seen from my bedroom window, and for miles around, the High Tor beacon blinked red and white, red and white, all night long for as long as I could remember.

"There's our mountain, Daddy," I said, squeezing my father's hand even more tightly. He nodded and smiled slightly, gazing at the mountain that he'd saved. I was very proud of him for that. It had happened in the late thirties, when I was too little to know what was going on. The local traprock company had come up with a dreadful plan. They intended to leave the part of the mountain that faced the Hudson intact and dig great quarries out of the back part, the Tor, that South Mountain Road and our houses faced. In a sustained rage, my father wrote the play *High Tor*. He depicted the traprock company as a bunch of money-grubbing fools, trying to displace the rightful owner of the Tor and the Dutch ghosts who, in the play, are waiting for their lost ship to sail back up the Hudson. The play starred Burgess Meredith and Peggy Ashcroft and was a success in every way—it won the Drama Critics' Award that year, and it saved the mountain. High Tor was turned into a state park; the traprock company couldn't touch it, and our star-beacon went on blinking red and white for years to come.

The road started winding downward after Conklin's orchards, where, during the summers, the trees grew together overhead. But in March they were still bare and as brown as the thick woods and the old stone walls that we passed. The walls had been built by the original Dutch settlers and marked property lines that no longer existed. We passed a mailbox that said Mowbray-Clarke, and a rutted driveway that led deep into the woods. My father nodded toward it.

"How are the Hyphen-Clarkes?" he asked, a hint of amusement in his tired eyes. It was a "road" joke, and I smiled and shrugged. Old Mary Clarke—with her two canes, her long, white braids—and her granddaughter, Sandra, lived in a rundown, eighteenth-century house beside a ravine at the end of that long driveway. Mary Clarke was proud of her aristocratic ancestry and insisted upon the Mowbray-hyphen-Clarke, which was shortened, along with amused glances, to the "Hyphen-Clarkes" by those who counted along the road.

After the thick patch of trees and the Clarkes' driveway, we headed down toward a cluster of those who counted. They counted as friends and as an elite little band of artists who had settled on the road. They had their own in-jokes, their own rivalries, their own histories, their own inbred snobbism, and they walked through the woods and in and out of each other's houses at any time of the day or night.

Anyone who didn't belong, and that included everyone except other successful artists, were spoken of with the same
kind of amused smile that my father and I had exchanged.
Amused smiles and slightly raised eyebrows were a kiss of
death on South Mountain Road.

Both the women and the men indulged in the snobbery,
but it didn't apply to the women in the same way. The only
thing that was required of a woman was beauty. An artistic,
successful husband helped a lot as far as status went, but
beauty was enough. Talent, even a woman's own success,
didn't count for much, and, if she were homely besides, it
barely counted at all. On the other hand, if she were homely
but married to "somebody," she counted to an extent. Those
were the rules, never stated out loud, of course, but as pervasive as the scent that came from the honeysuckle that tangled along the road, or the smell of the wood smoke that,
when I was a small child, drifted from the smokehouse and
entered my pores, and the delicately forming cells of my
mind.

I was thinking about this as we rounded a sharp curve
and passed the Poors' driveway, because Bessie Poor had always seemed a prime example of the road rule, of what not to
be. Bessie, gnomish and vibrant, with an acid tongue and a
cackling laugh, was tolerated because she was married to
Henry Varnum Poor, a distinguished painter, potter and ar-
chitect who had designed most of our houses—granite or
cinder-block castles, set deep in the woods. Henry was large,
handsome and warm, and no one could understand why he
had chosen Bessie over more desirable prospects. The story
that everyone told behind Bessie's back was that she won out
over the other single women on the road by coming down
with a case of flu at Henry's house and never leaving. No one
seemed to notice or be impressed by the fact that Bessie, as

Bessie Breuer, was a beautiful writer, whose short stories appeared regularly in the *New Yorker*, and in every collection of the best short fiction.

"Bessie's going to be a mess," I said aloud, picturing her at the funeral, or whatever was going to happen—I didn't know and hadn't asked yet. My father nodded and raised an eyebrow, giving me the "Oh-my-God-Bessie" look.

"And she's going to have to deal with Lenya," I added, as we continued down the hill and approached Brook House, nestled against the road, on the right. Brook House had belonged to Kurt Weill, the composer, and Lotte Lenya, his actress-singer wife, always called Lenya by those who knew her well. Bessie's house was only a short walk through the woods, but Lenya and Bessie had feuded for years. I'm not sure, but I think it was mainly about my mother, whom Bessie had loved and championed when the rest of the road had considered her an interloper and a poor replacement for Margaret, my father's beloved first wife. Bessie and my mother had been best friends, and then Lenya had moved to the road and my mother and Lenya became inseparable.

"There's Woolly's spot," I said, and my father smiled that same sad smile as we both remembered Woolly, Kurt and Lenya's sheep dog, who used to stretch out in the middle of the road and sleep and stop cars. Woolly was gone too but, amazingly, had made it to a ripe old age.

We passed the high, ivy-covered wall that shielded Brook House, and my mind wandered to the secret gardens behind it. I'd always loved knowing that they were there, gardens that I could escape to and pretend in whenever I'd felt like it. As a child I'd had the run of Brook House; the gardens were mine to play in, and the back door was always open.

The brook that flowed from the top of the road, through Mary Clarke's ravine, past the Poors', ran right beside Kurt and Lenya's, beneath an arched stone bridge and a huge, gnarled willow tree. It was another of my favorite spots. But the best of all, everyone's favorite spot, was the grape arbor at the back of the house.

We'd sit there, during the late summer and fall, shaded by the clumps of grapes and the thick vines that were as intertwined as our lives. My father and Kurt only wrote two musicals together, but they shared all their work with each other and with Lenya and my mother. The path between our houses, through the woods, was worn down to packed earth by the countless footsteps—Lenya coming to play canasta, Kurt coming with pages of sheet music. My father would write a lyric and give it to Kurt, and Kurt would appear the next morning with five melodies. He'd play them for my father, sometimes on the upright piano in his third-floor study, sometimes on the blond baby grand in our living room, then look up expectantly: "Vitch von do you like, Max?"

Sometimes, they even asked me. During rehearsals of *Lost in the Stars*, it was decided that a respite was needed between the heartbreak of the choral "Cry, the Beloved Country" and the quiet sadness of the ending. My father and Kurt played three songs for me, Kurt singing a South African boy's song in his thick German accent. I've forgotten the other two but I chose "Big Mole," and it went in and became a show-stopper.

"Kurt won't be there," I said, more to myself than to my father. He didn't answer, but his face sagged a bit further. Kurt had died three years before, also at the beginning of spring. It was sudden. He'd had a heart attack—he was only fifty, but he seemed to be getting better. In the hospital he and my father worked on *Huck Finn*, which was to be their next musical together. Only seven songs were finished . . . then a second heart attack, and Kurt was dead. That night my parents came in the glass dining room door, and I looked at them and said something really stupid like, "God what's wrong? You both look like somebody just died." They told me, and I felt both shock and foolishness. It hadn't occurred to me that Kurt would die; it hadn't seemed possible.

The next day I walked through the woods to see Lenya. She was drunk with grief—sodden, exhausted—and she held me and then took me upstairs to the rarely used front room where Kurt lay, white in a white turtleneck sweater. I didn't know what to say and murmured that the flowers were beautiful. "Kurtie is beautiful," Lenya said, and I nodded and stood there, as frightened by her grief as by my first sight of death.

"George will be there," I said aloud, and my father shrugged, saying silently that George, whom Lenya married a year later, was barely a replacement.

"I love George," I answered, a bit defiantly. George Davis was a gentle, witty gay man, who had been an editor at *Harper's Bazaar* and *Flair* and was now devoting his life to Lenya and the Weill music. It took all of his persuasiveness to get her back onstage, for the first time in years. He was the impetus behind the revival of *Threepenny Opera*, which opened in March 1954, at the Theatre de Lys, and in which Lenya once again became a star. For her, that wasn't the point; it was all for Kurt; and for George, it was all for Kurt and Lenya. He said to me one day, sitting under the grape arbor, a dry smile in his voice, "I am the husband of the Widow Weill."

I turned to my father and let it go—my fondness for George, the bit of defiance—it didn't matter right now. I looked past him, across the road, as we passed the Hargrove house, which was now the Mauldin house. For me it would always be the Hargrove house, with Marion's hand-lettered sign at the foot of the rutted driveway—THE OLD BAILEY. It was a nasty joke, to say to the world that your home was a Dickensian prison, but I thought it was funny. I'd been in love with Marion Hargrove for most of my eighteen years and, therefore, thought that everything he did or said was either brilliant, or funny, or both. It took me years to figure out that, after a time, I was the only one who thought so. Increasingly, Marion attracted a lot of stifled yawns and raised eyebrows from those on the road. He'd left the house and his marriage the year before Kurt died, and Bill and Natalie Mauldin had moved into the Old Bailey. It was odd that two young men, thrust into fame by World War II—Marion with *See Here, Private Hargrove,* and Bill Mauldin with his funny and poignant cartoons of the mud-splattered GIs Willie and Joe—both landed, one after the other, in a remodeled farmhouse, nestled against South Mountain.

I didn't mention Marion as we rounded the curve below his house. A burned-out chimney, covered with honeysuckle, stood next to the road, and near it a steep path that was a shortcut to Marion's back door. I glimpsed him on the terrace, a flash of him, a ghostly imprint, the sun reddening his hair, bringing out the light freckles on his arms, and then I turned away, to the other side of the road where the brook ran just below us, heading for our bridge and Alan's pond.

We both looked straight ahead, and I gripped my father's hand again as the road evened out and Lester swung the car left before making the sharp right turn into our driveway. He stopped the car and turned to us for the first time.

"Check the mail, Mr. Anderson?" he asked.

"Why not . . . ?" my father murmured, and Lester got out of the car and crossed in front of us to the mailbox beside the stone wall. The wall continued on the other side of the driveway, interrupted again by Alan and Nancy's front gate. My father was looking toward their house—his first house, the one he'd found in 1922—barely visible now behind the huge pines that he'd planted as saplings, thirty-some years before. He'd come, with his first wife, Margaret, and their boys, to visit Henry Poor, and Henry had shown them the small farmhouse on the edge of a ravine and a waterfall. They'd fallen in love with it and bought it, along with sixty acres of woods, for almost nothing. The house had no electricity or running water, and my father had showered under the waterfall, even in winter, he told me, with icicles hanging like crystal stalactites.

He'd written his first plays here. He was a newspaperman then, writing editorials for the *New York World*, and had never seen a play—or so the story goes—when a neighbor on the road wrote a play and had a reading of it at his house. My father went, listened, went home and said, "If that's a play, I can write one." He rode his bicycle five miles to the Haverstraw station, took the train to the city to work, wrote during lunch hours at the New York Public Library, took the train back, rode the five miles home and worked in the attic at night. His first play, *White Desert*, written in blank verse, won critical approval but none at the box office. His second play, *What Price Glory?*, written with Laurence Stallings, was a success, and my father finally quit his job at the paper. He and Margaret added onto the house and got indoor plumbing and electricity; and the original manuscript of *What Price Glory?* can still be seen, under glass, at the New York Public Library, where most of it was written during lunch hours.

Lester returned to the car, handed me the mail and sent the car rolling down the hill toward our stone bridge. The same brook that flowed from the top of the road flowed beneath our bridge, over moss-covered rocks, and emptied into Alan's dammed-up pond, our summer swimming hole, our winter skating rink. My father and the boys—even as older men they were always "the Anderson boys" on South Mountain Road—had built the dam themselves. Beyond the pond and the dam, the brook tumbled over the waterfall, through the ravine, past the old Indian caves on either side, then made its way into Lake Lucille and, finally, the Hackensack River.

We crossed the bridge, headed up the long driveway lined with low walls, brush and overhanging trees, and I glanced at the letters in my lap. The one on top was from me to my mother, mailed a few days before from Greensboro. It was like looking at her smiling picture on the front of the *Daily News*... My mother would never read this letter. It was just a silly schoolgirl letter, full of the drama club and a dance at Chapel Hill, but she would never read it ... she was dead.

I was afraid of the dead. I'd always been afraid of the dead. Even before seeing Kurt in his white sweater, I'd been afraid of cemeteries and the walking dead. I'd been afraid of the eighteenth-century cemetery with its slanted grave-stones, behind Mary Clarke's house, and wouldn't stay over-night with my friend Sandra. The couple of times that I did manage to stay there, I'd made sure that Sandra went down-stairs first in the morning. I was certain that one day we'd find Mary Clarke, with her canes and her white braids, dead as a doornail in her high, single bed. I'm not sure why I was so frightened. If you'd told me, as a child, reasonably, that the dead were dead and couldn't get up and couldn't hurt me, I wouldn't have believed you. I knew that Margaret's ghost haunted our house and would've killed me if I hadn't slept with the sheet tucked tightly over my head.

Margaret had died young, in her early forties, of a broken heart, so my brothers had told me when I asked them. I don't think I ever mentioned Margaret to my parents, but I knew that my father kept her ashes in a small urn in his cabin in the woods. But then one day I found the urn in a cedar chest filled with Margaret's letters in the attic storage room. An-other day I thought I saw the urn on the mantelpiece in the living room. I was secretly terrified, somehow sure that my parents had caused Margaret's death, which in a sense they had, and that Margaret's revenge was directed at me. Later, as a teenager, trying to develop a sense of humor about the whole thing, I referred to the wandering urn as "Margaret's floating ashes."

Now my mother was dead, also fairly young at forty-eight—another broken heart. Would she be in a casket? In an urn? Would I be afraid? I would know soon enough, because the car had reached the curve in the driveway, another spot where my heart skipped. Around the curve the house came into view—a sprawling, white, cinder-block castle. On the right, the huge lawn, dotted with birches and red maples, sloped up to the house. On the left were the fruit trees—cherry, apple, peach—and at the end was a circle formed by the driveway, its center filled with white birches.

Lester parked by the dogwood, just outside the flagstone terrace, next to the kitchen window and the dining room doors. To our left was the garage and the parking area—there were lots of cars there already. I got out on my side, while Lester opened my father's door, and I glimpsed Martha, our housekeeper, through the kitchen window. It took me a minute to realize that Little Terry, Martha's nine-year-old son, was perched above me on a limb of the dogwood, and he was crying.

"Hi, Terry," I said quietly. I didn't try to comfort him. I didn't know how, and I was surprised by the idea that he'd loved my mother enough to cry. I knew that she'd given him her little spaniel the year before, but I'd never noticed a closeness between them. Of course, I'd been away a lot that last winter, and my mother had been very alone. She'd written to me saying how silent the house was, saying that she'd give anything to hear my father's footsteps coming down the brick stairs, the sound of my voice, even if we were fighting, which half the time we were. She'd been left alone in the silent house with Martha, who cared for her and hated her, and Little Terry, a watchful, silent child, who had once killed a kitten.

My dog, Toby, a beautiful, ungainly golden retriever, bounded toward me from the woods, and I sank to my knees on the cold flagstone and let him lick me all over and hid my face in his tawny coat that smelled of moss and old leaves. He followed me in through the dining room door, the closest, most-used entrance, and I stopped briefly, savoring the empty room—I was home.

I reached up and touched the suspended circular staircase, Henry Poor's pride and joy when he built the house, and glanced at the round dining room table that had been made for my mother by Carroll French, a neighboring artist and craftsman, and noticed that something was slightly off. There were covered plates, napkins and silverware, but it wasn't set the way my mother would have done it. My mother knew how to entertain, how to arrange the silver and the flowers, and it suddenly struck me that we were entertaining today, and that my mother wasn't here to do it right, to make it all go smoothly.

CHAPTER TWO

MY FATHER entered the dining room behind me, and, out of habit, I put my mother's mail on the table beside the candles. Then my father and I both turned, automatically, into the kitchen. Martha turned from the sink, and I went straight into her arms. I felt the familiar heaviness of her breasts, smelled her musky, sweet smell and hid my face against her shoulder. Martha had been my nurse for as long as I could remember and had taken care of my brothers long before I was born. She was a tall, large-boned woman with beautiful, aquiline features and milk-chocolate skin. She adored my father, adored me and had done what she could to make my mother's life miserable. She waited on her, but always grumbling under her breath, and behind her back, referred to her as "that woman" . . . "That woman never lifted a finger a day in her life except to arrange a flower."

Once I was in school there was no need for Martha to stay on, but she was one of my father's stubborn loyalties, and she did stay, as our housekeeper. My mother tried, valiantly, to get rid of her, but she lost every attempt, and it struck me, now, as I kissed Martha and backed out of her arms, that she'd managed to outlive my mother.

"Mr. Anderson," Martha said warmly, and my father kissed and hugged her silently.

"I just made coffee . . ." But my father shook his head.

"I'll have some," I said. "Where is everybody?"

"The living room," Martha answered. "Where Mrs. Anderson is."

"Oh," was all I said, and my father was still silent. I helped myself to coffee, thinking that now I'll know whether she's in a casket, a box, an urn . . .

My father glanced at the doorway, girding himself, knowing that he had to go in there.

"I'd better see who's here," he said quietly, and there was another moment before he headed out of the kitchen, toward the family and friends that he'd left behind a few months before.

I took my coffee to the kitchen table with a momentary rush of contentment—Martha's baby in Martha's kitchen—and smiled at her.

"You're lookin' good, Missy," she said. "Lookin' more like your mother. That poor woman, didn't know what she was doin', didn't know—"

"I know," I said quickly, hoping to stop the flow of words.

But Martha was shaking her head, mumbling, "That poor little thing didn't know if she was comin' or goin'."

Lester came in through the kitchen door, his cap still pulled down, poured himself some coffee and joined me at the kitchen table. My mother had never been able to get rid of Lester either. She'd told my father for years that Lester was stealing them blind—liquor, tools out of the shed, cash—but my father just shrugged, as if it really didn't matter.

"You know your grandma's here?" Lester asked.

"She is? Oh, God."

"She came up from Florida this morning," Lester answered.

"Oh, God," I repeated.

In the stillness we could hear the murmur from the living room. It was a ways off, past the large dining room that had been the original living room, past the room that we called the pump room—I suppose because it had some kind of pump under the floor—that connected the two parts of the house, the original cottage and the large addition.

"Who all's in there?" I asked, nodding toward the low sounds.

"Mrs. Weill's in there," Martha said, while she fixed a tray. "And her husband."

"Mr. Davis," I interjected. Even Martha couldn't give George Davis his due.

"And Mr. Caniff and Mrs. Caniff and Wilhelmina."

"Willie," I said softly.

"That Wilhelmina," Martha went on, "telling me how she took Mrs. Anderson her last dinner—spinach and fillet of sole—and how they found spinach in Mrs. Anderson's stomach, as if I never fed her right, making it sound like it's my fault when Mrs. Anderson *told* me to go home for the weekend, *told* me she was going to the city—"

"I know she did," I interrupted again. "She told everybody, so they wouldn't look—"

"Yes, she did," Martha said emphatically, and I rose from the table, thinking that I could go in there now. If Lenya and George were there, and Bunny and Milton and Willie, I could manage to get myself in there.

Bunny and Milton Caniff were like another set of parents to me, and Willie, who'd run their house for twenty years, was another—less devious, less cantankerous—Martha. The Caniffs lived down the road, past Lake Lucille, a no-man's-land whose sturdy occupants looked upon us as a crazy bunch of Commie artists, past old Mrs. Mahoney, a hermit who lived up on the mountain, and just below High Tor. Henry Poor had built another cinder-block castle for them, with an enormous studio for Milton, where he could be found all night, every night, drawing his popular comic strips, *Terry and the Pirates*, and later, *Steve Canyon*.

I started to leave the kitchen, then stopped as a frightening sound—a screaming wail—came from the living room. The sound continued; I had no idea who or what it was, but it was what I imagined a werewolf might sound like, screaming at a full moon.

My brother Quentin appeared, crossed the dining room and stood in the kitchen doorway. Quentin was twenty-two years older than me, a tall, handsome, scholarly man with a deep voice who always chose his words as if he were teaching one of his classes at Columbia.

"Hesper, dear," he said carefully, "your grandmother is asking for a rabbi. We're not sure what to do."

"What in the world does she want a rabbi for?" I asked.

"Because your mother was Jewish," he said. "So are you." As I stared at him, he cocked his head toward the wailing sounds that were rising and falling like waves.

"That's your grandmother. She's inconsolable," he said. I nodded slowly and followed Quentin back through the dining room, passing Henry Poor's ceramic figures over the fireplace, through the pump room, where there was a bar and a phone, and into the living room. It looked just as it had the last time I'd seen it except, at the far end of the room, in the corner where the chess table usually stood, there was a casket.

I paused in the doorway, looking at the strangely familiar scene. It could have been any South Mountain Road cocktail party—the same faces, the same small groups, the hum of talk, the smoke rising to the high beams that were made of whole tree trunks. A few people sat on the brick steps that led upstairs, the spot where I used to imagine I saw Margaret's ghost. For a second I wondered if she was watching today.

My grandmother's wails had subsided to moans, and people were helping her, hefting her, away from the coffin and over to the sofa. She was small and pudgy, with long white braids that were coming undone, and I didn't like her now any better than I ever had. Her name was Anna Klein, but that hadn't meant anything to me. I'd never been aware of Jewish names, Irish names, any kind of names, because everyone on South Mountain Road had left all that behind. Kurt Weill was a cantor's son and had fled the Nazis, but Judaism wasn't a part of this, his American life. Lenya was Viennese and never mentioned religion. Milton Caniff was brought up a Catholic but had given it up long ago. And my father, the son of a redheaded, red-bearded Baptist preacher, told me that at eight years old, when Baptists usually consent to be baptized, he had refused. That didn't sit too well with his father, he'd said. Nor had the fact that he never went to church except when it was empty, and then only to play the organ. He loved music and had sent away for beginning piano lessons. He practiced on the church organ and, from then on, whenever my father played the piano he worked the pedals so that it sounded just like an organ.

As I've said, the only snobbery on South Mountain Road was artistic, so the idea of my mother's Jewishness, and my own, left my head as quickly as it had entered. I was sure that my mother wouldn't have wanted a rabbi, and, if my grandmother did—well, she didn't really count. I don't think the subject came up again, but then the whole scene was hazy for me, framed by moments of startling clarity.

I crossed the room and stood in front of the open casket. My mother looked terrible, wrong—more wrong than the table setting. Her face was puffy, her lips blue, her bangs brushed back off her forehead. She was dressed in one of her favorite dresses, a dark green Valentina, but dark green didn't go well with blue lips and the pallor of death.

In a moment, Lenya was beside me, an arm around my waist. Angry tears were on her face as she looked down at my mother, whom she'd loved so dearly. She shook her head.

"You are such a bad sport, Mabbie," Lenya said, the trace of Vienna in her voice. I knew at once what she meant. I'd heard her say, emphatically, to my mother that last year: "You are making an opera, Mabbie. If your husband dies, you grieve. But if your husband has an affair, that is nothing." It was Lenya's European view that neither of my parents understood at all. And now she was telling my mother, with that same impatience, her voice choking slightly, that my mother was such a bad sport for quitting the game altogether.

"Her hair is wrong," I said, as I reached down quickly and pulled a dark curl or two onto her forehead.

"She has no scarf," Lenya added. "She would not wear this dress with no scarf." I nodded as I stared down and realized that something else was wrong. Her breasts, which she'd bound in the twenties when it was fashionable to be flat chested, were lying flat, with no brassiere to lift them. She would have hated that, I thought, and I heard her voice telling me how stupid she'd been to bind her breasts, destroying the muscles, and that I should never do such a thing. At the time—I was eleven or so—breasts hadn't meant much to me. All I knew was that I wanted little ones, not big ones like Martha's, which floated on top of the water like large, brown puddings when she bathed.

"Maybe we should get a scarf," I said to Lenya, and she nodded and followed me into my mother's bedroom, which was just off the living room, near where we were standing.

The room was filled with windows facing south across

the terrace to the garden and the woods. The magnolia, just outside, would soon be filled with pink-and-white petals, and the birch tree that grew from an island among the flagstones would soon have new green leaves. I crossed to my mother's dresser, aware of the slight spring of the cork floor beneath my feet, and opened the top drawer.

"Which one? Do you remember?" I asked, and Lenya reached into the layers of silk and lace and pulled out the scarf that went with the dress. We went back into the living room, closing the door softly behind us, and Lenya put the scarf around my mother's neck, lifting her head slightly, and then tied the scarf in the somewhat rakish way that Valentina, the designer, had shown them. Lenya, when she wore a dress, which wasn't often, also wore Valentina originals. Bunny Caniff didn't—she was too tall, she'd said, and wore Adrian gowns and pantsuits with large shoulders.

"Hi, baby," Bunny said in her gentle Midwestern voice, suddenly beside us. She hugged me, stroking my hair, and then turned back to my mother, the scarf now in place, covering her bare neck and her flattened breasts.

"Poor you, poor baby," Bunny whispered, almost a purr. "We didn't think she'd do it. We didn't—"

"I know," I said, not knowing anything, not knowing what to say; and, in my mind, I saw an image of the three of them—my mother with her dark curls, Lenya with her carrot-red hair and Bunny, all blond waves, sitting at the chess table, in this spot, playing canasta till all hours, chatting, smoking, laughing. I'd watch them, secretly, at times, from the top of the steps—dark, red, yellow—just the tops of their heads, smoke curling up.

"She doesn't look like herself," I finally said. "She's all puffy and—"

"The carbon monoxide," Lenya interrupted. "The man from the funeral parlor—what is he?"

"The undertaker?"

"Yes, the undertaker—that one—he told me the carbon monoxide does this. He could do nothing."

"Oh," I said and nodded, quietly shocked, sure that my mother wouldn't have known that. She would have wanted to look beautiful in her coffin, would have wanted my father to think, "God, she was so beautiful. How could I have left her?"

Later—a minute, an hour—I stood beside my father as he said a few poetic words about my mother. Arranged behind us, almost in rows, everyone listened—Henry and Bessie, giving Lenya and George a wide berth; the Caniffs; the Lerners; the Mauldins; the Merediths; Alison Hargrove, whom Marion had left behind; and my brothers, who'd been through this before many years ago.

Those who loved my mother didn't say aloud how hypocritical they felt this was—my father's gentle speech—but the air was full of their disbelief, their animosity. How could he do this? How could he come back to where he'd left her, say a few words, bury her and leave again? There were others, naturally, who felt that it had all come full circle—my mother had displaced Margaret, and Margaret had died. Gilda had displaced my mother; now my mother was dead.

Tears ran down my face as I half listened to my father and looked at my mother, knowing that it was my last sight of her. But another feeling began to creep in—a sense of relief, a letting out of my breath. It was over, thank God, all the years of fights with my mother, of hopeless competition, and the last year of trying to keep her alive. It was over finally, and a momentary sense of triumph joined the feeling of relief. It was very fleeting—a sense that I'd won. I was standing here beside my father, young and alive, and she was dead. Not only was she dead, she wasn't beautiful anymore. I had the awful thought that for the first time in my life I was better looking than my mother. The feeling disappeared quickly, or I pushed it away, ashamed.

I took my father's hand, sad again, crying again, but he was with me, he would always be with me. Of course he wouldn't be. He would leave and marry Gilda, and I'd be left to flounder through guilt and loss, left to search for a home, for a mother I'd never known. I'd tried hard when I was little to know her, to reach her.

"Play with me, Mommy," I say. "Please play with me." But she doesn't answer. She doesn't even hear me. She's on her knees, digging in the perennial garden, wearing a sundress and dirt-stained gardening gloves, her face hidden by a straw hat. Beside her there's a basket filled with the weeds she's just ripped out. It's a June day, and I'm wearing a sundress too; I'm about three, and I really want something to do. More than anything, I want somebody to play with me.

"We could play with my dolls?" I say hopefully, a little louder, but she still doesn't hear me. She isn't deaf, I know; she answers when she's not doing something else. Our cat, Chaucer, is deaf, and I've learned to move in front of him or touch him, but my mother isn't like that. It's just that when she's doing one thing—gardening or a crossword puzzle or typing—she's so fully concentrated on that one thing, she's oblivious to anything else. I stand there, shifting feet, batting at gnats on my sticky skin, and I look at the freckles on her shoulders and across her back. They seem to make a bridge, reddish brown, joining together, broken by the straps of her sundress. I don't count very well, but I'm trying to count the freckles. I give up; there are too many.

"Can I help you, Mommy?" I ask. She turns, looking up at me, startled to see me, and I see that the freckles have made another bridge across her nose. I smile at her because she's so pretty—her small freckled nose, her large violet eyes, her natural ringlets, her perfect teeth—and because she's seen me.

"No, darling," she answers. "You wouldn't know what to do."
"You could show me . . ." I say.

"No, darling, it would take too long," she says, turning back to the weeds, once again totally absorbed. I stand there a while longer and then I give up, heading down the terrace steps to the flagstones, to the dining room door, to Martha's kitchen, where there's always something to do or something to eat.

Teppi is in the kitchen with Martha, on a break, and I run to her very broad lap. Teppi is the only person I've ever seen who is as wide as she is tall, and this fascinates me. I walk behind her whenever I can just to see the way her square hips, flat on top, click up and down, up and down, like a drumbeat. Teppi does our laundry once a week, in the damp basement where the machines are, and I usually follow her down the steep steps and perch on a table while she sends sheets and linens through a mangle that flattens them like cartoon characters that have been run over. I've only seen one or two cartoons because I've only seen one movie, Snow White, *and had to be carried, screaming and terrified, out of it. But I remember that's what happens in cartoons—everyone and everything gets flattened.*

Teppi starts to sing as I watch the mangle, mesmerized, wondering how I'd come out. She's from the Ukraine; she's told me all about it—the poor farm, the dry fields, the church—and she's singing a Ukrainian folk song that she knows I like.

She stops singing, shuts off the machine and asks me if I'm saying my prayers every day. I tell her that I am—a simple prayer she's taught me—and that I love my rosary. I have it hidden in a drawer next to my bed and take it out every night before I go to sleep. I love the pink beads and the little dead Christ on the little silver cross.

Teppi has introduced me to religion, her *religion, a primitive black-and-white Catholicism, where heaven and hell are real places, where the devil carries a blazing pitchfork, where Christ is the son of God, who has white hair and a long white beard. I love it all. I'm thirsty for it, since I haven't been allowed to go to church and, if God is mentioned at all in our house, he's dismissed with a raised eyebrow as something people who don't know any better like to believe in.*

Teppi is stacking the sheets, getting ready to carry them up-stairs, and I ask her to tell me another story about Jesus. She winks at me, wiping at the drops of perspiration that cover her reddened face, and says that she can do even better than that—she's brought me a book about Jesus, a picture book, but I have to promise to hide it and keep it a secret, like the rosary. I promise, excited, and follow Teppi up the cellar steps, watching her amazing behind as it clicks ahead of me.

In the linen closet on the second floor, Teppi hands me a small book, a child's catechism that's filled with pictures of Jesus— painted with gentle blue eyes, a vivid blue robe and a halo that's gold against the sky. I love him immediately, run my fingers over his face and beard; he's much easier to love than the little dead Christ on the rosary. I want Teppi to read me the stories, but she can't read any better than I can, so I take my precious book to my room and hide it in the drawer beneath the dollhouse people and the tin soldiers that I play with in bed when I'm sick. No one reads it to me—no one knows it's there.

The undertaker and his men moved the casket out of the living room before the party was over. Some people had left, but most were wandering from the living room to the dining room and back again, drinking coffee and eating the sand-wiches Martha had fixed. I heard part of a quiet conversation between my father and Lenya, about one of the notes my mother had left, asking to be cremated. They decided not to take it seriously; after all, she'd left lots of notes, several with each suicide attempt, crumpled in wastebaskets, saying dif-ferent things. One time there was an angry note, saying that I would never finish college and my father would never write another play. Another note said that my father had been right about everything, and that she had wronged him. It ended, "Why did I destroy Max and Mab?"

My father and Lenya decided that my mother would be buried, as planned, in the plot that my parents had bought next to Kurt and Lenya's. So my mother would lie next to Kurt forever—I liked that. But she couldn't be buried today; the ground was still frozen, they'd explained, so she'd be kept in a cold vault until Mount Repose, high up on the mountain, overlooking the Tappan Zee, began to thaw and the diggers could dig, and the wild violets would come up and the forsythia would begin to turn yellow.

CHAPTER THREE

I T WAS LATE afternoon and a few people were still in the house when my father left. Lester would drive him back to town and then he'd fly back to Los Angeles and to Gilda. I walked him out to the car, which was waiting in the driveway. He had a warm arm around me, and I felt the same safe feeling that I always had with him.

"You'll come right after school, won't you?" he asked, as we stood beside the car.

"Sure, for a while. Then I'll probably want to come home."

He nodded, looking at me, his eyes tired and sad, his jowls and shoulders heavy.

"Please love me . . ." he said, as if he didn't deserve it, as if he were afraid that I wouldn't anymore. I was startled by his fear and put my arms around him, hugging him tightly, saying, of course I loved him.

I waved as the car went down the driveway, and he waved from the backseat. It didn't seem that different from the other times when he'd left, when they'd both left, to go on the road with a play, to go to California to do a movie. I was sure he'd come home—maybe bring Gilda home, the way he'd brought my mother home after Margaret. It never occurred to me that he wouldn't. This was our place; these were our streams, our woods.

I turned and looked past the garden to the woods and saw an image of my mother as she'd stood, many times, with giant clippers, fighting back the woods that my father and I loved. They gave her claustrophobia, she'd said, as she'd hack away at the low branches and the thick underbrush, trying to push the encroaching woods back away from her perfect gardens. It was a losing battle, of course. One small, angry woman against the towering oaks and elms, the tangled vines and the strong saplings.

I didn't want to go back inside just yet, and I headed for the path that led to my father's cabin. I stopped at the edge of the woods, where the path began, and looked down at the rotting boards that covered the worst patches, the spots that were too muddy to cross during the warm weather. The mud was as hard now as the ground of Mount Repose, and I stood there, looking into the tangle of trees, seeing a summer morning.

"We just want the pepper mushrooms," my father says, "the little orange ones. Look, there's a bunch." He points to a cluster of orange-red mushrooms, growing out of the moss alongside the path, and I skip over the mud, from rock to rock, or along the boards, and carefully pick the little mushrooms. I carry handfuls to the basket my father carries and drop them in. He adds a few puffballs as we go a little farther into the woods, where the path becomes densely shaded, only glimmers of light filtering down through the dark leaves. We keep going, filling the basket, until we get to the clearing where the cabin stands. It's not much of a clearing, just room enough for the small log cabin that sits beside a wide, running stream. I know that this is where my father works, but I almost never see him work. This

becomes our secret. My father walks to his cabin every morning. My mother tells everyone that Max is working and can't be disturbed, and I'm the only one who knows what he really does, because I'm the only one allowed to visit him there.

*First, he turns on his rain machine. He says he can only write when it's raining, so he's rigged a simple contraption—pipes that lead to the roof of the cabin from the stream. When he turns it on, water sprinkles onto the roof. Inside, when he pulls down the green shades, it sounds and feels just like a rainy day. The cabin smells of mold and mildew, a smell I love because he smells of it too. There's a cot on which he spends most of his time, sleeping or reading, and a stack of well-worn volumes beside it—*Treasure Island, Kidnapped, Shakespeare, Keats—*that he reads over and over again. There's a wood stove for chilly days, orange crates with more books and a plain pine desk where, once or twice a year, for three or four weeks, he sits and writes a play in a delicate, nearly illegible hand.*

I wait outside the cabin, holding the basket, while my father goes in to retrieve a book or a poem from the day before. He takes a few minutes, and I decide to check on my castles to see if the fairies have been there. I know that they only come out at night and, sometimes, sleep on the fresh moss that I spread in their rooms and eat and drink from the hazelnut shells that I leave for them. I peer at the castles, two ancient tree stumps, whose rotting corridors I've cleaned out to make grand halls and chambers for the fairy princes and princesses, filled with stones and pink quartz from the bottom of the brook. I think they've been here—a shell is on its side, and a moss bed has been moved.

My father joins me, smiling at my handiwork, and we go back to the house, single file, stepping carefully on the boards and stones. In the kitchen, Martha's waiting, ready to scramble the eggs while my father washes the mushrooms, slices the puffballs and generally makes a mess sautéing all of it in gobs of butter. I eat in the kitchen, savoring the sweet, salty mushrooms, and then Martha puts a plate on my mother's tray and we go to wake her.

My mother sleeps with the sheet pulled up high, and only her dark curls are visible on the pillow as we enter the bedroom. I love her a lot when she's sleeping. Sometimes, after a nightmare, I wake up in the morning next to her, and she seems so quiet, so vulnerable, with just her curls showing. She's so different from the way she is the rest of the time—so busy, so quick, with so many things to do and nothing to do at all.

She sits up and, with a quick smile, puts on a fluffy bed jacket. My father places the tray across her lap, then he pours her coffee from the coffeepot, pours a cup for himself, and we both sit on the edge of the bed, keeping her company while she eats.

"We picked them, and Daddy cooked them," I say proudly, and she tastes them and murmurs that they're really good but she needs a cigarette first. She puts a cigarette in her holder, lights it, sips her coffee, and she and my father begin to talk about something that doesn't interest me—a book that she wants to read or a new play that she wants to see—and I wander over to her dressing table and try on the rings that she leaves there at night. They're much too big, even for my thumbs, but I love the deep red of the ruby with the little diamonds all around it, and the simple pearl embraced by gold.

"They'll be yours one day," she says, noticing me. "Now put them back, dear." I take the rings off reluctantly, trying to imagine that day, when I'll be a mommy and someone will bring me breakfast in bed and give me rings and I get to pick out all my clothes and never have to sleep alone in the dark.

It was cold, twilight beginning, and I turned from the woods, shuddering in the sweater set that I was wearing, the cashmere sweater set and fake pearls that all good college girls wore. I looked toward the garage as I started back to the house, then stopped again, thinking that she'd died there, alone in the dark, smoking a last cigarette that was found on the floor of the car. And she was even more alone now, in a cold vault somewhere; then she'll be in the ground. I stopped

my thoughts at that point—I couldn't stand to think of anyone being alone in the ground; they should have done what
she wanted, they should have cremated her—and I found
myself walking to my forgotten bird cemetery.

I reached it and knelt beside the large rocks where I used
to bury the little dead birds that Lester found for me. I collected cigar boxes, and when Lester found a small, wet-
winged bird with beady dead eyes, I'd place it in a cigar box,
dig a hole and bury it with an invented ceremony, then I'd
place a cross of two sticks above it. That was when I was fascinated by dead things, before I became afraid of them. I remember digging up a couple of the dead birds, months later,
examining their fragile white bones, holding them in my
hands before putting them back in the ground.

I got up, still shivering, and walked from the rocks, back
across the path and into the rose garden where I could look
into the house without being seen. I was looking for my
grandmother, hoping that she would leave soon, hoping that
she'd left without finding me. No such luck. She was sitting
at the dining room table, being enticed to eat, to drown her
tears in Nova Scotia salmon and cream cheese. I couldn't go
in yet, so I sat beside the empty fishpond, hidden by a hedge.
I gazed at the pond and saw it full, saw the water lilies, the
green, white-bellied frogs, the glimpses of bright orange as
the fish darted over the murky bottom.

*I lie on my stomach, in bathing trunks, one small hand, palm
up, just below the surface of the water. I'm very quiet, very patient,
and, after a long wait, one of the frogs settles on my palm. I wait
again, letting him get used to it, and then, very gently, stroke his
shining back with my thumb. He likes it; he just sits there, his throat
bobbing in and out, and I smile at him without moving.*

*"Hesper, for heaven's sake, put that thing back in the pond!" My
mother's voice cuts through the hot summer hum of insects, lapping*

water and warm breezes. The frog jumps off my hand, diving to the bottom, and I look up at my mother, totally absorbed in her war with the Japanese beetles. They ruin her roses, she says, and she hates them. I think they're beautiful—golden wings and bright emerald backs. She's picking them off the roses, dropping them in a jar of kerosene that she carries. I know they'll die in there, some immersed in kerosene, some suffocating in the fumes, and I wait until she's interrupted—a phone call from Lenya or Bunny—and she goes into the house. Then I run to the jar, take the lid off, free all of the buzzing, drowsy beetles and watch them fly back onto the roses. They attach, in clumps, to the roses, eating holes in the perfect petals, and I stand there, quietly gleeful, watching them.

After Pearl Harbor, I have even more fun. I know nothing about this war, but I've seen posters of Japanese soldiers, depicted as evil and bucktoothed, and I know that they're our enemy and that they bomb us and we bomb them. After I release the Japanese beetles from the deadly jar, I take a few of them, the really groggy ones, put them on lily pads and sail them across the fish pond. When they're about halfway—maybe two feet—I drop pebbles from above, bombing the "Japs," and watch them fly off the pads, disoriented as their ships sink, before going back to the roses.

"Hesper, doll face, come say good-bye to your grandma." It was my grandmother's wavering voice as she stepped out onto the terrace. It occurred to me, for a second, to stay where I was, but I knew I couldn't. After all, her daughter had just killed herself. I tried to work up some proper empathy as I rose and walked down the steps from the garden. Martha and my brother Alan were with her, Alan carrying her bag, and I smiled and walked into her powdery, tearful embrace. She powdered everything—her face, her white hair, her large shelflike bosom—and the powder smell was even more intense when wet. She held me, squeezing me against her until I thought I might suffocate. I finally managed to pull back as she patted my cheeks with both hands, repeating, "My doll face, my Gertrude's baby."

That sounded so strange to me. No one else ever called my mother by her real name, and I felt even more alienated from my grandmother. I'd never believed her, even as a little girl; there was something so phony, so unreal about her. Even her touch was unreal, and I'd never wanted her to hold me, never wanted to sit in her lap. She had visited once a year since I was born, and my mother had always admonished for weeks before her arrival to be nice to her, to let her dress me and brush my hair. I probably didn't. My brothers and my sister-in-law all said that I was terribly spoiled, rarely did what I was told and had tantrums when I didn't get my way. I could only remember a couple of the tantrums, but I was sure they were right.

I felt a sudden surge of guilt. My grandmother was leaving. Couldn't I be nice to her for five damn minutes? I put an arm around her and walked slowly with her to the waiting car, saying that of course she could visit me, that I might even be able to get to Miami. She was smiling now, creasing the wet powder, and I asked her to give my love to Aunt Libby, my mother's sister, and, after another long squeeze, she was gone.

I let out my breath and saw that Alan was grinning at me, his eyes full of conspiratorial laughter.

"Oh, cut it out," I said, laughing too, and he raised his eyebrows, looking hurt, his eyes still laughing.

"Me? What'd I do?" he said, and wrapped me in his arms. I hugged him, loving the feel of his hard chest and his arms almost as much as I loved my father's. "You'd better come in. You've got goose bumps," he said. After a moment, I walked with him back to the house.

There were still sandwiches on the dining-room table, and I took one and sat down, eating it by myself. Alan had gone to find his wife, Nancy; Martha was doing dishes, and there were still low voices coming from the living room. I was sitting at my place at the table, not my mother's or my father's, and thinking of the thousands of meals the three of us had had there. It wouldn't happen again. I looked at my mother's chair, her place, and remembered the hundreds of times I'd stormed away from the table. I remembered vividly the time at the table that I'd yelled at her, "You're not my mother—Martha is."

It was a rotten thing to say, but, in a sense, it was true, and I wondered what my mother had been like with her mother. What would it have been like to have Anna Klein for a mother? My mother almost never talked about it, and I sat there, trying to remember the little she'd told me, the little I knew. She'd been born in Montreal and had described the walls of snow to me, so high that she'd nearly got lost walking to school. She'd told me about the orphanage where her mother had left her and Libby after their father died. She didn't remember him—she'd been only three or four at the time—but she'd shown me a posed photograph of Anna and Benjamin Higger and their two little girls in ruffled dresses, wearing long bows in their hair. My mother looked just like her father—dark, tidy, with sharp features—and Libby looked a lot like her mother.

There'd been a scandal of some sort after her father's death—my mother had never told me what it was—and Anna Higger had taken the little girls to Cleveland. She may have tried to support them but ended up putting them in an orphanage. The main thing my mother had told me about it was that she had loved to study, got all A's and dreamed of going on to college and being a lawyer. But when she was fifteen, her mother had married Albert Klein and had taken her out of the orphanage, saying, "Now support me." And my mother had tried to, working at odd jobs, going to school at night.

No wonder I never liked my grandmother, I thought as I finished the sandwich and gazed at my mother's empty chair. It was dark now, and I rose and lit the candles—she would have lit the candles by now. I left the table, moved to the far corner of the dining room and curled up on the love seat in front of the television. On an ordinary night we would have watched the news and then *Kukla, Fran and Ollie,* but this wasn't an ordinary night—there hadn't been an ordinary night for the past year or so. I looked at the gray screen and wondered about the orphanage. I'd always pictured it as being Catholic because the only orphanage I'd seen was the one on Phillips Hill Road, where nuns, in their black robes, hurried groups of children from building to building. But Quentin had said that my mother was Jewish, and I knew that her father had come from Russia. So would she have been in a Jewish orphanage? Were there such things as Jewish orphanages? I felt stupid that I didn't know, and now I couldn't ask her.

"Hep, honey?" Alan called from the pump room.

"I'm in here."

"Well, come in with us. I got a fire going." He stood in the doorway, waiting for me. I got up, joining him, and he gently pushed me ahead of him into the living room. The chess table had been put back in its usual place, and only a few people were left sitting around the fire—the end of the party, the time when my mother, Lenya and Bunny would gossip about everybody, what they had been wearing, the bright or foolish things they'd said.

The fire picked up the gold in the Oriental rug and the dark gold of Toby's fur as he stretched out in front of it. Lenya was sitting in my mother's spot, at the end of the sofa beside the hearth, and Bunny was sitting in my father's spot, beside the radio and phonograph. The room was quiet; they'd stopped talking as I came in. Willie got up quickly, wiping the tears from her face, and said she'd see if Martha needed help. This was a concession; I knew how Willie felt about Martha. She was going to pass me but stopped, taking both my shoulders in her strong hands.

"I loved your mother," she said, looking directly into my eyes. "Mrs. Anderson was the best friend I ever had, and she'll always be the best friend I ever had till they put me in a grave beside her."

"Thank you," I murmured. I didn't know what else to say. I hugged her and crossed to the sofa, sitting between Lenya and Bunny. I put my head on Lenya's shoulder and reached out and took Bunny's hand—my two other mothers, who didn't fit the role any better than my real mother had. We listened to the fire and the night sounds—a whippoorwill, an owl—and I thought about Willie's words and how much my mother's friends really loved her. I could barely remember loving her that much.

She'd written to me after Christmas vacation, saying that, even though she knew that I needed my father more, she was there for me, always would be, and she tried to explain that the times when I didn't feel she was there, that she wasn't present, those were the times when she was just trying so hard to focus. Her thoughts jumped around so quickly, she'd said, that it took all of her energy just to focus on one thing. I was beginning to understand. That barrier, her monomania as I'd called it, that I'd knocked against until I'd given up knocking, wasn't a barrier at all—just a darting, troubled mind and soul, trying so hard to be quiet.

CHAPTER FOUR

NANCY SPENT the night with me, in the other twin bed in my room. They—I'm not sure who—had decided that, since Martha and Little Terry would sleep in the apartment over the garage, I shouldn't be left alone in the house. They were right. All the old night terrors began to form as I lay there in the dark. Moonlight touched the bark of the old birch outside the window next to my bed and dimly lit the rose pattern of the wallpaper. From the window on the other side of the room, red and white blinked in a familiar rhythm from the beacon on High Tor. I gazed through the open door toward the hall and the brick stairs, the spot where Margaret's ghost used to lurk, and wondered where her ashes were tonight. I called them "her floating ashes" to myself, trying to feel the irony and to distance myself from the fear that rushed through my body like a chill wind.

I turned to Nancy, beautiful as she slept, her breath peaceful, and I closed my eyes. But I couldn't keep them closed; something was watching me, as something always had when I was a child. I had to either keep my eyes open, ready for whatever it was, or pull the blankets tightly over my head, leaving only a small space for my nose. I kept staring at the doorway while I thought about the ashes. Would my father have taken them with him to California? That didn't seem likely, so they would either be in the cabin or up on the third floor in the trunk with Margaret's letters. And if her ashes were here, would she still haunt the house, even when it was empty? Another rush of fear hit me as I went further into the dark—would my mother's ghost, once free of the vault and the ground, haunt the house along with Margaret, or would she go with me, back to school, wherever I went?

I wanted to run, jump out of bed, run down the frightening stairs, run outside and down the driveway, run like lightning. Driveway images, real and only dreamed, blended in my mind—the first very real, very recent. I saw my mother running down the driveway at night, screaming that she wanted to die. It was fall; my father had left, and I'd been impatient with her tears. She'd run from the house, sobbing, and I'd followed her, even more impatient, catching up with her at the curve. I'd brought her home, her small arms fighting me off, her face wet and frantic. I'd calmed her down, got her to bed, but not with love. It was clear that I was sick of this; I was saving her but didn't want to. Silently, I was screaming back, if you want to die, go ahead and do it, for God's sake, stop just making scenes about it.

Maybe she hates me for this, I thought. Maybe she hates me now the way Margaret had hated me. Maybe they'll both get together and hate me together and kill me.

"No, she still loved me," I said to myself, trying to calm myself. "She left a note this last time, leaving everything of hers to me." I almost laughed; everything of hers—whatever that meant—her clothes, her jewelry? Everything else belonged to Daddy—the land, the house, the plays, the fame. But, still, it meant that she'd loved me when she died, lying on a lace pillow on the front seat of the car. Then I started all over again. Maybe she loved me but her ghost hated me. Maybe her ghost knew, but she didn't, that part of me had wanted her to die.

Nancy turned in her sleep, facing away from me: If I were little, I could climb in beside her, I thought, hide against her as I'd hidden between my parents on the nights that I'd made the mad dash down the stairs and into their bedroom. That was when it was still considered their bedroom, before my father moved, permanently, to the large, gabled room on the third floor. I'd felt safe in their bed, curled close to my father's warm, soft body. Sometimes, when I was there, he'd left the bed in the middle of the night to go sleep upstairs, and I'd wake in the morning and gaze, lovingly, at my mother's curls, her closed eyes, wishing she would stay that way, so very quiet.

There were nights when she wouldn't let me come in bed with them, and I'd scream, terrified, as she told me to go wake Martha up, go sleep with her—she couldn't stand another night of this. There was a fight one night, Martha pulling me to go with her, me clinging to my mother, my mother pushing me away. My father just stood there, helpless. It was around that time, between the ages of three and four, that I stopped trying to reach her.

The night sounds grew louder—the owls calling to each other, some close, some distant, and the katydids went on and on.

"Katy-did, Katy-didn't," Daddy says, sitting on the edge of my bed.

"That's not what they say," I answer, and laugh at his silliness.

"It is," he insists. "Katy did the laundry, Katy didn't do the ironing."

"Oh," I say, getting it. "Katy did the dishes."

"Katy didn't dry them." He smiles.

"Katy did drink her juice," I say proudly.

"Katy didn't eat her oatmeal," Daddy says.

"Katy did jump over the moon."

"Katy didn't jump with the spoon."

I laugh, delighted; I could go on all night, but Daddy kisses my forehead, saying, "That's enough now, time to sleep."

"Tell me a story, please?"

"About the mice?" he asks, with a slight sigh.

"Not the mice. Tell me about the farm."

He looks out the window at the moonlight on the birch tree and is silent for a minute.

"When I was eleven," he says, in his gentle, Midwestern voice, "my family left me at my grandmother's farm. They couldn't feed another mouth, they said, particularly a gangly, growing boy. I watched them leave in the wagon, my father and my mother, my two sisters, and never felt so alone in my life. I turned back to the farmhouse, where I'd be all winter, and saw my grandmother, smiling at me, holding out a pail. It was time to milk the cows, and I didn't have the foggiest idea how to milk the cows."

My eyes are closing and his story becomes sounds, blending with "Katy-did, Katy-didn't." He rises slowly from the edge of the bed and moves silently out of the room, leaving my door ajar.

A shadow appeared on the stairs, wispy as smoke rings, and then moved into the hallway. I lay there, my eyes wide open, frozen as in the nightmare when I tried to run down the driveway and I couldn't move. Gargantua was after me, huge with black fur and large, grinning teeth. They'd taken me to the circus, again at age three or four, and all I came away with was Gargantua, the gorilla, staring through the bars. I was fascinated; I loved him, didn't want to leave him, and then he began showing up in my dreams, my driveway dreams. It was a recurring dream, all through my childhood. I'd go into the large bathroom, off my parents' bedroom, filled with Henry Poor's tiles, and see my father in the shower. He was naked and soapy and, suddenly, he became a suit of armor like the ones I'd seen in the Metropolitan Museum when my mother took me to the city. The armor was empty, like a shell, like the skeletons of the little birds, but then it turned into Gargantua. It wasn't the Gargantua that I loved, but a ferocious, hairy creature that chased me out of the bathroom, out of the house, onto the driveway where I tried to run and became paralyzed, stuck to the ground. He never caught me. I'd wake then, run down the stairs, longing for the safety of my father's arms, wondering how he could be so safe, so gentle, like Gargantua, and then become so frightening.

The nuns chased me too, the ones I'd only glimpsed at the orphanage. They became evil in my mind, right along with the witch in *Snow White*, who appeared, on a regular basis, at my window, holding out her red apple and laughing her evil laugh. The other witch that I'd see in dreams was Norma Millay. She was my mother's friend and was, no doubt, a fine woman. I found out later that she was Edna St. Vincent Millay's sister, but to me, she was the witch who lived in an enchanted hut in the woods. She *did* live in a cottage in the woods, with her husband, Charlie Ellis, but I'm sure it was a perfectly ordinary house. I never went near it, just as I never went near Norma Millay. She'd visit my mother at times, and they'd sit on the terrace, having iced tea, and I'd peer down from behind a curtain at Norma's long, iron-gray hair, her sharp features and dark clothes. My mother would call me, ask me to come down, and I'd hide, not reappearing until I was certain that Norma had left. She never saw me, all the time I was growing up, and she must have wondered if I was a freak, or simply a figment of my mother's imagination.

I smiled to myself—what a weird child I'd been. No wonder I'd driven my mother crazy. Or was it the other way around, or both? We were so different in every way. She had a quick, logical mind, with little humor, that needed to always be busy. I had little logic, a lot of humor and could daydream the hours away.

My father put it another way, one day as we sat together, watching my mother charm the dinner guests. "Your mother is the dazzling, beautiful one," he'd said, "while you and I are the bumbling, homely ones, but we have the talent."

I'd hated that. Even though I wanted to be part of him, to be just like him, I already knew the road rules. Beauty, for a girl, was everything. Talent was the kiss of death.

For a second, my mother in the casket was vivid before my eyes—puffy and blue lipped, even ugly now. They should have cremated her, I said to myself again. No, no, they shouldn't, I thought as another image, long forgotten, jumped into view, blocking out the room and the night.

Teppi is folding laundry in my room and telling me about sin and hell. This is days or months after she's given me the rosary, and I want to know everything she has to teach me about Jesus, about saints and devils.

"If you make a sin," Teppi says, shaking out a towel, "like a lie, or you steal something, or you touch yourself there"—pointing to what Martha calls my Lou and my mother calls my vagina—"you go to hell and you burn all time."

"How do you burn?" I ask, and Teppi puts the towel down, gazes off and describes a cremation that she says she's seen . . . A naked body, all white, burns in flames, like leaves in a fire, behind a pane of glass. But it doesn't lie still; it sways in the fire and smoke, its limbs writhing, its hair on fire, before it collapses in the ashes.

I sat up, covering my eyes, thinking what a stupid woman she'd been to fill my mind with garbage, and how stupid my parents had been to let it happen. If I ever had children, I promised myself, I'd never leave them with anyone. I'd be like Nancy, I thought, uncovering my eyes and looking over at her. I'd wanted to be like Nancy from the time I was seven and she'd married my adored brother. She was blond and beautiful, and together they'd had blond, beautiful babies. Nancy looked like a Madonna to me—smiling down at a baby in her lap—or like a *McCall's* cover, the image of a perfect young mother. I'd helped her with her babies, her little boys, for years—feeding them, holding them, watching them at the pond, holding their small hands as we'd walked up the driveway. I'd shown them the blacksnake under the bridge, picked the ripe grapes for them and shown them how to chew the soft part of the sassafras leaves. I'd shown them all the things I'd loved when I was little.

I'm sitting on the stone bridge, Martha's arm around my waist, dropping pebbles one at a time, watching the circles they make on the water. The circles get wider and wider, and the blacksnake slithers out from behind a rock.

"There he is! There's my snake," I say.

"Ugh, he's an ugly thing," Martha says and shudders.

"No, he's a good snake. Daddy says he is. He kills the bad ones, the copperheads."

"The copperheads don't come down off the mountain."

"Sometimes, sometimes they do. Sometimes, they cross the road, then my snake eats them."

"Oh, he does, does he? You know everything about everything, don't you, Missy?"

"No, but Daddy says so. I want to get down. Can I jump?"

I turn around, and Martha holds my hands as I jump down

onto the gravel. We start walking back up the driveway toward the house, which is not visible from here. I skip ahead as Martha leisurely pushes my pink wicker stroller. I'm not allowed to ride in it anymore—my mother says I'm too big, almost three—but I still love it. The back and sides are woven pink wicker, and it has a soft leather seat. If I can't ride in it, I still want to take it on walks and push it sometimes.

We go up the hill and walk along the straight part of the driveway, the old stone walls on either side, the summer trees growing together overhead.

"Now don't touch the poison ivy," Martha says as I stop to pick a black-eyed Susan.

"It's on the wall," I answer, bringing her the flower.

"That's a pretty one," she says, putting it in the buttonhole of her white uniform. For a minute I help her push the stroller and then pretend to be suddenly terribly tired.

"Can I ride, just a little?" I ask, my legs buckling under me.

"You know you can't. You know your mother'll have ten fits if she catches you in the stroller."

"She won't catch me," I plead. "I'll jump out right up there. She won't see me, I promise."

"Oh, all right, get in," Martha says with a sigh. "And one sight of that woman, you jump, you hear me?"

"I promise," I repeat, climbing happily into the stroller. I stretch my feet out, looking up at the sky behind the leaves, and feel the familiar rolling of the rubber wheels.

"All right, out you go now." We've reached the curve in the driveway, where the sloping lawn begins and the house gleams behind the dogwoods.

"Just a little more," I say. "I'm sooo tired."

"That's it now!" Martha answers but, before I can manage to get out of the stroller, I see my mother racing toward us. She's furious, her small body filled with rage, her mules clomping on the gravel.

"I told you not to let her ride in that thing," she's screaming at Martha. She reaches us, panting, yanks me out of the stroller and starts shoving it toward the house.

"She's not a baby," she's screaming. "I've told you over and over again, she's not a baby!"

Martha walks slowly, not answering, an angry half smile on her face, as I run after my mother.

"Martha didn't want me to," I'm struggling to say, "I wanted to."

"I don't care," my mother yells at me. "You're not a baby!" and to Martha, "She's not a baby anymore!"

She's running with the stroller now, dripping perspiration and out of breath, and I'm running behind her. She gets to the garage, picks up the stroller and carries it, stumbling, to the rubbish pile, where Lester burns the garbage. She throws it on the blackened trash, douses it with a can of kerosene, finds matches in her pocket and sets it on fire.

I'm standing there, screaming now, or screaming silently, as I watch orange flames leap around the soft leather seat, lick around the pink wicker as it buckles convulsively and then disappears in a burst of flames that nearly reaches the trees.

"Please, God, let this night be over," I prayed to the morning star and to the first gray light that outlined the woods. I was still sitting up in bed, damp with sweat, waiting for the first sounds of morning—the robins and finches in the woods, a rooster on someone's farm. When I was little I used to listen to the slap of cards on the chess table, to my father playing the piano like an organ, and pray that nothing would ever change, that everything would always be just the same. Now all I wanted was to leave, to go downstairs to a spring morning, to drive away as my father had. Not forever, just for now. I'd come back in the summer, when the roses were blooming, and I'd swim in the pond with Toby, wander up the driveway in the sticky heat, walk into the cool kitchen and be home. I had no idea that this would be the last night that I'd ever spend in this house.

CHAPTER FIVE

THE NEXT MORNING I sat on the floor of my mother's walk-in closet, surrounded by her shoes. There was every kind imaginable, from silver evening slippers to lace-up ankle boots with fur around the top. None of them fit me. She was a narrow size five and I was a wide six and a half. I wanted all of them and tried to squeeze into a pair or two, but it was hopeless. They would all go to Lulu, my brother Terry's wife, another size five, who was trying on the dresses, heaped haphazardly on my mother's bed. I could hear her from where I sat on the floor, oohing and ahhing in her upper-crust New York accent to Nancy, who was also trying things on, and to Lenya and Martha, who were watching and pulling things out of drawers. It was every description I'd ever read of the carrion-eaters swooping in after death, picking at the spoils. And I was part of it—I wanted everything, and nothing fit me.

I picked up my mother's backless slippers and held them in both hands. She'd had a new pair every year, but they were always the same—lavender and pink and backless so that they clacked on the stairs in a certain way. I always knew when she was coming up to my room at night because I'd hear the click-clack of the slippers on the brick steps.

I'm in bed, mesmerized by the moonlit sparkle of the ice-covered trees. There'd been rain, a sudden freeze, and now every twig, leaf, branch is coated with a fine layer of ice. The tall birch glistens, almost dances, outside my window, and the usually dark woods are like a fairyland.

I hear my mother's backless slippers on the stairs and I call out, "Mommy, come see! Mommy, come look outside." Her footsteps reach the top step, cross the small hallway, and my door opens, swinging inward so that, for a moment, she's blocked from view. But because of the slippers, I know it's her, and I sit up, anxious to point outside at the magical night. But it isn't my mother who enters the room: It's a tall woman, wearing a long, full-skirted, green dress and an old-fashioned bonnet. I'm frightened at first, but then she smiles gently and moves to the bed. She sits on the end of it, and I can see that she's wearing an apron over her green skirt and her hair is dark blond beneath the bonnet. Her eyes are gray, her smile warm, and I'm not afraid anymore. Not at all. I smile back, thinking that she looks like the picture of Mother Goose on the cover of my book of nursery rhymes.

"Where's Mommy?" I ask, but she doesn't answer. She continues to smile, radiating sweetness, and then gets up and goes back to the door. She closes it behind her, but I don't hear her go back down the stairs. After a minute, I go to the door myself and peer into the hallway and down the stairs. It's dark and silent. Clearly, whoever was here to visit me has gone. I go back to bed and to sleep and I never see her again. I call her "The Green Lady" and keep her a secret, hoping that she'll come back. Some nights I hold my eyes open, trying to wait for her, but she never comes.

"Hep, Hep, what are you doing, sitting on the floor, crying with yourself?" Lenya said, dropping to the floor beside me. I was still holding the backless slippers, not aware that I was crying. I put them down, wiped my face and smiled at her, and at her phrasing.

"Crying *by* myself," I said, and she gave a wave of dismissal, her bright red nails catching the light from the one small window.

"What does it matter, darling—with, by?" and she rose, taking my hand, pulling me up with her.

"We go to my house now. Georgie cooks all morning, something fancy for you."

"What about the clothes?" I asked, starting to cry again. "Nothing fits me."

Lenya gave another wave of dismissal in the direction of Lulu and Nancy. "Let them take what they want. They always want Mabbie's things—now they have them."

"But she left everything to me."

"But, darling, nothing fits you," she said, putting her arms around me. "What are you going to do, put them all in the cellar for the mice? Let them have them."

"Okay, you're right," I answered, laughing. "But there are some things I want—scarves and gloves and—"

"We find them now," Lenya interrupted, and, together, we went back into the bedroom, went through the drawers and put things aside. I ended up keeping a few sweaters, scarves and some beautiful kid gloves that were also too small. Lenya said that it didn't matter—I could just carry the gloves, not wear them. There was also one silk suit with tiny roses on it that almost fit me that I kept. I gave my mother's new mink coat, the one she'd died in, to Nancy, and kept the old one for myself, thinking that it was rather inconsiderate of her to die in the new one. But then I remembered that she'd wanted to look as beautiful as possible when they found her, and who wants to die in a ratty, old mink coat?

My spirits picked up as Lenya and I walked, single file,

through the woods to Brook House. Noon sunlight warmed us through the bare trees, and we stopped several times to remove branches that had fallen across the path during the winter. The path itself was less worn than it used to be when my father and Kurt tramped it down on their daily walks between the houses. After a few minutes, we came to the fork where the path widened, protected by two of the old Dutchmen's stone walls. To the left was Ruth Reeves' house, one of Henry's first efforts, cut from local granite. She was a costume designer, whom we rarely saw, with three grown daughters. Straight ahead, across an open field, a path led to the Poors' driveway and their house, hidden by trees.

To the right the path led to Lenya's. We could walk side by side now, and I held Lenya's hand as we walked the short distance to the edge of the woods. The sunlight grew brighter as we emerged, touching the stone bridge, the clear, running brook beneath it and the huge willow tree that was a faint green against the sky.

We stopped on the bridge, and Lenya lit a cigarette. "You smoking, Hep?"

"Sometimes," I said, taking one and lighting it.

"I go to see Kurtie every week," Lenya said matter-of-factly. "I clean the weeds, I plant flowers, I talk to him. So you do not have to worry about Mabbie. I take care of her grave too, plant her roses."

"Thank you."

"I know Max will not do it," she went on. "He is such a coward. He will run, keep running."

"Well, he was very hurt," I said.

"Oh, hurt, yes." Again the dismissive wave. "Over and over, he says, 'Lenya, I am a cuckold, she has cuckolded me!' And I say, 'Max, this cuckold business, this is not serious, no one is dead.' And he moans, 'I am a cuckold!'"

She was spitting out the word, impatience hitting the two

syllables. "And Mabbie too," she adds more softly, "making an opera."

"I know," I said, and we were quiet, blowing smoke across the brook.

"All this to-do about affairs," Lenya said, breaking the silence. "Did I ever tell you what I do when I think Kurt is serious about his affair?" I shook my head, and she smiled her mischievous, toothy smile. "I invite her, his mistress, to come here for the summer. So she comes and she stays with us and by the end of the summer, Kurtie is so bored with her."

"No, I never heard that," I said, laughing. We put out our cigarettes and headed for the house and the kitchen door, which was wide open.

George was busy cooking, an apron tied over his paunch. His silver hair was damp, his good eye smiling, while his other eye hung, expressionless, in the side of his face, which had been partially paralyzed by his accident. (It was always called "his accident" by those on the road.) I hugged him, taking in the pungent smell of aftershave and frying onions as he sat me down at the kitchen table with a steaming cup of coffee.

"I'm sure you haven't really eaten," he said with his soft, slight drawl. "And I know Miss Lenya hasn't. So—Spanish omelets, potatoes, hot sausage from that little market on Second Avenue." He turned back to the stove, juggling pans, and Lenya kissed him quickly before running upstairs, saying she'd be back in a minute.

I sat at the familiar pine table, half seeing George, half seeing Kurt and Lenya and my parents crowded around this table. I smiled to myself, understanding what George had said to me once: "Do you know what it's like to come down in the morning, have coffee and read the paper with Kurt looking over my shoulder?"

I saw Kurt again, for an instant, standing in the doorway, snow piled behind him, wearing the Russian fur hat that covered his bald head, his pipe in his smiling mouth. And then Lenya, years ago, as she'd danced for me across the kitchen, imitating her washing machine that had a way of jiggling across the floor. It had been my first glimpse of Lenya the performer, Lenya the star, because on South Mountain Road, she'd insisted that all she wanted to be was Kurt's wife.

I looked back at George, beating the eggs, and asked him if he'd managed to avoid Bessie yesterday? He looked over his shoulder at me, a baleful look in his good eye, and nodded in the direction of Bessie's house.

"There's a tiger lives over in them thar woods," he said, his voice hushed, and I laughed. He turned back to the eggs, saying that breakfast would be ready in a minute, and then we could gossip to our heart's content. I loved gossiping with George; he'd tell me things that no one else dared tell me. He'd told me about Truman Capote's lovers and Carson McCullers' hypochondria—both were writers he'd discovered and published back in his young glory days. And he'd told me about the New York that he loved and that I'd never seen—the Bowery, the old Third Avenue bars, the junk shops, the nightlife and the dark side. His own dark side, the side that nearly killed him, he left out.

It was a June morning, a Sunday, a couple of years before, and Lenya and I were at the Caniffs', having a late breakfast, reading the Sunday paper, when a call came for Lenya. I assumed that it was George, because he was in town for the weekend, at their Second Avenue apartment. But Lenya came back from the phone, shaking, her eyes glazed with shock, as she told us that the call had been from the police, that George had been robbed and beaten the night before and left on the street to die. An ambulance had taken him to Welfare Island because he'd had no identification on him. It had taken this long to find out who he was.

For some reason, it was decided that I would drive to

Welfare Island with Lenya. Maybe everyone else had been too busy—Milton worked round the clock, with naps in between—or, maybe, they had no idea what we were in for. At any rate, I drove into town with Lenya, who was speeding most of the way, gesticulating as she drove, and pouring out George's other life that so frightened her. I knew that George was a homosexual; that was nothing new on South Mountain Road, but the homosexuals we knew were couples. And I knew that George and Lenya slept in different rooms, but so had Lenya and Kurt, so did my parents, so did Bunny and Milton.

I didn't think of that generation sexually; to me they were all parents, in a way. But Lenya was telling me about George's weekends alone in the city, going to bars in the worst neighborhoods, walking the piers at night, bringing home the roughest, most unsavory characters he could find. It seemed that George—so erudite, so gentle—had a taste for thugs, for tattooed sailors, for an underworld that we knew nothing about. Lenya told me that she tried to stop him by not giving him any money, and she said I had to understand that it was for his own good. It wasn't that she minded affairs—she'd had plenty herself, with both sexes—but what George was doing was dangerous. She'd lived in fear of this phone call.

It was very hot that day, and as we took the ferry across the East River to Welfare Island, Lenya's red hair looked pink in the sunlight. We pulled up in front of the hospital; it was a hospital for indigents, run by the city, and the outside steps were jammed, like a tenement stoop, with aged, shrunken men, who stared silently at the brick buildings, at the grassless ground, at the slow, dirty river that separated them from any other life. And I knew, like a stab, that these men had been left here to die—hopeless, forgotten, together.

Inside the building, the hallways were as crowded as the

steps outside. Beds were lined up on both sides of the hall, leaving only a narrow passageway between the dying. Lenya and I tried to get the attention of a too-busy nurse, who ignored us, so we searched on our own, peering at the gray or bandaged faces. After a time, we found him. His bed was in an alcove, once part of a waiting room, with six others. One old man was sitting up in bed, reading a comic book, another had both legs suspended in casts and another I was sure was already dead.

George was barely recognizable. Half his head and one eye were wrapped in bandages; his ear was matted and raw, and the one eye that opened and looked at us was streaked and purple and nearly swollen shut. He reached out a hand, and Lenya dropped her head on his chest, her face against his gray, spattered hospital gown. He patted her back—short, tired pats—and, after crying quietly for a few seconds, she got up and took off.

"We get you out of here, Georgie," she called back, before disappearing around a corner. George's hand reached out for me, and I took it and drew close to him. He opened his mouth to speak, and I saw that his front teeth had been knocked out, leaving gutted, blackened gums. His one eye was trying to smile at me, and I waited.

"Leave me here," he said painfully. "I like it here with these old boys. It's where I belong." Then his good eye closed, and he lapsed back into sleep or unconsciousness. Of course, we moved him that afternoon to a hospital in the city, where he recovered, his old self, except for the drooping eye and a new set of teeth.

"I am famished," Lenya announced, returning to the table, her hair combed, her lipstick reddened, and George piled our plates with food. We ate for a while, in familial silence, and then chatted about everything except the strange funeral, my father's departure, my mother's absence. It was a warm afternoon, the first real spring day, and we took second cups of coffee down to the lawn chairs beside the stream. We talked about a short story that I'd sent George from college, then talked about Marc Blitzstein's translation of *The Threepenny Opera*. He'd sent a new lyric for "Pirate Jenny," and George and Lenya were looking for a better phrase to use instead of "the ship, the black freighter." We tried all sorts of things—"the ship, the old trawler"; "the tugboat, the old Annie"—until we got sillier and sillier and were soon laughing at nothing.

Lenya leaned forward on the lawn chair, wiping the tears from her cheeks, and then suddenly looked at me with such softness that I found myself blushing.

"What? What is it?" I asked.

"You looked—just that one second—you looked just four years old again, Hep, with your long curls and your big eyes."

"Oh, please," I laughed.

"You do," Lenya insisted. "I can see you at three, four, backstage at *Knickerbocker Holiday*, all dressed up, a bow here, and you are in love with the dead fish."

"What?" George asked as I laughed again, shaking my head.

"She always have bad taste in men, starting with the dead fish," Lenya teased, and I explained to George that my first crush had been Richard Kollmar, the young lead in *Knickerbocker*, who had gone on to host a morning radio show with his wife, Dorothy Kilgallen.

"Everybody hate Dick Kollmar in the part," Lenya interrupted. "He is so bad, and, behind his back, we call him the dead fish. So Hep, she sooo loves him, and she stamps her feet and she cries, 'He is *not* a dead fish, he is not!'"

"It's true," I said to George, "I did."

"And then that one," Lenya said, giving a relentless gesture up the lawn and across the road to the old Hargrove house. "Then she falls in love with that one."

"I saw him last year," I said, not sure whether she knew or not. "For the first time since he got back—some dinner or something."

"I know. Mabbie told me. So stupid they were, your parents, to send him away, like *Romeo and Juliet.*" She rolled her eyes and clutched her heart, mocking the whole concept of romantic love. And then she looked directly, forcefully into my eyes.

"Do not see him, Hep," she said gently. "For God's sake, do not marry him. You are too vulnerable." I looked down at the ground beneath the chair, at George, who wasn't about to interfere, at the wet quartz, like diamonds in the bottom of the brook, and didn't answer, knowing that I would marry him in a second if I ever had the chance.

I walked back through the woods by myself and stopped at my mother's rock garden. It was my favorite of her gardens because it was shaded and wilder, clumps of flowers spreading over the rocks that Lester had hauled for her years ago. There was no sign of her Johnny-jump-ups, miniature pansies that flourished during the summer, and I wondered, for a second, where they went in the winter, beneath the cold ground and the snow, and then thought, Wouldn't it be nice if people were like that, if they too went into the ground and then came up again, all new and refreshed? But people weren't like that—they came up as weeds or flowers, an idea that I didn't find the least bit comforting. I knew that Lenya did, though; she'd told me that nature was her religion, the seasons and the cycles, and that we were all part of it. Then why did she go to Mount Repose to talk to Kurt every week? If he was now just grass and flowers, why bother? I was obviously trying to make sense of death, and it wasn't working. I shrugged it off and went into the house, quiet now, except for Martha in the kitchen.

She told me that I was supposed to take my mother's jewelry to the insurance man, Carl somebody, and leave it there in a safe. I asked her to come with me, and we traveled the few miles to Suffern, Martha driving, while I went through the jewelry box, holding it between my knees. The things that I'd coveted for so long, the ruby and diamond ring, the pearls and the sapphire bracelet, I found that I didn't want anymore, or I didn't want yet—they'd look foolish on a college sophomore. I decided to keep, to take with me, her simple pearl ring, a pair of earrings and her wedding band, which she hadn't worn in years. Maybe it had grown too small for her, I thought, as I tried it on—it would fit only my little finger.

CHAPTER SIX

IT WAS LATE AFTERNOON by the time we got back, and the Caniffs were expecting me for dinner and to spend the night. I walked through the house, all of it so quiet, so empty; I grabbed my overnight bag. Toby was lying on the rug in front of the cold fireplace, and I decided to take him with me. Bunny loved dogs, all kinds of dogs, but since Blaze, her great Dane, had died, she hadn't been able to get another. Blaze used to sleep with us, when I was nine or so, and had loved to sleep in Bunny's big bed. Her sheets were softer than any other, her perfume sweeter, and I'd wake in the morning to Blaze's huge tongue, licking my face. The neighbors on the mountain were afraid of him, and old Mary Clarke sued the Caniffs once, claiming she'd been bitten, but to me, Blaze was an oversized kitten. When he got old and his back legs became arthritic, Bunny carried him down the stairs herself when he had to go out, and then she'd carry him back up again to her bed. When he died, she mourned terribly, as I'd watch her mourn for others.

Bunny never seemed to get over anything. If she lost someone, she never stopped grieving; if someone slighted her or anyone dear to her, she'd hold a grudge forever. Second husbands and wives, with the odd exception, like George, were not welcome in the Caniff house. A few people found that out the hard way. Bunny hadn't known Margaret, my father's first wife, so her loyalty was with my mother. Bunny never spoke to my father again after my mother's death. And, as far as Bunny was concerned, Gilda never even existed.

Toby jumped into the gray Jeepster, the car that I usually drove, and we headed down the road to the Caniffs'. I loved Jeeps; I learned to drive our army-surplus Jeep—it doubled as a snowplow—when I was thirteen. I'd turned it over a couple of times, on the side of the mountain, but no damage was done, and no one seemed to care. At fifteen, I got my learner's permit and drove everywhere—out of the state and into the city, which was illegal—my father could have been sued for a fortune if I'd had an accident, but, again, no one seemed to care.

It was dusk, the mountain shadowing the familiar road, as we passed Lake Lucille, old Mrs. Mahoney's place on the mountain and then the Hope house. The Hopes had built their house in the eighteen hundreds, but there hadn't been any Hopes living there for years. I knew it as the house that Elmer Rice lived in for a while, with his first wife, Hazel. There was a South Mountain Road/Elmer Rice story that always made me smile. It was told that my parents, the Weills, or someone, had dropped in on the Rices one day, and Hazel had come to the door, a finger against her lips, and had whispered, "Quiet. Elmer's thinking." It was a story that could have been told about any of the road's "creative men," but most of them liked to think that they didn't take themselves that seriously.

Milton Caniff *really* didn't. He referred to his comic strips as his "paper dolls," and he was an unassuming and generous man. There was ego there, of course; he'd fought his way to the top of his field, working inhuman hours, to become "the Rembrandt of the comic strips," as he was called, but he took a loving interest in everything and everyone around him. His spacious studio, where he worked all night, first on *Terry and the Pirates*, and then on *Steve Canyon*, was open to any insomniac, any blocked writer, or to anyone who just wanted to talk.

The Caniffs' house, halfway up the mountain, beneath the tor, was another Henry Poor castle, with curved walls and full-length windows overlooking the valley. Milton never bought the house, though; he paid Henry and Bessie an exorbitant rent, saying that he didn't want the responsibility of owning anything. He said the same thing about having children—it was just too much responsibility, and yet he and Bunny took care of all the road's mixed-up children for years. The Caniff house was our place of refuge, the place where we could go and be totally accepted. They took us in, fed us, put us to bed and sent us on our way with no questions asked.

The road snobbery extended to the Caniffs, led by Bessie, but it wasn't the distinction between artists and nonartists—it was the distinction between artists who were commercial, those who made money, and the real artists, those who didn't. My father fell somewhere in the middle because he was considered a real writer, who, at times, made money. Kurt Weill and Bill Mauldin fell into this category, real artists who got lucky, but Milton was, definitely, at the other end of the scale.

The fact that Milton had invented the adventure comic strip, that his drawing style was impeccable, meant nothing to Bessie—he was commercial and rich and didn't count. Of course, part of Bessie loved "rich"; she would have sold her soul for a hit play or novel, which never happened, and she courted successful artists, at the same time that she put them down. I remember meeting John Steinbeck, weathered and quiet, at the Poors' house; Julie Harris when she was young; and Carson McCullers, stretched out on a chaise, looking like a book jacket.

Bessie courted and mocked them all, but Milton got the worst of it. She compared his work to the Camels sign in Times Square that puffed out one large smoke ring at a time. She said that there was all that machinery behind the sign, just like the machinery that ran the Caniff household—Bunny, Willie, secretaries, assistants—just to produce that one puff of smoke, a comic strip.

I was laughing to myself, remembering this, as I turned into the Caniffs' driveway. It was very steep, going straight up the mountain, and, during the winter, they kept a Jeep at the bottom, transferring to it from the station wagon to get up and down the icy hill. I parked in front of the garage, crossed the terrace, glancing at the mountainside that I knew would soon be white with dogwood blossoms, and entered the kitchen with Toby right behind me.

"Well, if it ain't dirty babies, it's dirty dogs," Willie said, looking up from a paper at the kitchen table. She turned to Adelaide, Milton's secretary, who was just about to leave.

"This child's been draggin' dirty babies after her just as long as I can remember."

"Alan and Nancy's kids," I explained to Adelaide, laughing.

"*And* the Hargrove kids," Willie added. "And who knows who else. Sometimes, she'd have six or seven of 'em trailing after her."

"I loved taking care of them. And Bun won't mind Toby—she loves him."

"Did he eat?" Willie asked, rising from the table, ready to feed any living creature that entered her house.

"I think so."

"Well, I'll find him something. Come on, Toby boy, we'll fix you a treat."

"Thanks." I smiled, waved to Adelaide and pushed open the swinging door that led to the dining room and the large living room with Bunny's peach walls. Bunny had had all the walls painted in varying shades of peach and pink and, somehow, it worked. She was having her before-dinner vodka-on-ice—several of my contemporary Caniff refugees keeping her company. One of them was the son of old friends who'd been in junior high in Dayton with Bunny and Milton and remembered them as high school sweethearts. Milton had fallen in love with Bunny, a perfect flapper girl, when he was fifteen and she was sixteen. Now in her forties, Bunny liked to tell people that she'd been teased for going out with a younger man.

They stopped talking as I entered and hugged Bunny. Even though they'd all been at the funeral the day before, today was awkward. We couldn't just chat and tease the way we usually did, and I realized, suddenly, that while everything was just the same, it was not the same at all.

I went up to the studio to see Milton, who was at his drawing table, inking in a strip. A small television, turned to the news, was in front of him, and his left leg was propped up on a folding stool. He had phlebitis in that badly scarred leg and had to keep it elevated.

"Hi, baby," he said, smiling at me. "Welcome home."

"Hi," I said, kissing the top of his head while he worked, and I pulled up a stool to sit beside him. For a while, I watched him draw. "Jerry Stagg called me this morning," I said finally, out of nowhere.

"He did?" Milton asked, and turned down the television.

"Yeah. He was nice—sounded really sad—said to let him know if he could do anything for me." I trailed off, wondering why I'd told Milton this and no one else. I'd thought of telling Lenya, but Lenya would have disposed of Jerry with another wave of her red nails.

"Jerry was way over his head," Milton said quietly.

"I guess so," I answered. "But I think he really loved my mother. And it seemed, for a while, she loved him." Jerry Stagg was the attractive young producer who had started all this. When my mother had gone to work, finally, after pleading with my father for years, she had got a story editor job on *Celanese Theatre*. It was the early fifties, the time of *Playhouse 90*, of fine television drama, and my mother was a good editor—she'd edited my father's plays for twenty years. He'd been having financial problems—an IRS debt that wouldn't go away, plus no hit plays—and my mother had convinced him that she could help support the family. In her first thrall of freedom, she'd met Jerry Stagg on *Celanese Theatre*. She was forty-seven, Jerry in his early forties, and my father was sixty-three.

"She got so mad at me," I said, "because I couldn't figure out why she was so unhappy. We were in the dining room, just us, and she was crying, and I said if I loved someone who loved me, I'd be so happy. She yelled at me that I didn't understand anything and ran out of the room."

"It's hard to understand," Milton said.

"Yes, and Daddy was telling me everything," I went on, "like he always did, about her and Jerry, and all about Gilda. My mother was really furious about that."

"Mm-mmm," Milton said. He'd just put the pen down and was looking at me, his sky-blue eyes gentle and perfectly neutral.

"She said that Daddy had no right to burden me with it all, and that she was just trying to protect me. Then I got really mad and asked what she thought she was protecting me from—I knew it all already!"

I jumped off the stool, getting angry all over again, and we heard Bunny's voice, drifting up the stairs. "Hep?" she called. "Mee-ul-ton? You coming down?" In Bunny's voice Milton's name was at least three syllables.

"Coming, Bun," Milton called and got up and hooked my arm through his. "Shall we?" he asked, his voice soft and comforting.

We ate on trays in the television room, watching the news and then *Kukla, Fran and Ollie,* just the way we used to at home. After dinner, Milton went back upstairs and the rest of us helped Willie clean up, then set up the Scrabble game and played for a while. The other lost teenagers went home to their unhappy families, and Bill Mauldin arrived, escaping from his. After the war, after being the voice of the GIs with his irreverent cartoons, he was having a hard time finding a niche in the civilian world. Bill had been young, seventeen, when he'd joined the army; he had no formal education to speak of and, by the time he was twenty, had found himself world famous. He was wiry, pugnacious, with a devilish grin and a Southwestern drawl. He was the sort of person that, when he told you he'd started smoking at three, you believed him. He'd married Natalie, a dark and lovely Vassar girl, and they'd bought the Hargrove house when I was fifteen and Marion had left. Natalie and Bill had had four boys right in a row; Bill couldn't find a new career, and Natalie was falling apart.

Playing Scrabble and joking around with Bill, it made no sense to me. Natalie Mauldin had everything I'd ever dreamed of having—a successful husband, a house I loved, four beautiful babies. I couldn't figure out why she kept having breakdowns.

Bill went up to the studio to chew the fat with Milton, as he said, and Bunny and I said good night. I'd get to sleep with Bunny in her wide bed, the way I used to as a kid, except that tonight we'd have Toby instead of Blaze. I took

Toby out before going upstairs, and Willie came with me. She was holding back tears and, clearly, wanted to talk. We hadn't talked about my mother tonight—no one had. We stood in the moonlight beside the mountain, while Toby sniffed the night smells, and Willie told me again about the last dinner she'd taken to my mother.

"I told her I'd stay with her, spend the night with her, with Martha off and all," Willie said. "But she just thanked me, saying she was just fine. And she was, real calm, not like other times."

"She'd made up her mind," I said.

"And she told me why," Willie blurted out, the held-back tears spilling out of her eyes. "And I promised her—I promised Mrs. Anderson on my mother's grave I'd never tell what she told me."

"Why?" I asked. "What'd she say?"

"She made me promise," Willie answered, shaking her head. "But she loved you, baby—you gotta know that—and she was protecting you."

"Protecting me? Oh, Willie, she wasn't protecting me! She was miserable—she tried eight times—she wanted to die, Willie."

"She was protecting you," Willie repeated, "and she loved you that much."

"If she loved me that much she wouldn't be dead!" I answered, getting angry again. "She *always* said she was protecting me—she'd lie to me and scream at me and all the time say she was *protecting* me!"

"I don't want to hear you say anything bad about your mother," Willie answered quietly.

"Okay," I said, taking a deep breath. "Sorry." And I knew there was no use trying to explain what I felt to Willie. She adored my mother, and that was that. I hugged Willie, wiped her tears, called Toby, and we went inside together.

I curled deep into Bunny's sweet sheets, wondering for only a minute what Willie was talking about. Was there really some secret that I didn't know? I doubted it. Toby was on my feet, stretched out on Bunny's down quilt, and I drifted off to the sound of Milton's voice and Bill's infectious laughter.

CHAPTER SEVEN

I T RAINED during the night and was still cloudy and
cool when I got home the next morning. Martha told me
that the funeral home had called to say that it might be
another week or two—they weren't sure—before they could
dig my mother's grave.

"But it's getting warmer," I said.

"Maybe not up on the mountain," Martha said. "Oh, I almost forgot—they wanna know what you want on the headstone."

"Me? Why are they asking me?"

"Well, who else are they gonna ask?" Martha said with a
look. "Your dad's long gone, and you're her only child."

"Tell them . . . tell them I'll have to think about it," I said,
walking back out the door.

"Where're you goin' now?" Martha called after me.
"Lester's waiting to take you to the airport."

"My plane's not till three," I called back and headed down
the driveway with Toby running ahead of me. The lilac and
rhododendron bushes were bent and dripping. Thunder rum-
bled over the Hudson, across the mountain, and I listened to

it, thinking that my father would have loved this day. He loved fog, rain and thunderstorms, and there he was in that California weather that he'd always despised. "One goddamned blue sky after another," he'd said.

When I was small, he'd take me for walks during thunderstorms. My mother would stand at the door, protesting that it was dangerous to take a child out in a storm like this—lightning could strike and trees could fall. Her voice would disappear into the rain as he walked away, not answering, my hand in his.

"It's a hurricane, Daddy, a real hurricane!" I say, holding tightly to his hand.

"It's the tail end of one," my father says, his face rain splashed and happy. A tree branch lies across the driveway, and he helps me over it as lightning slices the sky. I grab his hand again and count the seconds, waiting for the thunder. It comes quickly, a crash and then a roar, and I laugh with excitement.

"It's Thor, Daddy," I shout. "He must be mad."

"He must be terrible mad," my father says, grinning at me. He's been reading the Norse myths to me at bedtime, and I've been immersed in Odin's world. It's my favorite time with my father, tucked in bed, feeling his weight next to me, listening to his voice as he reads aloud. Sometimes I understand what he's reading—myths or fairy tales or Winnie-the-Pooh, *but sometimes I don't understand at all. Sometimes he reads Keats and Kipling and Shakespeare's sonnets to me, the things that he loves, and then I just listen to the rhythm of his voice and watch his shadowed face and large, spotted hands as he turns the pages.*

There's another flash of lightning, more thunder, and a birch tree topples, missing us, falling across the stone wall. I screech and splash ahead, gripping his hand, totally unafraid. As we approach the bridge and the stream, we see that it's become a torrent of churning, muddy water, overflowing its banks and hurtling over the dam. The pond has risen to cover the bathhouse beside it, and we stop and watch, not attempting to cross the bridge.

Logs, tangled in vines, and bushes from upstream wash under our bridge, and I spot broken pieces of furniture being carried along.

"What's that?" I ask, pointing, and my father peers through his spattered glasses and laughs. "It's Lenya's lawn chairs," he says, "going all the way to the Hackensack." He's still laughing, exhilarated by the storm, and I'm happy too—soaked, with lightning flashing and trees falling at my feet.

Toby barked as we neared the bridge, and I glimpsed a deer bolt into the mist. A light rain was falling now, pebbling the brook and the pond. We crossed the stone bridge and walked along the edge of Alan's lawn. The crocuses that Nancy had planted beside the reeds were starting to bloom, white snowcaps, and for the first time I missed them terribly—my parents, our home—everything that was, everything that used to be. I wanted my father to walk beside me, my mother to storm around the house. I wanted to be five and six again, when it all seemed as magical as walking unharmed through the lightning.

When I was five, and Martha became our housekeeper instead of my nurse, I began to wander our property by myself. My parents didn't want to send me to school yet, and I only had one friend, Sandra, whom I rarely saw, so I spent most of my time in the woods, the gardens, the ravine, being somebody else. My father called me Rima, after the bird girl in *Green Mansions*, and he smiled at the leaves in my hair and the poison ivy on my legs. But I knew that I wasn't Rima—I was Christopher Robin, and our woods belonged to Pooh, Piglet and Eeyore. Or I was Princess Margaret Rose—not Elizabeth, because she wasn't pretty enough—wandering in our gardens beside Buckingham Palace. On other days, I was a young Indian mother, and I'd pass the pond and the dam and climb down to the caves beside the waterfall. It was cool and dark, and I'd slide down the slippery moss, holding onto branches, until I felt the spray on my face and the wet rocks beneath my feet. There was one deep cave, where water always dripped, and a flat rock in the center where I'd sit and grind pieces of rock into cornmeal for my handsome Indian husband's supper when he'd return from the hunt.

On rainy days, or if I was sick, I'd be Jane and Michael, stuck in the nursery, and Mary Poppins was our governess. She'd bring stars down from the sky for us to play with, and she could talk to the birds outside the window and they would understand her.

I didn't just read these books—I lived them. I filled notebooks with drawings of the characters, made up new chapters and gave everyone a happy ending. My world would change as my reading level improved. By seven I lived with the March family, pined for the Christmas with no presents and made up a whole new ending—Beth, miraculously, recovered, and Jo changed her mind and married Laurie. After that I discovered The Little Colonel, devoured all thirty-two books, said my name was Lloyd after my grandfather, the Confederate colonel, and drove my parents crazy by playing "My Old Kentucky Home" on the piano, over and over again, with tears running down my face.

In the more or less real world around me, the country was heading for war. Most of the fears my parents felt were kept from me, but I heard snatches of their conversations and saw the defiance in their eyes when South Mountain Road began to pull together: Hitler must be stopped at all costs; Roosevelt had to find a way to override the isolationists and must declare war.

Horror stories drifted back from Europe, and Kurt and Lenya told everyone about the Nazis, the persecution of Jews and their own narrow escape. Before this, my father had been, politically, an anarchist. He'd distrusted governments and their powers, and had voted for Willkie instead of Roosevelt. *Both Your Houses* and *Winterset* had been antiestablishment and anti–big government. *Knickerbocker Holiday* had been a satire on Roosevelt and "government by professionals," as my father had deemed it. He'd called for the government of amateurs, no matter how stupid or corrupt. But when Nazi Germany began marching through Europe, when rumors of atrocities began filtering back, he became a firm believer in democracy. He even began to preach, and to believe, that the theatre was the temple of democracy, just as his red-bearded father had preached the divinity of Christ.

My father's first war play was *Candle in the Wind,* in 1941, months before Pearl Harbor. It was an attack on Fascist Germany; it starred Helen Hayes, and it had a successful run. I wanted to see it because my father had given Lenya a small part—she'd played a maid—but I wasn't allowed to go. They kept me as sheltered as possible. This became more difficult when my parents decided that it was about time I went to school. The fall that I was seven, I entered the second grade at Street School, the local elementary school that was only about three miles away. Lester drove me, wearing his chauffeur's cap, past the neighboring farm children and the children of Lake Lucille as they walked to school.

I was eager at first. I greeted my friend Sandra with hugs and giggles, tried to be smart for the teacher, tried to make friends with the other girls. I *was* smart for the teacher, but I never made any friends. They shunned me because I came from the crazy artist's colony that wanted to go to war (most of Lake Lucille was of German descent). They shunned me because I was driven to school in the black Packard, wore clothes that my mother bought at Best & Co., and, worst of all, because my teeth were coming in large and crooked.

"Look, she's got big buckteeth," they'd say, and I'd try to hide in the girls' room. One day, at recess, I was hiding in a stall while three or four of the popular girls were washing their hands and giggling. In the stall beside me a fat girl named Winifred was actually going to the bathroom. This sent them off into fits of giggles, and they began to chant, "Winifred goes plop, plop, plop. Winifred goes plop, plop, plop." I stayed hidden until they left, continuing to chant in the hallway, and vowed to myself that I would never do anything that they could make fun of. At home I pleaded for braces, refused to wear the beautiful clothes my mother bought and insisted on walking to school. When the rain was too heavy or the snow too deep, and Lester *had* to drive me, I'd make him let me out where no one could see me, and I'd walk the rest of the way.

The artists and liberals of Rockland County came together in 1941 as they never had before. Sidney and Madge Kingsley, Herta and Will Geer came from Suffern; Helen Hayes and Charlie MacArthur, Rose and Ben Hecht came from Nyack; Burgess Meredith and Paulette Goddard came from Mount Ivy. Even Robert Sherwood, who was writing speeches for Roosevelt, came from across the river. There were meetings and rallies, speeches made and telegrams fired off.

My father would sit, night after night, beside the radio in the living room, the paper at his feet, listening to the news as Europe fell to Hitler's army. He'd always been somewhat distracted, as if part of him was listening to the characters in his head, or wrestling with issues more important than our daily lives, but this air of distraction became more noticeable, more pervasive. He still got me up in the morning for school, checked the outside thermometer and sat with me at the kitchen table while Martha gave me breakfast. He still read to me at bedtime, or told me stories about his boyhood or the mice that lived in our garage and went to California in a box-car, but I felt that he was waiting to get back to the radio, waiting to talk anxiously with friends—waiting to go to war.

I started up the sloping lawn to Alan and Nancy's house, to say good-bye, and stopped halfway and gazed at the gnarled cherry tree in front, at the rough stone steps that led to the Dutch door that Carroll French had carved years before I was born. This had been Margaret's house; my brothers had grown up here—an earlier generation, a different South Mountain Road. And now Alan and Nancy's boys were growing up here, the babies I'd tended, the generation after mine. I knew this house, inside and out, as well as I knew my own—the steep staircase with no railing, that no one had ever fallen from; the dark beams, all carved by Carroll; the uneven white plaster and huge stone fireplace.

Alan came around the side of the house, carrying a ladder. I stayed where I was, halfway up the lawn, and watched him, smiling to myself as he positioned the ladder, climbed it and began to repair a loose shingle. Alan always made me smile—always had—and he had the same effect on others. He didn't seem like an Anderson at all—he was outgoing, charming, fun loving, while all the rest of us seemed to have inherited a heavy strain of melancholia. Alan's genius for fun must have been an exceedingly recessive gene, I'd decided at some point, because Quentin and Terry tended to be even gloomier and more introverted than my father and me.

I never lived with my brothers because they had stayed in the first house, Margaret's house, after her death. My father, in the throes of guilty despair, had made a deal with Quentin—if Quentin would marry Meg, his girl at the time, my father would give them the house and they could finish the job of bringing up Alan and Terry. Martha would be there, of course, as she had been while Margaret was alive, and my father would be free to start his new life with my mother. Quentin accepted, partly to help, partly because he loved his home and family, and partly because he couldn't stand my mother. Terry, the youngest, had a hard time with her too, even though she really tried with Terry. She reached out to him, again and again, in her own overly charming, overly eager way, and each time he withdrew further, leaving her to feel more and more hopeless about her place in my father's family.

Alan was good to her, but, then again, Alan was good to everybody. Lenya said once that Alan should have been a politician, and I'm not sure that she meant it kindly. I didn't care what anybody said. Alan was my first memory—holding out a glass of juice for me on the Christmas morning when I was two—and my second father, my young, athletic father, who taught me to swim in the summer, to skate on the pond in the frozen winter and built bonfires beside the bathhouse so I could thaw my mittens and toast marshmallows.

Alan was seventeen when I was born, so at the time of these first memories he was living in the city and working as an assistant stage manager. He'd show up, unexpectedly, for a day or a weekend, and I would leave whatever fantasy world I was in at the moment and join him in his exuberant reality. I'd follow him down the slide into the black water, rippled with gold, at the bottom of the pond. I'd clutch him fearlessly, as he tobogganed down the steepest part of Zukor's golf course. I'd let him toss me high over his head and then rest against his shoulder while he danced with me around the living room. I'd follow him around, probably driving him crazy, particularly when he brought young women home.

There were lots of young women, but I only remember the redheaded chorus girl and Nancy. I remember the chorus girl because I'd watched her doing the high kicks, third from the left in *Knickerbocker Holiday*, and decided that that's what I wanted to be. Then I watched Alan chasing her through our house, leaping over chairs and sofas while she ran and screeched, her red hair flying. I was genuinely frightened, started to scream, and Alan had to come and comfort me and explain that it was just a game, that he hadn't meant to scare me.

Nancy I remember because she was so perfect, and Alan was so in love with her. Her name was Nancy Swan, and she was from an old Suffern family that didn't think Alan was good enough for her. She was refined, lovely and had a wonderfully stinging tongue. From the time Nancy appeared there were no other young women around, and I dropped the idea of being a chorus girl and decided that, above all, I wanted to be a bride, preferably my brother's, but if that wasn't possible, then I wanted someone of my own just like him. But mostly I just wanted someone of my own. My mother had my father, Nancy had Alan, Lenya had Kurt, Meg had Quentin—everyone had that one special person that belonged to them, except me.

When Alan and Nancy were around, I wanted to do everything they did, go everywhere they went—a walk in the woods, a game of tennis—anything. When I was six or seven, Nancy gave me a children's book called *Me Too*. There was a pink baby pig on the cover, and his name was Me Too. Wherever the pig family went he ran after them, crying, "Me too, me too!" I knew that was me, but I didn't mind because Nancy had given it to me.

Toby was barking somewhere down in the ravine. I called to him, and Alan heard me and waved.

"We were just coming up to the house," Alan said, climbing down the ladder, as I continued up the hill and across the lawn.

"I beat you to it," I said as we met on the terrace and hugged.

"How are you doing?" Alan asked gently.

"Okay, I guess. Ready to get back to school."

"What happened to the play?"

"Oh, I missed it. They had to get somebody else," I answered, and we walked together toward the ravine.

"Mother and Lenya were going to drive down. Did I tell you?"

"Yeah," Alan said quietly. We stood at the edge of the ravine, just listening to the waterfall. Toby saw us and scrambled up the side, sending small rocks cascading down into the dark pool at the bottom. Alan threw a stick across the lawn for him, and we watched him as he chased after it.

"It's a shame Mab didn't get to see you," Alan said finally.

"I know. I thought she was getting better." Then, before Alan could answer: "Keep an eye on Toby for me, okay?"

"Sure," Alan said. "He'll be fine. And I'll talk to Dad—I'll call you when we've got some idea—"

"I'm supposed to visit him," I interrupted. "Right after school. But then, I'm sure he'll come back. He hates it out there."

"He followed Gilda out there," Alan said with a shrug, which seemed to mean it was hard to tell.

"So he'll bring her back with him," I said, and then added, with a touch of sarcasm, "now that the coast is clear."

"I suppose," Alan said, wrapping me in a bear hug, avoiding my eyes.

CHAPTER EIGHT

I LOOKED BACK at the house, as I always did, when we rounded the curve of the driveway. I always waited for that last glimpse of it, white behind the trees, before turning forward in the seat. Lester drove me to the airport, and before I knew it, I was on a plane to Greensboro, headed back to "Marion country" as I called it to myself. Marion Hargrove had described it to me years before I'd ever seen it—red clay hills, flat towns, wide, lonely beaches and islands to the east, pine-covered, snow-capped mountains to the west. He'd described the delight of the springs—the March spring in North Carolina, when the crocuses, forsythia and jonquils bloom, and just as the magnolias, lilacs and dog-woods began to bloom in April, you could go north and ex-perience the beginning and flowering all over again.

My eyes closed on the plane, I heard his voice, his faint accent all around me. It was more an inflection than an ac-cent, a gentle rise and fall, a way of hitting certain conso-nants—*singing* was pronounced as if there were two interior *g*'s, "sing-gin'," and the final *g* was forgotten. My roommates would hear the downstairs phone and call out, "Ma sweetie's callin' me!" And there were the phrases that Marion loved: "Well, shut my mouth with a hot biscuit!" . . . "She's jes' a particular friend of mine." That's what I was to Marion, he'd said. He'd sing the song to me as we sat in his beat-up black Plymouth, tapping the rhythm on the steering wheel with his long, freckled fingers . . . "You can tell she's not my sister, 'cause my sister's too refined, you can tell she's not my girl-friend, 'cause my girlfriend's something-something—she's jes' a particular friend of mi-ine."

I fell in love with Marion Hargrove when I was seven, the spring after Pearl Harbor. The country had, finally, gone to war in December of 1941, and South Mountain Road was galvanized into action. Everyone tried to enlist, even Kurt Weill, a citizen by then, and Milton Caniff. They were both 4-F, Kurt because of his bad eyes, Milton because of his phlebitis. Quentin was turned down because of a childhood accident which left him with one leg shorter than the other. My father, too old at fifty-four, became a war correspondent, but Alan and Terry did join the army.

At home, my mother had the best time of her life. She be-came head of civil defense for Rockland County, and all of her pent-up energy and organizing skills went into the job. Everyone was very serious about this effort. For the first few months we were losing the war, and it was believed that our coasts were vulnerable to attack. There was a civil defense post in New City, with a first aid station attached, and I'd go there sometimes with my mother or Bunny and play alone in the makeshift hospital—I'd be, in turn, the dying wounded and then the nurse and doctor saving me. But my favorite place was the airplane tower, set in a field on the way to Spring Valley. Everyone, including me, passed tests to recog-nize enemy aircraft, and all the adults took turns in the tower at night, spotting planes—ours and, possibly, theirs. There were great poker games in the tower during the all-nighters. Even my father, who rarely played, would join in for Red Dog. They'd let me watch, at times, and I became pretty good at the game by sitting behind my mother or Lenya, who almost never lost.

There were other changes. Gas rationing meant that we took the train to the city instead of driving. I didn't like going to the city, but it became more fun because the train went as far as Weehawken and then we'd take the ferry across the Hudson. At home, my mother and Lester planted a victory garden at the end of the lawn, and we grew all our own vegetables. Then came the barn. My parents decided that we should help the war effort by being totally self-sufficient, and the barn was built right beside the curve in the driveway. We had a couple of cows, a few pigs and chickens. I didn't like the chickens; their yard was smelly, and they pecked at me when I tried to gather eggs, but I fell in love with one of the pigs, which I named Zorina, after the dancer, because she was so graceful, and when a calf was born, I called him PFC, because Terry had just become a private first class. I was stunned and heartsick some months later when I found out that they'd killed the calf. I had no idea what these animals were for. I pleaded for Zorina, whom they allowed to live. She became a very large, very graceful pig, and I became a vegetarian.

Lela Chambers was my father's favorite sister, and she and her husband, Dan, had four sons. Lee was the oldest, and he was killed in the crash of an army bomber—the first death to hit us, to hit home. Their second son, Keith, was killed a year or so later, flying over Italy. My father was devastated by Lee's death and frightened for his own sons. This was the motivation behind *The Eve of St. Mark*, a play about a young soldier, dedicated to Lee Chambers: "One of the first to go, one of the first to die."

My father's trip to Fort Bragg, North Carolina, was a research trip, to get the feel and the sound of the young soldiers about to go overseas. This is where he met Marion Hargrove—as charming and wise as a young serpent, he said—and then brought him into our lives. Marion had shown my father, while guiding him around the army base, some humorous pieces about basic training that he'd been publishing in the *Charlotte News*, and my father was as taken with the writing as he was with Marion's Southern charm and quick wit. He showed the pieces to Bill Sloane, our neighbor up the road, at the time an editor at Henry Holt, and Bill, equally impressed, wanted to meet Marion and do what he could to get the collection published as a book.

I didn't know any of this when Marion walked into our living room. I just knew that he was a soldier, about my brother Alan's age, and my father had invited him for a visit. I was seven and a half and Marion was twenty-two. I looked up at him—tall, thin, pale—and he held out a hand and smiled down at me, really looking at me, not just passing over me as most people did. I took his hand, saw the yellow flecks in his gray eyes, the reddish cast to his short, curly hair, heard the lilt of the North Carolina hills in his voice and fell in love. His gaze didn't waver; I had his full attention, his interest, even his love, it seemed, and he had mine a hundred times over. All of me poured out to him as if he were a newly discovered sun and I needed his light just to exist. And, as he became the light, everything else dimmed. Everything that had mattered to me for the last five conscious years didn't matter anymore. The fairy castles and Indian caves didn't call to me in the same way; the pepper mushrooms and purple grapes weren't as enticing. Being Princess Margaret didn't interest me—Marion wasn't in her life.

Of course, I wanted to show him everything. I took him for long walks during that first visit, through the woods and down the driveway, and I didn't feel that I was driving him crazy by wanting to be by his side every second. I didn't feel that he was just being nice. I felt that he *wanted* to be with me. It was that which made it so different. He wasn't my father, waiting to get back to my mother, or to the voices in his head. He wasn't Alan, waiting to get back to Nancy. He wasn't Terry, tolerating me, or Martha, paid to take care of me. He walked with me, talked to me, read to me as if there were nothing else he'd rather do.

I knew that he had a girlfriend somewhere, but the idea didn't bother me. I was seven; I'd have to grow up to be his girlfriend—I knew *that* much—but I felt that my love for him and his love for me (or whatever it was) was so special that no one else could really compete. He rarely touched me, and that didn't matter either. I'd simply bask in his light, listen to his voice, his laughter—more a cackle than a laugh—and watch the yellow flecks in his eyes become bright when he smiled.

We're almost at the bridge because I want to show Marion the blacksnake if he'll come out for us. It's chilly, and Marion's wearing his khaki jacket and his army cap pulled down on his forehead. He's talking—he talks a lot—and sometimes I don't know what he's talking about. Sometimes he laughs at something he says, and I laugh too, though I don't know why. Sometimes I say that I don't understand, but most of the time I don't say anything.

"Did I tell you I have a poltergeist?" Marion asks. I shake my head and he goes on, "She's like a muse. Do you know what a muse is?" I shake my head again. "Well, a muse inspires you. She gives you ideas, things to paint if you're a painter, or to write about if you're a writer."

"Does she give you ideas?" I ask.

"Oh, she gives me lots of ideas," Marion says and laughs. "She's got long, red hair, gorgeous long legs, and she sits on the

edge of my desk and files her nails. You see, the problem with my poltergeist is that she's not too bright. She tries to stay with me, but she gets lost a whole lot."

"Is she real?"

"Sure, she's real. She's a poltergeist," Marion answers, then smiles at me. "That's like a ghost but not scary. She's a wraith—a beautiful wraith—and she lives on a diet of wood smoke."

"Oh," I say, understanding finally. "You made her up."

"No," Marion says seriously, looking around, a finger to his lips. "Hush your mouth, child, she might hear you, take offense and run off, and then I'd be left without an idea in my head."

"Is she here?" I whisper and giggle.

"Around here somewhere," Marion whispers back, "unless she got herself lost again."

We've reached the bridge, and I grab some pebbles, scramble up and sit with my legs dangling. Marion swings his legs over, sits beside me and watches as I toss one pebble at a time into the brook, watching the widening circles.

"He doesn't always come out," I say.

"That's okay," Marion answers. "I've never been too partial to snakes." There's a silence before he asks, "Have you read Mrs. Wiggs of the Cabbage Patch yet?"

"Uh-uh," I murmur, still watching the circles.

"I'll send it to you," Marion says. "What about the Miss Minerva books?" I shake my head. "Oh, my God," Marion says, "nobody told you about Miss Minerva?" Before I can answer, he adds, "There are about thirty of them, the Miss Minerva books—I'll send 'em all if I can find them."

"You will?"

"I will; that's a promise. Oh, Hep, you will love Miss Minerva."

I turn to him and he's smiling, the yellow flecks dancing and, for a second, I wonder why . . . why is he doing all this? But the thought disappears as he tells me more about Miss Minerva and I

watch his Adam's apple go up and down, study his long, freckled
fingers, the curve of his chin, and simply take in his light.

Marion went back to Fort Bragg, then came back again
and left again. The light dimmed when he was gone, and I
spent most of my time waiting for the mail. I'd walk to the
mailbox at the end of the driveway, long before the mail was
due, and sit on the stone wall and wait. His letters to me
were either block printed or typed, and I'd sit on the bridge
and read them slowly. They were long, not just notes, as if he
really wanted to write all this to me. They went something
like this . . . "Dear Hep, I'm sitting at my desk, typing, and
the Sergeant is happy because he thinks I'm working. He
doesn't know that what I'm really doing is writing to you.
And I have a terrible problem—I can't think of anything to
write about because that fool girl poltergeist of mine got
herself lost again. If you see her wandering around in your
woods, would you, for heaven's sake, give her a good meal of
wood smoke and send her home to Fort Bragg?"

It took me hours to answer his letters—ruled paper and
carefully printed words. My letters weren't that long, but I
tried to tell him what he was missing on South Mountain
Road . . . "I walked to the cabin with Daddy in the rain.
Daddy said he is writing you into his play. He gave you a new
name." The play was *The Eve of St. Mark*, and my father
based the character Francis Marion on Marion Hargrove.
He read some of the scenes with Marion in them aloud to me,
and I was as much in love with my father's version of Marion
as I was with the real thing.

My mother and her friends thought that my crush was
cute and that Marion was sweet to pay so much attention to
me. My father took my feelings more seriously; the stories
about his grandmother's farm began to include Hallie. Sitting on the edge of my bed at night, he told me about the

beautiful, blond little girl who lived on a neighboring farm. He was eleven when he first saw Hallie and fell in love—as much in love, he said, as he'd ever been in his life. He used to sneak out of his attic room at night, cross the fields and sit on a tree branch where he could see a candle lit in Hallie's window. She was his light, his dream, he told me, and when Hallie first noticed him and began to walk to school with him and hold his hand, he thought the sun had come down out of the sky and was walking beside him. His eyes were melancholy as he looked out at the beacon. He hadn't told me the rest of the story yet—what it's like when the sun disappears—and so I'd drift off to sleep as dreamy and heart filled as he'd once been.

Marion became famous in the background of my love for him. His book was published as *See Here, Private Hargrove* and moved quickly to the top of the bestseller list. It stayed there for a couple of years, and the book was bought for a movie that would star Robert Walker. Everyone knew Private Hargrove; everyone laughed with Private Hargrove, but his fame made very little difference to me. Everyone I knew was famous and it seemed right to me that Marion would be too, and for me it didn't change anything.

Marion visited as always, wrote long letters when he was gone and sent me all thirty Miss Minerva books. I read them and everything else that he suggested. Actually, I read *only* what he wanted me to read, listened *only* to music that he loved and laughed at whatever he thought was funny. He took me to see Abbott and Costello movies, read King Arthur stories to me, and Oscar Wilde's *The Happy Prince.* Although Marion's formal education was negligible, his informal education was extensive and eclectic. His mind dazzled my parents, the road and the New York literary world. At the peak of his fame he was on *Information, Please,* and we all sat around the radio in the living room and listened as he competed with Franklin P. Adams, Clifton Fadiman, some of the best minds in the country, and answered as many mind-boggling questions as they did.

I sat on the floor in front of the radio, awed by the idea of anyone knowing that much. I thought that my father did—he could quote Shakespeare, Keats and Shelley backwards and forwards—but his was a quieter sort of knowledge. I'd heard my father say that the Algonquin Round Table had terrified him, that he had the kind of mind that came up with the perfect retort twenty-four hours later. That's probably why he was so charmed by sharp, facile minds like Marion's, and like my mother's.

During that fall, *The Eve of St. Mark* toured the country before opening on Broadway. My father wanted it to have a chance before putting it in front of the New York critics' firing squad. That's how he thought of them—a small group of men who were out to kill his play. And he was right to be wary. During the late twenties and thirties, based on the strength of *What Price Glory?*, *Both Your Houses*, *Elizabeth the Queen*, *Mary of Scotland*, *Winterset*, the critics had built him a throne. "The bard," they called him, "the new Shakespeare. Anderson has brought poetry back to the theatre," they wrote.

Winterset, especially, brought accolades from the critics, the public, even the scholars. It was a contemporary play, a modern *Romeo and Juliet* based on the injustice of the Sacco-Vanzetti case. It starred Burgess Meredith and Margo, and when it opened at the Martin Beck Theatre in the fall of 1935 my father was compared, not only to Shakespeare, but to Sophocles as well. But by the forties, the critics were busily tearing his throne apart. His poetry became "verbiage," his high drama "out of touch with reality."

No one was more surprised than my father when the critics applauded *The Eve of St. Mark* and it became a hit. It had a good run, a movie sale and left my father with a tax debt that he never got rid of. His lawyer had told him to save enough to pay the IRS in case the film sale was considered income instead of capital gain. This was ludicrous on the lawyer's part—he knew my parents and should have realized that they had never been able to save a dime. What my mother didn't spend, my father gave away. He virtually supported his brothers and sisters, my mother's mother, his sons, his nephews, certain neighbors and various hangers-on. He gave them land, houses, set them up in businesses and goodness knows what else. And not all out of the generosity of his heart—my father found it much easier to write a check than to sit down with someone and give them his time and energy.

During the winter of 1942, after the success of Marion's book and the success of *The Eve of St. Mark*, Marion began bringing a new girlfriend, Alison, to the country. She was tall, almost six feet, blond and beautiful, and, of course, I wanted to be just like her. I wasn't jealous though. I still felt that Marion belonged to me in a way that no one else could touch. I didn't understand it, didn't even try to—I just *knew* that in some indefinable way Marion was mine and I was his.

The plane landed in Greensboro, and I took a cab to the campus. The Women's College of the University of North Carolina was sprawling and beautiful—brick buildings, green hills, heavy trees. Everything was blooming, as Marion had said, a month earlier than it would up north, and, as I walked to the dorm, I heard the lilt of his voice all around me. I'd lost my virginity the past fall to a boy named Jimmy because he'd had Marion's voice. He'd wooed me at a drunken party at Chapel Hill after a football game, and I'd left my date and gone with him to a basement room. I kept telling him that I was a virgin, but he didn't believe me—

there were very few eighteen-year-old virgins in North Carolina. There was a lot of blood, and his face was white with shock as he looked down at me. I reassured him, telling him that it didn't matter, that I'd wanted to lose it anyway, which was true. I didn't want to be a virgin if Marion ever came back to me again. There wasn't much pleasure in that first encounter, and I didn't repeat it. I'd been brought up to believe in love—romantic and total—and I was waiting for it.

I didn't think that Alison had that kind of love, when I was eight, and she married Marion. He'd brought her to the country a few times, and he didn't seem to know her as well as he knew me. He didn't seem as gentle, as intimate with her as he was with me when we took our walks together, or laughed at private things like lines from W. C. Fields movies. Marion would say something like, "Has Michael Finn been in here?" and I'd know that it meant: "Please give this boring person a Mickey Finn." We'd exchange looks, secret smiles, leaving Alison out, just the way my father and I would trade awful puns, irritating my mother and shutting her out.

Then, unexpectedly, I realized that I was wrong. One weekend, soon after Alison and Marion were married, I decided to take them breakfast in the large room on the third floor. Martha put muffins and juice on a tray for me, and I carried it very carefully up the brick stairs. I was about to cross the landing when I suddenly heard low, soft sounds—whispers, murmurs, sounds of tenderness and touching—a closeness that I knew nothing of. The pain hit me in the stomach. I managed to put the tray down before I sat on the top step and threw up on the stairs.

After that I let Marion go—for a time, anyway. I hadn't liked the pain and had to accept that I'd have to grow up before Marion, or someone, could totally belong to me. Letting go wasn't that hard, because Marion was sent overseas. He was a corporal now, working for the magazine *Yank*, and was sent to China as a correspondent. He sent long letters from the Far East that I didn't answer, and a whole collection of Chinese money that I glanced at and put in a box. I stopped reading his books, stopped listening to the music he loved and tried to be a child again.

My dormitory room was on the third floor of an older building. I'd chosen it because it was a corner room with a gabled window like the one on the third floor at home. I climbed the steps to the room and found everything just as I'd left it. My roommates were sympathetic, if not particularly understanding. Jerri was sweet, inviting me to go to the coast with her; and Brooks, when I started to cry, said that she thought I hadn't liked my mother, that I'd been so angry when she had sent me Girl Scout cookies. I tried to explain that just because I didn't like the cookies my mother had sent didn't mean I didn't care about her.

I don't remember too much after that. My memory goes into one of those blank patches of time that kept interrupting my life like empty rooms. I must have gone back to my classes, the drama club and dates with the two sweet, boring boys at Chapel Hill who thought they were in love with me. But the only thing that I remember clearly is the letter from my father saying that he was selling the house. He said that he couldn't go back there, couldn't take Gilda there, and that he was so looking forward to me coming to California in June. I called him to say that I understood, and I did—I wasn't just saying it. I felt that to leave it all behind was the right thing to do. He'd said that it would never be the same, and he was right. When Alan and Nancy sent me the inventory of everything that was in the house—the paintings, the piano, the Carroll French furniture—saying that I could choose what I wanted, I wrote back saying that I didn't want anything.

It was only in my dreams, nearly every night, that I cried, sometimes screamed, "Daddy, please don't sell the house! Please, Daddy, you can't . . . you can't." I'd be on my knees, pleading, holding the walls, the birch tree on the terrace, the old dolls on my bed. But he didn't hear me. And my mother, the times that she was also in the dream, couldn't help either. She'd stand, somewhere in the background, silent and insignificant.

CHAPTER NINE

FOR SOME REASON that I've never figured out, I decided to leave North Carolina that spring. I'd had a good time there, made friends, done well in my classes, even though most of my attention was focused on the plays that I was in and the short stories that I worked on. The Women's College, at that time, was known for its writing department, and my first attempts at writing were in short-story classes taught by Lettie Rogers and Robie Macauley. They were both good writers, wonderful teachers, and my friend Arlene Croce and I were the two students that they encouraged to be professional writers. I knew that being a writer was the last thing I ever wanted to be, but I enjoyed the attention. Arlene *did* want to be a writer and, above all, wanted to leave Asheville, her hometown, and get to New York. She applied to Barnard, so I did too, even though for me it didn't make much sense. Why transfer to Barnard and New York when I'd just lost my home there?

I think the decision had more to do with changing my life in the wake of disaster than with anything else. I'd done it before. When Marion had left me—or been sent away—

when I was fifteen, I'd left Miss Hewitt's and the city, where I'd been happy, and, in the middle of the year, transferred to Nyack High School. I hadn't been able to stand the loss of Marion in all the familiar places. I didn't want to face an empty doorway where he'd stood, or walk a street that I'd walked with him, so I'd left the place itself. I'd thought that by leaving a place I could leave the feelings behind. It hadn't worked completely, but it had helped. And now Greensboro—the dorm, the classes, the friends—had become a place of loss, and I wanted to leave it. I wanted a place where the losses hadn't happened.

Arlene and I were excited when we were accepted at Barnard, and we planned ahead to a fall reunion. She would spend the summer in Asheville, languishing in the stupor, as she put it. I would spend the summer in Los Angeles with my father and Gilda and then return to a new New York life.

At home they were still packing things up, dividing the furniture, the art work. A good deal of it was put in storage for my father, for whenever he wanted it. Lester would soon be out of a job, and, once the house was empty, Martha and Little Terry would join my father in California. He'd rented the Lapworth house in Agoura Hills for the summer. I'd seen it before, on earlier California trips, and thought that it must have reminded him of Henry Poor's houses. It was a romantic house, an unfinished fortress on top of a hill that overlooked an expanse of valley. The Lapworths, old friends of my parents', had built it themselves. There was a staircase that led nowhere, a room without a door and a room without a roof so that, on a summer night, you could sleep upstairs under the stars.

Gilda would be there with my father, although she had her own apartment in town. At least I know that she had the apartment the following year when I visited them there, but, as I've said, this period of time was filled with blank patches, a bit like the Lapworth house—rooms with no doorways, stairs that led nowhere.

I went home first, taking it for granted that I could go to Lenya's, to Alan and Nancy's, to the Caniffs'. I showed up on their doorsteps, and they took me in as they always had—the road was home, and I thought it always would be, even if our house sat empty. I didn't go to the house. I still thought, consciously, that I wanted nothing to do with it. Only the dreams still held on to it. I'd search frantically in empty closets for lost clothes. In my dreams I'd be back in my room as it was, and I'd cry with delight as I found an old toy, an old book. I'd call Toby everywhere and run through the woods looking for him.

Bunny had taken Toby after the house had been emptied, so I went first to the Caniffs'. Toby was in the kitchen when I came in the back door, and I sat on the floor with him, holding him, kissing him while he wagged and squirmed and licked me all over. He was fine, his coat shining, and I felt the relief of waking from a nightmare—he wasn't lost, he wasn't wandering, hungry, looking for home. He was here with Bunny and Willie, and as happy to see me as he'd been all the other times, whenever I'd gone off and come back.

I didn't stay long, a couple of days with the Caniffs, a couple of days with Lenya and George. I was still numb with loss and guilt, and, like my father, just wanted to run from it, wanted to go forward to a new life, new family, new landscape. I couldn't avoid the guilt around Lenya and Bunny because they were so heavy with it. They had been as impatient with my mother during those last few months as I had been, and now they agonized over it, agonized over what they could have done but didn't do. They could have listened to her more, even though they'd grown so tired of listening. They could have been more compassionate, not begun to avoid her, as everyone did, because she seemed to be wallowing in melodrama. They could have believed her suicide attempts, instead of saying that they were only staged to get attention, to bring my father home.

They went over and over the last night when they could have saved her but didn't. They'd gone to the theatre in town—Lenya and George, Bunny and Milton—and they hadn't invited my mother. They were home by midnight, and some instinct told them to check on my mother. They drove up the driveway, but the house was dark and peaceful and they'd driven home and gone to bed. She was probably in the car, in the garage, at that time. They might have saved her, but they didn't know. They said it over and over again—they didn't know; they didn't know.

Clearly, I hadn't known either, and their voices blended with my guilt that lay beneath the surface, stirring it up like a slotted spoon, until I'd agonize too: I shouldn't have left her alone. I should have gone home for the four-day break in February. (Instead I had gone to my roommate's home in Baltimore because hers seemed to be a happy family.) I should have told my mother that I'd come home that summer and be with her instead of wanting to run off to my father and Gilda. I wore my mother's wedding ring, that small gold band that I didn't remember her wearing, on my right hand, and I twisted it with guilt and promised that I'd never take it off.

After saying good-bye to Alan and Nancy, who were down at the pond, weeding and raking, getting ready for the summer, I walked part way up the driveway. I stopped at the curve, before the house became visible, and gazed at the duck pond that hadn't had ducks in years and at the barn that, after the war, had been turned into a small house. We'd rented it out at times, but now it was empty too, blank windows where the two cows and my horse, Tony, had been. They'd given me a pony when I was eight and trying to be a child again after Marion got married. I didn't know too much about being a child, having spent very little time with other children, but I knew from books the things that children liked to do. They liked to ride ponies, swing on swings, play in tree houses—things like that—so Lester nailed a board up in the willow tree for me where I could sit and read. I'd sit there, swatting mosquitoes, smelling the skunk cabbage below, and wonder why anyone thought this was fun.

I was excited about the pony, but he turned out to have a mean streak that outweighed his cuteness. When I'd walk him, he'd purposefully put one hoof to the side and step on my bare foot. I liked racing him up and down the driveway, but one day he tore into the rose garden, skidded to a stop and threw me over his head into the fishpond. I landed sputtering and yelling in the lily pads, and my parents decided that he was too much for me and traded him for a gentle chestnut mare named Tony.

I looked past the lawn at the wide, sloping field that ended at the pond and, for an instant, saw myself once again on Tony's bare back, cantering across the field, long braids flying. Tony was careful of me, avoiding low branches when I'd ride her through the woods, but by then I'd learned how to roll off her, as loose as a rag doll, so falling didn't frighten me. I should have taken care of her, groomed her and fed her, but I didn't, or I did it only when I felt like it. That was all done by Lester and someone else, who I don't remember, who milked the cows and cleaned the barn.

No one asked me to be responsible for anything, and there were no rules to speak of. I knew that I didn't have to listen to my mother because my father would always take my side, rendering her expectations useless. I was supposed to go to school but I played sick so often that even school wasn't taken seriously. When I had trouble with spelling in the third grade and asked my father for help, he laughed. He said that spelling didn't matter much, and he quoted Mark Twain: "I have absolutely no respect for a man who can only spell a word one way."

I turned from the barn, going back down the driveway, thinking how quickly all the animals had disappeared after the war. The chickens and ducks that had been raised in incubators in the garage—so fluffy and adorable—and then been killed by Lester behind the garage, on the stump that always stank of blood and feathers, were gone. The cows, pigs and my horse were sold or given away. The victory garden was eaten by deer, rabbits and raccoons before being overtaken by weeds. It had all been about the war.

Everything was geared toward winning that hellish war. Patriotism verged on fanaticism because if we lost we would all be dead, or worse, lose our freedom and live in Nazi slavery. My father was a great believer in "freedom or death," and I overheard conversations between my parents and their friends about all of us being lined up and shot. My father said that our family would be first because he was such an outspoken believer in the democratic process. I wasn't supposed to hear any of this, so I'd go silently to my safe bed, stare at the rose-covered wallpaper and picture all of us, everyone on the road, being lined up against the mountain and shot.

Another horror story seeped through the shield that they tried to keep around me. I must have heard this at Street School, and the image stayed with me—someone said that the Nazis would toss foreign babies into the air and impale them on their bayonets. The impaled baby would flash before my eyes at odd moments of the day or night. The image would sicken and horrify me. How could someone possibly do something like that to a baby? I'd cried my eyes out over the dead calf, the chicks that would die and the suckling pig that my mother made the mistake of cooking one Christmas—I'd screamed at her to take it off the fire, and the impaled baby and the baby pig, going round and round on a spit, became one in my nightmares.

It had been hard enough to get my mother's attention before the war; during the war it became almost impossible. She had that fierce look of concentration—dark eyebrows knit to the fine lines in between, cigarette holder clenched between her teeth—as she ran the civil defense, spent nights at the airplane tower, worked on Red Cross drives and USO parties. There was a party at the Poors' one night, for sailors on leave, and I sat on the steps above Henry's studio and watched my mother jitterbug with one sailor after another, her forties dirndl skirt whirling, that same look of concentration on her face. My father wasn't there. If he ever danced, I never witnessed it. His entire focus, at the time, was a new play about our troops in Europe, and he was traveling more than usual, interviewing soldiers, and going back and forth to Washington, trying to get overseas.

Both my parents, and every artist in the county, worked on the Russian War Relief Benefit, which later stamped many of them as Communist sympathizers. During the McCarthy era, many were blacklisted and several were actually indicted, although Russia, during the war, had been our ally.

My parents noticed me long enough to put me in the benefit, and I was terribly excited. I had just turned eight and had decided that I wanted to be an actress, or at least that's what I wanted until I was old enough to marry Marion. Helen Hayes was to be in a scene with Zita Johann (I think from *Elizabeth the Queen*), and it was decided that Helen and Charles MacArthur's daughter, Mary, and I should open the whole show in a skit with Ed Wynn. Mary, who was twelve then, was known as Helen's act-of-God baby, because Helen had broken the contract committing her to star in my father's play *Saturday's Children* because of her joyous pregnancy, which she had declared an act of God. Mary *was* Helen's joy, and a joy to be around. I didn't know her well because of the age difference, but she was pretty, unspoiled and fun.

Mary and I practiced and practiced our lines for the skit with Ed Wynn. We cued each other, were word perfect, and, during one of these sessions, Mary taught me to smoke. The MacArthur house was on the Hudson in Nyack, a beautiful Victorian with screened porches, and terraces that went down to the river. The shore was lined with boulders and flat rocks, and we took a couple of my mother's red-tipped Marlboros, her father's filled pipe and a box of matches down to the rocks. Hidden from view, we smoked it all. I loved the taste instantly, probably because my mother chain-smoked before and after my birth, and I smoked the pipe until there was nothing in the bowl but ashes.

On the big night, Mary and I were confident. We hadn't rehearsed with Ed Wynn yet, but we knew our lines and our moves. We went out on the open-air stage in white dresses and hair bows, said our opening lines to the sea of faces, the stars above and Ed Wynn himself, and he answered with something else entirely. Apparently, he had decided to ad-lib the whole thing. We stared, confused, tried to get our lines in, but each time he'd fire back a quip that had nothing to do with the scene. The audience laughed, loving it, and, finally, after what seemed like a very long time, it was over. The lights went out, there was lots of applause and two confused, angry little girls ran off stage, saying, "But he didn't say what he was supposed to! He didn't even know his lines!"

Mary's sudden death at eighteen from polio was devastating for Helen and Charlie and everyone close to them. Helen never fully recovered; Charlie sank into alcoholic despair, and Jamie, their adopted little boy, felt the survivor's guilt for just living. To me, Mary's death was both shocking and unimaginable. Someone like Mary just didn't die. She wasn't the type, like Beth or Camille. She was too mischievous, glowing and funny to die so young.

I passed the mailboxes at the end of the driveway and turned left on the road, deciding to leave the car at Alan's and walk up to Lenya's. As I passed the stone wall where I used to sit and hope for a letter, I thought about the time when they were all gone—Alan, Marion, Terry, my father— and our only contact was the unpredictable mail. My father left for Europe in March of 1943 and was gone until July. Robert Sherwood, who was at the Office of War Information, had made it possible for him to travel as a correspondent. He went to England and North Africa, where he mingled with troops at the front and met with Eisenhower, who he said suggested the title for his new play, *Storm Operation*. It turned out to be one of his biggest flops, but he was exhilarated by the trip.

He wrote long, loving letters to my mother all the time he was gone, and she read bits and pieces of them to me, being careful to avoid anything that might scare me, like the war itself.

London, April 15, 1943 . . . Darling, I begin to get terribly lonely! Just no news at all since that one cable in the Azores. Maybe I'll get some word from you tomorrow. They say any cable the censors find suspicious or that sounds as if it were sent by a new arrival is held about ten days—At last—your cable came!

London, April 18 . . . Darling, Today I went out to Keats' house in Hampstead with Willy Wyler. It was very nice to see the house and garden again, uninjured in the midst of a pretty badly bombed London . . . I've talked now with a lot of men who have been here nearly a year, leaving wives and children in America. They are all pretty unhappy about it. One feels really cut off. I feel it already my-self—and even though I'm seeing and experiencing the most exciting things I could hope for here, there's always an ache in me that keeps wishing for home and you and Hesper.

1:30 A.M.—There's just been another air raid by moon-light—guns going off all around. A small raid—nobody pays attention.

He wrote several times about possibly staying in London for a while if my mother could join him. He'd been offered a screenplay, and the producer had said that he could arrange for my mother to join him as his assistant, but there were problems with her passport. I remember her fretting and carrying on about delays and red tape, but I didn't know what it was about. I didn't want her to go. Certainly, *I* didn't want to go. I just wanted my father to come home. I wrote to him every week, and finally a letter came just for me.

London, May 11 . . . I've had three letters from you and it's beginning to be high time you get at least one from me. It's hard work to write letters but it's lots of fun to get them. Imagine me sitting in a small hotel room with noth-ing in it but a couple of tables and a couple of beds—one I sleep in and the other is covered with books—and I'm just sitting here trying to remember what you look like while I write you a letter.

I went down to the British Museum today because I wanted to see the Elgin Marbles again. They are Greek statues that Keats wrote about. But the museum is closed now . . . Mother tells me that you've been learning some poems. I'm glad you're learning to skip rope. If you ever want to be a prize-fighter that will be invaluable . . . Love, Daddy.

And then to my mother from North Africa:

June 3, 1943 . . . My first impressions were just a North African blur—made up of dust, heat, sunshine, crowded streets, military cars dashing up and down, ships in harbor, veiled women, more dust, more heat, delay, crowded offices, lifts that won't work, ten men in one billet, mosquitoes, no water in the taps, no baths, cold water shaves saved in a Johnny Walker bottle, French officers, British officers, American officers, salutes, Moorish castles taken over for supply depots . . . Crowded buses, paper francs, misdirections, desperate attempts at French, getting lost, walking miles in the heat to get money changed, dinner with American soldiers at their stand-up mess . . . The Kasbah, the native market, dirty Arabs in white, dirty white veils, never by any chance anything clean, except the officers' uniforms on that day when they first put on their summer tans. I saw General Eisenhower on that day and he was really clean and cool . . . Oh, darling—I'm so weary of traveling about. I want to see you and home.

I wanted him to come home almost as much as he did. The house felt strange with just my mother and Martha there, as if its center were missing. They would go at each other as they always had, but without my father's quiet voice to intervene, or just his presence to calm them, and I felt unprotected. Anything might blow up at any minute, like the sudden raids that he'd written about that set the sky on fire. I missed him in the kitchen in the early morning, missed his thick fingers on the piano keys, missed his stories at bedtime and missed curling up in his broad, safe lap.

I spent most of my time with the animals and the two new babies. Quentin and Meg, still living in the first house by the waterfall, had a little girl, Martha, who had had some kind of birth injury. "Little Martha," as she was called, was bright and sweet, but the left side of her body couldn't keep up with the right, and speech was difficult for her. Each day Meg laid her on a soft towel on the dining room table, exercising her small limbs for an hour or two. I visited and played with her, but Meg and Quentin, understandably, didn't let me take care of her the way Nancy let me take care of Little Alan.

When Little Alan was about a year old, and Alan went overseas as stage manager of *This Is the Army*, Nancy moved into the red barn just across the road from our mailbox. I glanced at the barn now, still painted bright red, and realized that I'd been standing still just beyond the mailbox. I started to walk quickly up the road, seeing in my mind Nancy's blond head bent over the baby's gold curls and pudgy, compact body. The image represented everything I'd wanted when I was eight years old, and everything I'd wanted to be.

I walked past the stream and the marshland on the left side of the road, which in June was filled with tiger lilies, and looked up at the Mauldin house, the old Hargrove house, on the right. I never looked at the house from this angle, from below, without seeing Marion's image on the terrace, his eyes cold and full of pain as he'd shattered all those eight-year-old dreams. It was another June, June of 1948. I was thirteen, almost fourteen, and I'd stammered, "But I thought—I thought it meant you loved me." And he'd answered, "It was body chemistry, nothing more." While I'd looked into his gray, pained eyes, I'd seen a shadow pass behind him—Alison's heavy, pregnant figure moving past the living room windows.

Looking up at the house, I felt the same jolt in the pit of my stomach that I'd felt when I was eight and had thrown up on the stairs, that I'd felt on his terrace at thirteen and felt again at fifteen, when they'd sent him away. He'd been cruel, wanting me to hate him, I guess, which was foolish because nothing could have made me hate him. When he made it clear that he wanted to be rid of me and talked about his new girlfriend and her beautiful long legs, I simply felt rejected, ugly and not good enough for him or anyone. Lenya was the only one who told me the truth. She wasn't supposed to, she'd said, but she couldn't stand to see me so miserable.

Brook House was ahead of me, and I looked away from the terrace and up at Lenya's third-floor windows. I'd been in that room, the low-ceilinged guest room across the hall from Kurt's study on that last New Year's Eve—Kurt's last New Year's Eve—when Lenya had come upstairs to find me on one of the twin beds, crying. I'd cried outside for a while, holding on to the old willow tree, and gone inside just in time to see Kurt pull his melted lead out of the fire. It was a ritual that Kurt and Lenya had brought from Europe—everyone melted a piece of lead before midnight on New Year's Eve and then let it harden. Whatever symbol the lead formed would repre- sent the coming year. Kurt's piece of lead formed a bird, a phoenix, rising from the ashes. I'd watched it harden, seen it clearly, thinking that it meant a new success. None of us thought for a second that Kurt might die that year.

At midnight, January 1, 1950, we stood in a circle, hold- ing hands, and sang "Auld Lang Syne." My tears started again—for years Marion had been part of this circle—and I'd run up the steep stairs to the guest room. Lenya came up a few minutes later, sat beside me on the bed, stroking my hair, and told me that she had to tell me the truth—she wasn't supposed to, but she had to.

"What? What truth?" I asked.

"Marion is a fool," Lenya said, "but he didn't hurt you be- cause he wanted to."

"What?"

"Well, he did not have to do it the way he did, be so mean," she added. "But it was not his idea."

"But he has a new girlfriend—"

"Oh, that. That is nothing serious."

"And he's gone to France—"

"But that was not his idea," Lenya interrupted. "Alan and your mother and father had—what do you call it?—a pow-wow. They decided it was not good for you, this Marion business, and they went to see him in town."

"All of them?" I asked.

"Yes, Alan too," Lenya answered. "They told him that he was seeing you too much in the city and that he should not see you anymore—he should go away."

"You're kidding!" I said, stunned, starting to get angry.

Lenya shrugged. "They should have done it a long time ago, if you ask me," she said. "But then nobody ask me."

"How could they do that?" I said, sitting up straight, really angry now. "They ruined my life!"

"No, darling, not your life," Lenya said with a gentle laugh and reached out and held me while I cried again, betrayal added to the mix of hurt and loss.

Reliving that awful moment, I walked quickly down Lenya's short, steep driveway, thinking how grateful I'd been to her for telling me. I didn't tell my parents or Alan that I knew about their talk with Marion, and once my anger lessened, it helped me to know that Marion hadn't simply rejected me, that they'd told him to stay away. After a year or so I'd been able to let him go again, keeping only his old letters and a secret hope that one day he'd come back.

"Hep, I'm out here," Lenya called, and I found her carrying a flat of summer flowers up to the terrace. She was wearing loose slacks and a kind of coolie hat that she wore for gardening. "I thought we take these up to the cemetery for Kurtie and Mab," she said lightly, and I froze for a second, unable to move. I'd avoided the cemetery until now. I'd been back at school when the ground had thawed enough for my mother's body to be buried, and I still hated cemeteries, hated the idea of bodies in the ground.

"Come now. You take these," Lenya said, hustling me to the car, pretending not to notice my stricken face. I carried the flat of snapdragons and daisies as Lenya continued blithely: "Mabbie's stone is up now, and you know she *has* to have her flowers."

"Does it look all right?" I managed to ask as we put the flowers and trowels on the backseat and got in the car.

"It is nice. It is simple," Lenya answered. "I like what you choose. It fits with Kurtie's."

"It means so much more than it seems," I said. "I hope people understand."

"Oh, people," Lenya said, with a flash of red nails. "Who cares about people?"

I laughed, and then we were quiet as Lenya drove down the road toward Haverstraw. We passed High Tor, drove through the old quarry road that cut through the mountain and came out on 9W, the two-lane highway that ran parallel to the Hudson. The Tappan Zee was gray green in the afternoon sun, the small town of Haverstraw below us, as we turned left through the gates of Mount Repose. We wound through the cemetery, on the other side of the tor, until we reached the top and parked. With Lenya leading the way, we carried the flowers to the graves at the crest, beside the woods.

After a few winters and springs, Kurt's headstone had a seasoned look, with lush grass and plants all around it. My mother's seemed spare and new beside it. The inscription that I'd chosen while still in North Carolina was also spare, and recently chiseled. It read: MAB ANDERSON, 1904–1953 . . . STAY WELL. Those were the words that I worried wouldn't be understood, but they meant so much to us. In *Cry, the Beloved Country,* and then *Lost in the Stars,* it was the greeting of love and farewell—"Go well, stay well, come well."

In the haunting song "Stay Well," the lyric began, "Stay well, oh keeper of my love, go well throughout all your days." When Irena, the young black woman, said good-bye to her husband, Absalom, for the last time before he was to be put to death, she said, "Go well, stay well." It meant—go with love, with peace, sleep well. On Kurt's headstone there was a passage from *Lost in the Stars*, part of another lyric:

> This is the life of men on earth;
> Out of darkness we come at birth
> Into a lamplit world, and then—
> Go forward into dark again.

I knelt beside the graves with Lenya and began planting the flowers, trying to dispel my fear of the dead, my sickening thoughts of worms and maggots, and realized that I didn't know how to plant the daisies that I held in my hand. I suddenly saw my mother kneeling in our garden—weeding, concentrated; her sundress, her freckled shoulders—and heard myself saying, "Can I help you, Mommy?" and heard her answer, "No, darling, it would take too long." I started to cry, with three-year-old love, because she'd never taught me how to garden. After a while, I'd stopped asking.

CHAPTER TEN

MY FATHER had sent me a train ticket for my trip to California, and I boarded happily at Grand Central Station. I was eager to see him, eager to leave the grief that was surfacing back on South Mountain Road and erupting from beneath my skin. He and Gilda would meet me at Pasadena, he said, with the car he'd just bought for me. We had wrangled about the car. My father was in love with foreign cars; he'd bought a Hillman Minx for himself and another for Gilda. I wanted something simple and American—a Ford convertible or a Jeepster like the one at home. We'd left it that he would keep that in mind. It would be a surprise.

There was another reason that I was happy to board the train, to settle into a compartment that was like a miniature hotel room. Some of my favorite times had been spent on trains, going back and forth to the West Coast. I loved how confined the compartments were, everything neat, shiny and in its place. The stainless-steel sink pulled down from the wall. The seats turned into enclosed bunk beds during the night; the top berth, where I usually was, had its own porthole window. And best of all, the train rocked all the time, like a moving cradle. Between my mother's edgy, smoke-filled womb and the Scottish nurse who didn't believe in picking up babies, I was left with a longing for small, en-closed places like little rooms with low ceilings, or curtained beds—and if they rocked like backseats and Pullman cars, all the better.

The other wonderful thing about a train trip was that there was nothing to do except read, look out the window and eat every once in a while. Since reading and staring out windows were my two favorite things to do as a child, I could have spent my life riding trains. But only in style, of course. I didn't know about trains where people sat up all night, or about people who rode boxcars, although I'd watch, counting the cars, as endless freight trains went by. I knew about the Twentieth Century and the Atchison, Topeka, where kindly black porters in white jackets took care of us, and where breakfast was served in a dining car, with fresh linen and a rose on every table.

There was one moment one night that frightened me, when I came face to face with the real world that I knew so little about. It was at the end of the war, early 1945, and we were going to Los Angeles so that my father could work with Ingrid Bergman on *Joan of Lorraine*. I was alone in the compartment, reading *The Secret Garden* by a night light. It was a dark night outside—no moon, no stars, no town nearby—when suddenly another train hurtled along the track right beside us. It was full of shouting, hooting black faces, only about two feet away, packed against the window, and, at first, I thought they were angry, thought they wanted to take over our train. And then I saw that they were grin-ning as they shouted and waved caps in the air. I realized that it was a whole trainload of young black soldiers, on their way to some front somewhere. By the time I smiled and waved back, their train had sped past us. I sat there, the book open, thinking about them, wondering where they were going and whether I'd ever meet up with any of them again. A quick smile, a shout—is that it for a whole lifetime? Questions like that could occupy me for hours, especially on a train, thinking, dreaming, rocking.

I barely remember the first trip. I was four, and Kurt and Lenya went with us. My father must have taken a screenwriting job, but I don't know which one. They all went pretty much the same way. My father would clutch, take a job for the money in Los Angeles, get terribly depressed as soon as we'd cross the Mississippi, complain bitterly about the sunny weather, the studio system that thought he should write by the clock, everyone he worked with, the general terrain: "It's all as ephemeral as the great mud hills," he'd say. "One good rain'll wash it all away." Sometimes he'd quit the picture; sometimes he'd just take his name off it, but he'd always leave as miserable as when he'd arrived and barely smile, or straighten his stooped shoulders, until he felt the rain on his face and smelled the wet woods of Rockland County.

Kurt was much more sanguine about the whole thing. I remember him trying to cheer my father up. "Max," he'd say, as my father sat on the beach, draped in a wet towel, wet handkerchiefs on his balding head, topped off by a jungle helmet, "you come out here, you take their money and you go home." But my father couldn't do it that way. He'd try, but he'd end up either going off in a sulk or blowing up at somebody important to his welfare. He'd tell Kurt that it wasn't as easy for him—he didn't pluck melodies out of the air, as Kurt did—he had to believe completely in what he was doing, and how could he believe in a picture that he was just doing for money with a bunch of idiots? Kurt agreed that they were, primarily, dealing with idiots; he just didn't take it as seriously. I never heard him say this, but I think he felt so deeply grateful for being in this country, instead of Nazi Germany, that a few idiots in the theatre or the movie business couldn't get him down that much. For him, the trips west were not such an ordeal.

I watched as the train slid past backyards, blowing soot on lines of laundry, skimming past eastern towns as the day darkened. I closed my eyes and tried to picture the house on the beach the summer that I was four. It was close to Pacific Coast Highway in Santa Monica, and I could see the picket fence and the car burning out of control on the shoulder beside the house. It was my most vivid memory of the summer—flames shooting up against the midnight sky and the hill opposite, fire trucks screaming to a halt and everyone running outside.

I could picture the beach in the early morning, the only time that my father liked to swim, because the fog still hung low. And I could see him later in the day in what we called his "Arab Chieftain" outfit, wet handkerchiefs framing his face like a headdress. The only other memory of that trip was going with my parents and Kurt and Lenya to the Venice Amusement Park on my birthday. I loved the revolving tunnel, the hall of mirrors and the roller coaster, and couldn't understand why they didn't want to ride it with me over and over again.

Once the berth was made up and I could lie there in the dark and gaze out the window, I let my mind wander to the next trip, the year I was ten, the end of the war and the brief encounter with the trainload of soldiers. We were going to visit Virginia Maynard, and I couldn't wait. Of course, my father was going to work and was in his usual doldrums, but I didn't pay much attention to that—I just wanted to see Virginia, to feel her thin arms around me, to see her sweet, crooked smile. Virginia had married my mother's first husband, Charles Maynard, after he and my mother were divorced. They became friends, all of them, my mother and father and Charles and Virginia. My mother saved some yellowed photographs of the four of them fooling around at the beach before I was born.

Virginia, whom we mostly called Diddy (a niece's mispronunciation of Ginny), had come into my life earlier that year. Charles had died suddenly that fall, and Virginia was grieving. They'd been very happy; they'd wanted children but Charles had died too soon. He was only forty, my mother had said, when she'd explained that Virginia needed a change, needed friends, and would I please be good to her when she came to stay for a while. I found that she was easy to be good to. She was gentle and warm, with a soft voice and an unassuming presence. She was, obviously, everything that my mother wasn't, and I took to her the way the duckling automatically wobbles after its mother. I didn't want to *be* Virginia, the way I'd always wanted to be Nancy. Virginia wasn't even pretty, not by South Mountain Road standards anyway. I simply wanted to love her, to help comfort her and to let her love me.

Staring at the blackness of the countryside going by, I pictured Virginia's tear-stained face as I tried to amuse her with my dolls, puppet shows, or by pulling old costumes out of the trunk that we kept in the third-floor guest room where she slept. She did get better, after a month or so, and would dress up with me and put on plays that we made up, go for walks when the leaves were turning, read with me, or invade Martha's kitchen and cook special desserts. I loved her as much, or more, than I'd loved Marion, but it was different. There wasn't the physical longing that I'd felt for Marion, even at seven. I wondered, drifting off to sleep to the rumble of the wheels, whether I loved her so much because she was alone. Was it that same thing of wanting someone just for me? Everyone was a couple and I was by myself, outside looking in, the little pig that cried, "Me too." Was it that selfish?

It probably was. I squirmed in the cozy berth and shut my eyes against myself as I realized that I'd cared more about my mother during those last months when she was alone than I had for years. Maybe I just needed to come first with someone. Maybe, because my father was gone and no longer playing my mother and me against each other, we could break through to an extent. It had just been a beginning. "Beginnings end," I whispered to myself, "endings begin."

Or maybe it had been because my mother's pretensions had dropped away, leaving her so vulnerable, a raw nerve without skin. I'd heard from her friends, and from Martha, that about a month before she died, she'd become irrationally happy. She'd called everyone up and said that she was giving a party because Max was coming home. She even called people in town, people that she wanted to impress, people who only came because of my father's status: "Max is coming home, and I'm giving a big party for him!" It seemed that she really believed this even though, at the time, he wouldn't answer her letters or give her his new address. With all her energy she prepared for a party. It was embarrassing, everyone said, and heartbreaking. "Oh, God," I whispered to my version of Christ in his sky-blue robe, "forgive me, I should have gone home. I should have put out her cigarette, laid her on the grass, spooned hot coffee into her mouth . . ."

She's in the dining room, wearing her black velvet pantsuit, clunky gold bracelets dangling as she rearranges the table.

"You'd think after all this time," she mutters, "Martha would know how to set a table. And you, darling," she says as she glances

up at me, speechless in the doorway, "don't you know yet that the salad fork goes on the outside?"

"You're not dead," I manage to say.

"Of course, I'm not dead," she says impatiently. "Now help me with this. We're having a party for your father and Gilda."

"Why didn't you tell me you weren't dead? Why didn't you let me know, Mommy?"

"I just went away for a while, darling," she says more softly. "I didn't think you'd care so much."

"Of course I care." I run to her, repeating, "You're not dead! I'm so glad—so glad!"

The dream was still vivid in the first light as I realized, with a thud in my chest, that she *was* dead—it was just a dream. I went back to sleep and then was jolted awake by the train as it lurched unexpectedly. I opened my eyes to see the outskirts of Chicago, but my senses were engulfed by the smell of eucalyptus, a California tree, a California smell. At first I didn't know what it was. Then I remembered waking up the same way, back in my bed at home, missing Virginia. Her sloping gardens, even her house, were permeated by the smell of the eucalyptus trees that surrounded them.

Virginia's house was on Woodrow Wilson Drive, near the intersection of Laurel and Mulholland. It was set against the hillside, dark and woodsy, and the gardens, on different levels, went all the way down to a high fence at the edge of Laurel Canyon. It was a small house with two bedrooms upstairs and a guest room and bath downstairs with a separate entrance. My parents stayed downstairs, and I was given the small, dark bedroom next to Virginia's that faced the street. Almost no sunshine came through the trees, the bed was set in a paneled nook, and on the wall above my feet was a large crucifix, as if Christ were nailed to the wood of the room. His body was bone white and very dead—not the living image that I loved—and because I found the room depressing, I spent most of my nights beside Virginia in her canopied double bed.

Her room was bright, with windows on three sides and a view of the hills and Mulholland Drive. I loved waking up in her bed, hearing the calls of mourning doves, smelling the eucalyptus leaves and the trace of night-blooming jasmine that still lingered in the air. Virginia and my father were usually up first, my father puttering in the kitchen as he did at home, and they'd give me a cup of coffee that was mostly milk, and some cereal, and get me ready for school.

I'd gone into the middle of the fifth grade at the Wonderland School, which was farther down the canyon, and to get there I took a school bus for the first time. The bus stopped at the corner of Woodrow Wilson, and I walked there by myself and joined the three or four other children who were waiting. It made me happy to be like everybody else, to live in a small house, to ride the bus without the Street School stigma of coming from the "rich Commie nudist colony." I even made friends at Wonderland, another first, and there was a boy who liked me. He shyly asked me to be his partner in folk-dancing class and sat on the bench next to me at lunchtime, under the huge, shady trees.

In February it began to rain, which improved my father's mood, and I sloshed my way to the school bus, in rubber boots and a yellow slicker. I'd never seen rain like that. It came down in sheets, almost walls of rain, and it didn't let up. It was like standing under the dam at home. The garden was too soggy to walk in; Laurel Canyon had a river of mud running down it, and the paneling in my room smelled damp and musty. Virginia would light a fire in the living room fireplace, and I'd dry off in front of it after school, then curl up on the sofa beside it and read or do homework. It was probably the most contented I'd ever been.

I'm not sure what my parents were doing during the time at Virginia's. I barely remember my mother being there. She'd dash in for a change of clothes and makeup, then dash out again. My father was still working on his play about Joan of Arc—he'd started it the year before—and he might have been doing a screenplay too. He spent most of the time holed up in the downstairs room. Every once in a while he'd go meet with Ingrid Bergman about the play, which she had agreed to do, and he'd take me along to play with her daughter, Pia. Bergman was still with her husband, Peter Lindstrom, who was only spoken of derisively. According to my parents, he managed her money, doling it out to her a dollar at a time. They also said that he'd been a dentist in Sweden and now called himself a brain surgeon—"The drill slipped," my mother had said, laughing.

I didn't want to play with Pia any more than I ever wanted to play with the three or four other children of my parents' friends that they insisted I be nice to. Pia was pleasant, as I remember, and I liked her beautiful mother and the house, high up in Benedict Canyon, but I would have much rather stayed at Virginia's, warmed by her fireplace and her sweet smile.

We changed trains at Chicago, and I settled into my compartment, looking forward to two more drifting, dreaming days and nights. After the train pulled out, I took a walk through the cars, opening and closing the heavy, metal doors between them, until I reached the lounge car at the back. The drinkers and gamblers were already going strong, and I sat in a corner and watched a poker game. I couldn't help envisioning my mother there, bracelets dangling, cigarette holder clenched, her eyes squinting against the smoke that drifted up through her curls. She spent almost all of her time on the train playing poker. We'd have to go get her to take her to the dining car, and then she'd hurry back again. She loved the ruse of looking so small and pretty and rich. The sharks would look at her and think, "We can take her, that's for sure," and then she'd bluff them out of half their money before they caught on.

She'd been particularly excited on this trip to Virginia's. It had been a monotonous year back home. We were winning the war; it would end soon, and all of her focused energy, once more, had nowhere to go. She was back to gardening, crossword puzzles, canasta with Bunny and Lenya. On top of that, my father had no new play that year, so there were no handwritten pages to criticize and then type, no rehearsals and out-of-town tryouts. My father had been very depressed after the failure of *Storm Operation* and had spent most of his time in the cabin, moping around the house, or in the woods, smoking fish.

He'd built a smokehouse near the cabin and there pursued his love of smoked fish, particularly mackerel. It began as part of the war effort and took on a life of its own. He'd buy the mackerel in bulk—the same way that he'd buy twenty shiny shirts and twenty Anderson-plaid ties from the Sears catalogue—and spend days smoking it, a few fish at a time, in the small smokehouse. He'd go up and down the road, giving fish to everyone, until they could no longer stand the sight of a mackerel. The thing that really drove my mother crazy was that he *smelled* like a smoked mackerel. Between his cultivated hayseed look, his shirts and ties from Sears and the fact that he smelled like a smoked fish, she couldn't take him anywhere. They were invited to all sorts of fancy openings and parties in town that my mother wanted to attend, but how could she go with a hayseed husband who smelled like a mackerel? Was that part of his plan? Probably. It was even better than his trick of staying in the cabin, saying that he had to work or think, when she invited socially desirable people to the country for parties or weekends.

My mother was, understandably, craving people and excitement by the time we boarded the train for Los Angeles. While I loved it at Virginia's, I think it was too tame for my mother, and by mid-March she'd convinced my father that we had overstayed our welcome and should move to a hotel. Of course, I didn't want to go, but by the beginning of April we'd moved to a cottage at the Bel-Air Hotel. It was simpler then than it later became. The grounds were smaller, though just as beautiful, with low-hanging sycamores and a stone bridge over a wide stream filled with swans. It was owned, at the time, by Burton Schutt and his wife, a couple whom I vaguely remember as a tall, blond man and a small, dark woman. My mother made friends with them and was in her element—maid service, room service, glamorous people all around her. She went to the races with Lee and Ira Gershwin, sometimes taking me along, placing a bet on a horse I'd chosen because I liked the name. I actually picked a few winners for her.

I was transferred out of Wonderland to a public school in West Los Angeles at which I lasted three days. The school was large and low, with what seemed like acres of concrete. Several languages were spoken; English seemed the least useful, and I was totally lost. By the end of the third day, back at our cottage, I sobbed so miserably that my parents agreed that I could go back to the Wonderland School. The main problem was that I would have to be driven—the school was in a different district—but my father agreed to drive me in the morning and pick me up later. It was one of the sweetest things he ever did for me. He'd wake me at seven, fumble around in the small kitchen, finding something for breakfast, and then drive me all the way to Laurel Canyon so that I could be at school by eight-thirty. In the afternoon he'd either pick me up at school, or I'd take the bus to Virginia's and wait for him there.

Sometimes, if my father was in the midst of Hollywood woes, I'd spend the night at Virginia's, tucked in her canopy bed, breathing in the eucalyptus.

"Diddy," I ask, in the middle of the night, above the sounds of crickets and coyotes, "can I always come back here? Will you always want me?"

"Of course I'll always want you," Virginia says sleepily. "You're my little girl."

"You will?" I ask, suffused with happiness.

"I promise," Virginia says, turning to me, her eyes gentle, her fingers gentle as she pushes back my hair. "I couldn't have my own little girl—we tried and I couldn't—so you're it." She's smiling, her gray-green eyes teasing, and I go back to sleep, feeling a safety I'd barely imagined.

We went home in June, and I missed Virginia terribly. I wrote to her often and, at times, lay in bed at night, reaching out my arms, calling her name. But new things came into my life. I went to a private school in the city, and Marion came back to South Mountain Road. I fell in love with him all over again when I was eleven, but I still longed for Virginia. We finally went back to California two years later. I was twelve by then, and even though I didn't want to leave the road and Marion, I couldn't wait to see Virginia.

A visit was arranged soon after we arrived. I knew that Virginia had remarried and adopted a baby, a little boy, but I didn't expect it to make any difference. She still loved me; I could have my old room with the dead-white Christ on the wall and still curl up in her bed in the middle of the night. But it wasn't like that. My old room was now the baby's room, the paneling painted white, the crucifix nowhere to be seen, and when I asked if I could still sleep in her bed, she explained that her husband slept there now.

She offered me the guest room downstairs, but I didn't spend the night. I was glad that she had a baby and was happy, but I'd been replaced. "But you promised," I wanted to cry, as I suppose most children want to cry at times, and I felt a terrible loss that I couldn't express. I told my parents that the visit was nice and I went back to see her again a couple of times that summer, but it was never the same. My love for Virginia gradually withered until, back home the next winter, it was as if she had died and all I had left was a sweet memory and scent-filled dreams of Laurel Canyon and eucalyptus trees.

When I was sixteen, and a senior at Nyack High School, Virginia did die. There's a lifetime between twelve and sixteen, and when my mother came down the stairs and into the living room, her face covered with tears, and told me that she'd just spoken to Virginia's husband and that Virginia had died of cancer, I must have looked at her blankly for a moment, because she went into a tearful tirade: "What's wrong with you? You loved Virginia so much and you're not even crying! Are you just going to sit there and look at me? Don't you care?" She dashed back up the stairs before I could begin to explain that of course I cared. I felt badly for Virginia's husband, for her little boy, but, in a way, she'd died for me a long time ago. I *did* cry, alone in my room, but it was for the memory of that rare time of contentment when I was ten and walked home from the bus stop in the rain and dried off in front of Virginia's warm fire.

After the train rolled past the flat fields of the Midwest, we entered the deserts and mountains of the real West, vast expanses of nothingness, and then tunnels and trestled bridges cutting through the Rockies. I had one more night in the berth to dream and rock, and I knew that the next morning I'd wake up to the sight of orange groves. I'd always been excited by the rows of trees, bright with oranges, sometimes with smudge pots glowing along the rows. It meant that we were almost there.

I woke early—it was still dark—and lay there, half watching the real world slide by, half wondering about my father and Gilda, about the house in Agoura. Would I like it as much as Laurel Canyon, or the cottage in Bel-Air? After I'd stopped missing Virginia's so much, I'd really liked it at the Bel-Air. It was a perfect place to play princess. It looked like a castle to me, and I could wander beside the stream and the swans and pretend that it was Buckingham Palace and I was Princess Margaret. I'd make up games for my homely older sister to play with me, and we'd tease the imaginary guards.

There was no pool at the Bel-Air then, and as the days got warmer I was allowed to cross the road and swim in Greer Garson's pool. I don't remember her—I think a maid watched me—but I do remember Katharine Hepburn vividly. A couple of times a week she'd pick me up in the afternoon and take me to her house in Beverly Hills to swim. She'd wait for me next to the side gate at the Bel-Air so that no one would see her and annoy her. I don't think they would have recognized her anyway. Her face was all freckles, her chestnut hair falling out of the bun on top of her head; she always wore large sunglasses, and a kind of army-surplus jumpsuit covered everything else.

She'd drive me to her house, which reminded me of Rockland County houses, give me a sandwich and milk on the brick terrace that overlooked the lawn and then go down to the pool with me. Sometimes Spencer Tracy was there, on the terrace or beside the pool, although I don't remember saying more than hello to him. I don't remember saying much to Katharine Hepburn either, or her to me. We swam together, played badminton, and she gave me diving lessons.

My parents in Malibu before I was born.

My mother (Mab Maynard)—as an ingenue.

With my mother.

With Martha.

With my parents on the lawn at the back of the house.

With my father.

My mother and Lotte Lenya at the tower. My mother was then head of the civil defense for Rockland County.

From left to right: Martha's husband, Willis; Jules, who worked for the Weills; my father and Kurt Weill at the tower.

Nyack Trots Out Sock, Buskin for Russian War Relief...

With Mary MacArthur. The Russian War Relief Benefit caused
a great deal of blacklisting later.

The dining room.

My mother and father playing chess in the living room.

With my father.

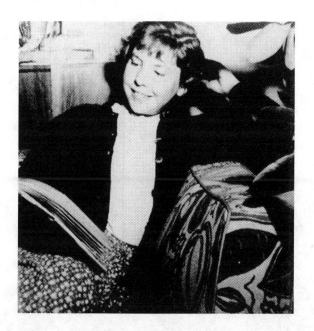

At fourteen and in love—

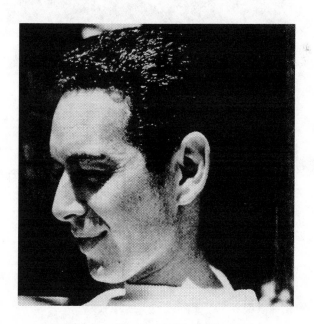

—with Marion Hargrove, Prince Charming.

The last photograph of my parents together.

I called her Kate, because everyone did. I knew that she was a movie star, but I didn't know how really famous she was, because I rarely went to movies.

At home the nearest movie theatre was five miles away, in Haverstraw, and someone would've had to drive me. Also, since I'd been carried screaming out of *Snow White*, and, later, out of *Pinocchio*, movies had been restricted for me. Marion had taken me to some vintage comedies when I was seven and eight years old, but that was about it.

So, at ten, I'd never seen Greer Garson, Ingrid Bergman or Katharine Hepburn on the screen and wasn't as impressed as I might have been. And, as I've mentioned before, nearly everyone we knew was famous in one way or another, so I tended to take fame for granted. I also took for granted the fact that they were all so nice to me. I was aware that some people were nice to me because they wanted to ingratiate themselves with my father, but there were others, like Katharine Hepburn, who seemed simply to like me. She didn't want or need anything from my parents; she didn't even spend time with them.

Lying in the berth, remembering, with the darkness rushing past outside, I thought about Bunny's open door, Lenya's open heart, Virginia's love, Katharine Hepburn's generosity, and wondered if they'd sensed my yearning for a mother's love that I didn't even know was missing. They may have seen my mother, rushing here and there, focusing on everything except me, and their maternal instincts had kicked in. They were all childless, and I was, in a way, motherless. By that time, it was as much my fault as my mother's, because I was keeping her at arm's length, but there was still a void that cried to be filled.

Ingrid Bergman had a daughter of her own, didn't need to fill any void of mine and was as nice to me as she was to everyone. I idolized her beauty but didn't ask anything of her during the couple of years that she was around us a lot. I treasured a gold charm that she gave me for my charm bracelet—a royal flush poker hand that said on the back, "Love and luck, Ingrid." And, in my usual way of mixing fantasy and reality, I believed that she *was* Joan of Arc. Actually, she came to believe it too, which made things difficult for my father, because he certainly didn't. It wasn't too bad at first when she rehearsed and starred in *Joan of Lorraine* on Broadway. She was wonderful in the part—radiant and ethereal—and wasn't any more temperamental than stars tend to be. But this was New York and the theatre, where the playwright was king, had veto power and could fire anyone, including the director and the star.

The play opened in November 1946, at the Alvin Theatre, and got rave notices, the first raves that my father had seen since 1942 and *The Eve of St. Mark*. The play had a good run, and everything went well until the next summer when my father began working with Bergman and Walter Wanger on the screenplay. Back in Hollywood, on her own turf, Bergman was queen, and the writer, my father, was a lackey. My father always resented this treatment, but Bergman's belief that she was the reincarnation of Joan made the situation even more difficult.

Things weren't going well for Bergman at home—she was about to toss away Dr. Lindstrom and her career for Rossellini and Italy—and if she was suffering certain delusions, who could blame her? Such was my parents' attitude, which I overheard a few times, but when it came to the script, that was something else. Bergman thought she knew better than anyone else what Joan would have thought and said and, even though my father disagreed vehemently, she had the final say.

My father became increasingly miserable and defiant that summer, until he finally woke us in the middle of the night, told my mother to pack our bags, and we hit the road. He left messages for Bergman, Wanger and everyone else involved, saying that he had quit, but he left no forwarding numbers. He simply said that we were driving up the coast, then heading east and couldn't be reached. We drove slowly up to Seattle, following the coast road, stopping at inns and motels and, at nearly every stop, there were frantic messages waiting for my father. They must have called every motel along our route. My father didn't answer any of the messages or accept any of the calls that happened to catch us, and we proceeded—very slowly, it seemed to me—across the northwest, heading for North Dakota.

I didn't mind the first part of the trip. The Pacific coastline—rock cliffs and churning ocean—was breathtaking, and I was cozy, with pillows and blankets, in the backseat of the station wagon that we were driving, but I got restless as we headed east. I wanted to get home—to Marion, to the road—but my father was determined to make this trip last as long as possible, avoiding phone calls all the way. I remember looking forward to seeing the Blackfeet Indians and then being disappointed when I discovered, in a diner on the reservation, that they didn't have black feet. After that, I slept most of the way to North Dakota.

We stopped first in Minot, on our way to Grand Forks and the university, my father's alma mater. It was late when we arrived, and we couldn't find a place to stay. We finally ended up in the basement of a rooming house. My mother complained bitterly about the pipes above and our lumpy beds, but I thought it was exciting. I'd never slept in a basement before. Early the following morning we headed for Grand Forks, where we spent the next couple of days. My father visited former professors, old friends, and everyone made a huge fuss over him. He was, by far, their most successful alumnus, and the attention that was lavished on him eased his mood a bit, but he was still quietly fuming over his latest Hollywood disaster.

My father rarely lost his temper. I remember it happening about once every five years, and when it did, it seemed to me that our mountains would shake. He was usually so good at avoiding conflicts—a master at disappearing before a fight could happen—that I kind of looked forward to the occasional blowup. His explosions were never directed at me, so I could watch and wait and, in a perverse way, hope that I wouldn't miss it.

I watched and waited for the rest of the trip. He was still avoiding phone calls from the West Coast and fuming more and more as he prolonged the trip. While he fumed and my mother complained, I got more and more restless. My father decided that he had to swim in each of the Great Lakes, which took another few days. I remember putting my feet in Lake Superior and thinking I was going to die. By the time we passed Niagara Falls, I was so homesick and in such a bad mood, I wouldn't even lift my head off my pillow to look. My mother pointed excitedly at the spectacle and then was furious with me for being such a pain. I didn't care; I knew I was being a pain, but by then all I wanted was to get home.

We reached upper New York State and then headed south. Finally, the roads narrowed, the woods were my kind of woods, and we were almost home. I was ready to jump out of the car as we reached the road and our driveway. I was joyous as we rounded the curve and the house came into view. It was evening; lights were on in the kitchen and the dining room, and I bolted from the car as soon as it stopped. Martha was coming out to meet us, and the phone was ringing in the kitchen. My father got out of the car and walked straight to the ringing phone. He picked it up, listened for a second and then shouted, "You big, dumb, goddamn Swede!"

The explosion had happened, and, standing outside the window, I looked at South Mountain to see if it was shaking.

At dawn, the orange groves became visible, miles and miles of them, and I stayed in my berth, watching the California sunrise, brighter than in the East, and tried not to remember the worst summer, the one at Zuma Beach when I was fourteen. It was the summer that Marion spent a lot of time with a redheaded starlet, while Alison was at home with the babies. It was the summer that I was so miserable that I barely left my room, even though the broad beach was right outside our door. It was the summer that Carole Landis killed herself over Rex Harrison. He was at our house that day, talking with my father about *Anne of the Thousand Days,* when the police arrived and told him that Carole Landis, a young actress who was his mistress at the time, had committed suicide. I'd watched from my window as Harrison, shaken, left with the police.

I threw back the blanket, jumped out of the berth, pulled down the sink and began splashing water on my face. It wouldn't be like that, not ever again. I would never again feel as much hurt as I had that summer. I dressed quickly, packed and then sat by the window as the train moved out of the orange groves and headed slowly for the city.

CHAPTER ELEVEN

MY FATHER and Gilda were waiting at the station. I saw them from the steps of the train as we came to a gradual halt. My father was leaning against the car that he'd bought for me, a shy smile on his face, and I knew right away that it wasn't what I'd asked for. I didn't know *what* it was, not knowing or caring about cars, but I could tell that it was the kind of sporty, foreign car that he loved and I didn't. Gilda was standing off to the side, as if not wanting to intrude, and I jumped down from the steps of the train and ran right into my father's arms. We hugged for a minute, and I turned to Gilda, including her, hugging and kissing her too. I barely knew her, but I was trying to make this as easy as possible for my father.

"I missed you, I missed you!" I said to my father, and then turned to the car, trying to keep the dismay out of my voice. "What's this, Daddy?"

"It's for you," he answered, his smile hopeful now, "a Sunbeam Talbot."

"It looks great—thanks. I don't think I've ever seen one."

"It's better than the Hillman," my father said, encour-

134

aged. "Better pickup, and it's a convertible, did you notice?"

"Oh, it is, yeah. How d'you get the top down?"

"Um, let's see," he said, and we struggled with various knobs and levers but couldn't budge the canvas top.

"Let's try later," I said finally, and we piled my bags in the back of the car and took off for Agoura. Actually, I don't think we ever got the top down, but I gradually became fond of the car—it was mine, and my father had given it to me.

I drove while my father gave me pointers and directions from the passenger seat, and Gilda drove the Hillman by herself. We met outside the Lapworth house, high on a Valley hill, and carried my bags to the front door, where Martha and Little Terry were waiting for us. It was strange to see Martha here instead of at home, and I realized, as I hugged her and went inside, that my father was trying to make this place seem like home to me. It was sweet of him, and I tried hard to fit in with his hopeful plan, even though we both knew that this arid hill and imitation castle couldn't compare with the damp woods and cinder-block castles of South Mountain Road.

We ate at the long library table in the living room, an area with a stone floor and high beams. The candles were lit, and Martha served us—me, my father and Gilda. I kept glancing at her as we made small talk, thinking how much she looked like my mother—a somewhat distorted version of my mother. Gilda was five feet tall, weighed about a hundred pounds, had short brown hair and a pretty face, but the whole effect was marred by a wandering left eye. She'd turn to me and smile, with one eye focused and the other eye looking at the wall. I got used to it after a while, but it was disconcerting at first.

Gilda was wearing an outfit that my mother had given her—a full, forties skirt and a white blouse. It had looked sexy on my mother; on Gilda it looked girlish. Gilda probably didn't remember that this had come from my mother or she wouldn't have worn it. After all, my mother had given her lots of clothes. When they'd both worked on *Celanese Theatre*, my mother as story editor and Gilda as a production assistant, my mother had liked Gilda and felt sorry for her, a young woman alone, supporting two children. My mother had invited Gilda and her children, Laurel and Craig, to the country for weekends, given her clothes she no longer wore, books and dolls that I'd outgrown. I think that was when my father and Gilda first noticed each other.

Aside from her looks, Gilda didn't seem to be like my mother at all. She was soft and sweet, almost sugary, and she adored my father. Where my mother would prod and criticize, Gilda simply gazed at my father and murmured, "Oh, you're so wonderful, Max." I figured that he needed this kind of devotion—after life with my mother and her ultimate betrayal—and I found it rather soothing myself.

As I went upstairs, then went to sleep in the room that used to have no ceiling, I entered one of those blank spaces of time that I've mentioned. I have only two memories of the month that I spent at the Lapworth house. One is of a day that I spent at the beach, and the other is of a day in early July when I received a letter from Lenya and knew that I had to go home. It wasn't that anything had happened, or I don't *think* anything had happened—I don't remember. I just know that as much as my father tried to create a new home for me, it didn't work. I longed for my old one.

The day at the beach was a day of searching. It was an overcast, June day, the low tide seeping into the fog as I drove my new car to Santa Monica and up the coast to Zuma, looking for the houses that we'd stayed in. I didn't have much luck. The house in Santa Monica, on Pacific Coast Highway, had been nondescript from the front—just a garage and a high picket fence—and there were rows of houses like that.

The house at Zuma Beach was right next to the Coast Guard Station—I remembered it vividly, with the flag flying out front—but when I found the station there was no house beside it, just the dunes that we used to cross to get to the water's edge. I wondered how a house and garden could disappear so quickly, but it had—there was nothing there. I parked anyway, and the sun began to break through as I crossed the dunes and then sat in their shade, seeing the shadowy figures of the recent past, flashes of the summer that I didn't want to remember.

I'm thirteen, almost fourteen, and I'm sitting on the beach beside the dunes, almost all of me covered by a favorite summer dress. I have braces, chubby cheeks—called Anderson cheeks by the family—and new breasts that I don't know what to do with. My inclination is to hide them, to pretend they're not there. Everyone else here is beautiful. Even my mother is intimidated by how beautiful everyone is. She went into town last week and came back with yellow-blond curls. My father took one appalled look and sent her straight back to the beauty parlor.

Elizabeth Taylor rides her horse on our beach, even more beautiful in real life than she was in National Velvet. *Her horse is beautiful too. She lets me ride with her one day, on a horse that I've borrowed from the Viertels, and she's very nice to me. Peter Viertel and Irwin Shaw are friends of my father, and their wives are beautiful. The Viertels have a canyon house and a stable, and I sometimes ride with their daughter Victoria, who at my age is already beautiful.*

Marion brings the redheaded starlet to the beach nearly every day. She's very beautiful, with long, red hair, and she gives me about fifty packets of bobby pins that all have her picture on the covers. She doesn't say very much and she giggles a lot, and I want to be her more than I've ever wanted to be anybody, even Nancy. I feel a bit sorry for Alison, at home with the babies, but no one seems to expect the Hargrove marriage to last. I certainly hope it doesn't. I want Marion to be free when I'm old enough for him.

My father is on the beach for a change, wearing his jungle helmet and being morose with Irwin Shaw and Peter Viertel. They're lamenting Hollywood and saying that this is the last time—they'll never come back again. Then they begin laughing about Irving Lazar, their mutual agent. Lazar likes to show up at the beach in costume—a cowboy hat and boots, or something black and flamenco—and since he's round, bald and five feet tall, he looks a bit ridiculous. My father is laughing, tears in his eyes, as he tells them how he always knows when Irving is coming—when he sees a large Cadillac heading up Pacific Coast Highway, with nobody in it, Irving is on his way.

Marion and the starlet approach me, hand in hand, and stand above me in the shadow of the dune. My feet are bare, my long cotton skirt tucked around my ankles, and Marion studies my feet for a minute as I play with the sand.

"You know, Hep," he says finally, "you have very beautiful toes." They amble off down the beach, and I sit there, wishing that I were a clam or an abalone, and that I could pull my shell around me and be pulled out to sea beneath a breaking wave. No one reassures me that it will get better. No one says, "You'll bloom, you'll see." People say, "Well, you'll lose your baby fat one of these days"—things like that. I didn't notice Elizabeth Taylor having any baby fat, or Lee Remick, who was in my class at Miss Hewitt's. Lee Remick was so perfect at thirteen that the rest of us gaped at her in awe.

One day in May, the spring before this awful summer, my mother had found me crying in front of my bathroom mirror. She asked me why I was crying, and I didn't want to tell her. I didn't trust her with my confidences, but she wouldn't leave, and finally I said, "I think I'm really ugly."

"Don't worry, darling," my mother answered, "lots of really homely women marry very handsome men." She went on to give

me a few examples, but by then I was too devastated to listen.

One evening I leave the beach house to go with my parents to a screening of Joan of Arc. *It's just us, Marion and his friend, and a few others. The movie is long and dreadful, and at the end there's an awkward silence. Marion breaks it by muttering, "It just goes to show, a woman's place is over a hot stove." Nobody laughs. His starlet doesn't even giggle. Of course, I think it's funny.*

Back at the house in Agoura, the sun setting over the dry hills, I found the letter from Lenya waiting for me. Lenya wrote just the way she spoke. She typed, the words running off the edge of the page, and then she'd add in the margins whatever she'd forgotten.

July 6th, 1953

Hesper dear,

Thank you for your letter. I could just see you there, sitting having your coffee in a living room, which had no roof when I saw it last. It looked lovely with stars shining right into your cup. And I remember the stillness of the place. Well, I guess all that has changed by now. I cant tell you, how happy I was that you spent a few days with me. I know darling, how you feel about So.Mt.Rd. I cling to it too and have less reason than you have, having been born here. It holds so many happy memories, that one hates to leave them and not knowing where to find new ones . . . But darling, don't look back too much. It's different with me. I know it sounds maudlin to say, you have your life before you, but you have and you should never be afraid of new people. You have a rare gift, the gift of being loved on first sight. You don't have to do anything. I am sure, you will leave California with many new friends and I hope, you will get good parts to play. So you have already two very definite talents to choose from. One is acting, the other writing. Maybe you can do both. I rarely have seen George as enthusiastic about a story as he was about yours. And you know, he is too serious about writing and his taste is impeccable. He would not flatter at any price. And he does love what you have done. So Hep, be happy, go lucky!

Julie Sloane had a 4th of July party. A bonnefire, with hamburgers and marshmallows cooked in the open. It was a damp and chilly evening, no mosquitoes though (George said, they have too much sense to come out on an evening like this one). One lonely firecracker tried to create some illusion, but gave up in the dampness of the evening.

This is about all darling. Your wish for my happiness is a sweet thought and I wish it too. But it seems that I have run out of pennies for that wishing well . . . It might still happen . . . Write again if you find time. And all my love darling from us both.

kisses, Lenya

I put the letter back in the envelope, smiling, tears in my eyes, and wondered what she'd meant about me being loved at first sight. I went immediately to, "What about second sight? What about third? What then?" And my talents—I knew that I had them, but what was the point of pursuing them? They wouldn't get me what I wanted. They wouldn't make me beautiful, even though I knew that I'd improved since that thirteen-year-old summer. They wouldn't make Marion love me or turn me into a *McCall's* cover.

In the album that my mother had put together, with pictures of me from infancy through high school, there was a photograph of me at six or seven, wheeling a baby carriage filled with dolls and wearing a bride's veil made out of cheesecloth. I could see that it was silly—the mommy bride—but it was still my dream, still the only thing I really wanted.

Lenya so clearly wanted me to go forward with my life, but her letter made me so homesick that I sat there in the Agoura twilight, thinking about summer on South Mountain Road. It would be warm and sticky, with an occasional thunderstorm, and I'd spend my days at the pond, watching the toddlers—as I had Nancy's and Alison's—play in the shallow water and the sandbox. I'd give them a boost to the top of the bathhouse, only about four feet, and we'd lie on towels on the tarred roof until we were dripping and had to go back down to the cool water's edge. There was a rope that marked the drop, from the shallow water to the deep, and I'd watch them carefully so that no one went out too far.

I was supposed to go forward, and all I wanted was to go home. There would be different toddlers at the pond— Nancy's babies were young boys now, and after Marion left, Alison had moved to Nyack with the children. But there would be other, newer babies. My father told me that Joan and Sidney Simon were in the process of buying our house and they had four small children. I heard the words but didn't really take them in. I couldn't imagine another family in our house, the Carroll French furniture replaced, Henry Poor's paintings off the walls, strange children playing in my mother's gardens. I wondered if the Simons would take care of the gardens—the weeds could grow so quickly.

I told my father that I had to go home. I didn't want to upset him, so I made excuses—there were so many things that I had to take care of before starting at Barnard. He said that he understood, that he would probably be moving in with Gilda soon anyway, that the house was inconvenient, that it was hard to have Martha here. I left my car with my father, promising to come back, making him promise that he would come and visit me in New York. I called Nancy and Alan, asking if I could stay there for a while, and then I flew home, leaving everything to dismantle behind me.

With me gone, my father left the Lapworth house, moved in with Gilda and sent Martha and Little Terry back to their small house in West Nyack. Martha had bought the house some time ago, when she was married to Willis Jackson, no doubt with help from my father, but now she would be back there without a job, for the first time since she'd come to work for my father when she was eighteen. I was surprised by how easy it was. My mother had tried to get rid of Martha for twenty years, without making a dent in my father's stone wall, and now Gilda had managed it in a matter of weeks.

The next thing I heard, when I arrived at Alan and Nancy's, was that the Caniffs were planning to take in Martha and Little Terry. Martha would cook and they would sleep there during the week, going home on weekends. This was practically over Willie's dead body, but in the end, Willie didn't have much to say about it. So Bunny and Milton had taken in my Toby, and soon Martha would be there too. I cried when I heard all this, and cried again when I saw three of my mother's prized rose bushes planted and tended in Nancy and Alan's front yard.

The Simons moved into our house—always our house to me—sometime during the summer, and the whole feeling of the place changed. It became a "young-family house," a child-centered house that thrived on its disarray. Joan was a Lewisohn and had grown up with money, estates and the family art collection. Probably in reaction, she seemed to have a carelessness about things. She hung a Picasso in the downstairs bathroom, a couple of Renoirs in the girls' rooms; antiques were covered with toys, and small children were everywhere.

Joan herself was the epitome of expensive bohemianism. Pregnant again, she had long, dark braids and wore peasant blouses, skirts and sandals. She turned the apartment over the garage into a studio for Sidney, and they built a huge playroom off the pump room. The original design was obliterated, as were the gardens. Untended and trampled, the gardens grew wild even faster than I'd imagined they would.

It struck me, on my first, cautious visit to the house, that my mother's upbringing, in loneliness and poverty, had caused her to value beautiful things and flowers above all else, while Joan's upbringing, in the midst of wealth and beauty, had left her with a desire to toss it all away. I empathized with Joan; when given the opportunity, I tended to toss things away as well. It was people and babies and animals that mattered to Joan and me—we'd kind of had it with the worship of things. Still, it made me terribly sad to see the pride of my mother's life—the beautiful house and its gardens—disappear beneath the weeds and the normal, human disorder.

The barn was furnished, but empty that summer, and the Simons suggested that I stay in it until school started. I accepted, moved my suitcases from Alan and Nancy's and found it weird to be sleeping in what once had been the chicken coop. It was an oblong, cement room that had been added on to the back of the barn, and it had no charm whatsoever. Neither did the barn itself. Lester had remodeled it in a workmanlike way—a small, square house with small, square windows and a redone chicken coop sticking out the back. At moments, going off to sleep or just waking, I was sure that I could still smell the chickens.

I was alone for the first time in my life, in the small house that sat beside the curve in the driveway. I didn't feel lonely; I felt shut out, cut off, rootless on this same piece of land that held my roots. It began to sink in that it wasn't mine anymore. The big house, as people called it, was bustling with a new family. Terry's house, the unused studio that my father had given him, belonged to Terry and Lulu and their two little boys. Alan and Nancy's house, beside the waterfall, was theirs as always, and Quentin and Thelma had built a house on the mountain side of the road on some acreage that my father had given them.

My house had disappeared, taken over by happy strangers—at least they seemed happy from the outside. I felt that I was seeing everything from the outside; that old feeling of being outside looking in increased dramatically. Not only was I alone and they were couples, but I was outside their windows, looking into their homes, something I no longer had. I had no idea how much I would miss it all—my parents, Martha in the kitchen, my room with a view of the tor, my rose-covered wallpaper that the Simons had painted over. Everything that I had so taken for granted had suddenly slipped away, as if an ice floe had moved across it. Even I was missing. Hesper, the Andersons' girl, Max and Mab's daughter, wasn't there anymore. She wasn't anywhere.

Little Nora Simon seemed to be lost too. She was three and a half or four, the fourth Simon child, and she loved to run down the driveway and wake me up in my chicken coop room. She was tiny with big black eyes and wavy black hair, and she liked to do the things that I used to do. I took her into the woods to turn a tree trunk into a castle, down to the pond and into the ravine to play in my old Indian cave. I took the other children too, sometimes, but Nora was the special one—I wanted to show her everything before I left.

I had to leave the barn in early September and move into the dorm at Barnard, so I was also getting ready, getting my books and clothes together. I had no idea where most of my things were; my room had been cleaned out while I was still in North Carolina, some things given away, some things put in storage with everything else. There weren't many things that really mattered to me, but I missed the gilded icon—the angel Gabriel—that had always hung over my bed, and the carved bedside table where I used to hide my rosary. My mother had given away my favorite thing, the antique doll-house with tiny lights that turned off and on—to a cousin I didn't like, while I was away in college. I'd been furious because she hadn't bothered to ask me. I was still furious; I'd wanted to save it for the daughter I'd have one day.

Barnard was in the city, on upper Broadway, opposite Columbia. I hadn't lived in the city, or even thought much about the city, since I'd left Hewitt's when I was fifteen, so I found myself remembering. Lying on top of the bathhouse, or walking back up to the barn, I'd see in my mind the brownstones on Seventy-ninth Street between Madison and Park, clusters of girls in smocks or Hewitt blazers rushing between them—Lydia, Toni, Jane, Estelle, Silvia. I found myself smiling—they'd been my first real friends.

My mother had really pushed for Miss Hewitt's, a proper girls' school where, hopefully, I'd acquire some manners and wouldn't be able to run wild anymore. She'd had other, less obvious, hopes—that I'd make friends with the daughters of New York society and, through me, she'd join their circle; that I'd go to dancing school, in white gloves and Mary Janes, and that I'd become a debutante one day. Remembering my mother's vain hopes, I laughed as I walked up the driveway, back to my chicken coop.

I realized something else as I pictured the Hewitt's girls: there were only white faces—blond hair, brown hair, brown eyes, blue eyes. There had been one Spanish-looking girl, Giselle Sanchez Machado, but her father had owned all the sugar plantations in Cuba. There may have been one or two Jewish girls, but if they were there, they probably were Roth-schilds or something. I hadn't been aware of things like that at the time, but I thought about it now and wondered if my mother had kept her Jewishness a secret for my sake or for her own.

Lenya and Bunny said, when I'd asked them about it, that she was protecting me from anti-Semitism before and during the war. But I enrolled at Hewitt's the fall after the war ended. There was nothing to be afraid of anymore, nothing to hide, so I had to assume that my mother's social ambitions kept the lie going. Hewitt's might not have accepted me if they'd known that I was Jewish. We weren't rich enough, old-money enough, social enough. As it was, Margaret Perry, a friend of my mother's, and an old Hewitt's girl, had to pull hard on a few strings to get me in.

My father hadn't cared one way or another about my schooling, considering it relatively unnecessary in the first place, and I went along with the Hewitt's idea after reading *The Little Colonel Goes to Boarding School.* It sounded like fun, and I definitely didn't want to go back to Street School. I was almost eleven and had just finished the fifth grade at the Wonderland School. The war had ended, and there had been jubilant parties up and down the road, celebrating first VE Day and then VJ Day. Alan had come home to Nancy and Little Alan, after taking *This Is the Army* around the world, and Marion had returned to Alison and an apartment in the city.

My father was working on *Truckline Cafe*, a play about newly returned veterans, which ended up having only one thing to recommend it—Marlon Brando in his first major role. My father had begun the play in Los Angeles in the spring of 1945, while taking breaks from *Joan of Lorraine.* He'd drive up the coast and hole up in a dingy motel to write, think and escape. The motel was attached to a diner, a truck stop, and he'd decided that it was the perfect setting for his new play. He was still waiting for Bergman to be free to star as Joan, so he wanted *Truckline Cafe* to go into rehearsal that fall. The time frame coincided with my going to Hewitt's, and since there wasn't yet room at the boarding department, my mother talked my father into staying in the city for a few months.

She must have been beside herself; she'd been wanting this for years. She bought new, city-style clothes for herself and dragged me in and out of department stores, looking for just the right plaid skirts, knee socks and oxfords. I also had to have a navy blazer with the Hewitt's crest on the pocket and a bunch of plain, cotton smocks. The smocks had been old Miss Hewitt's idea. She was an ancient English woman with gold curls piled in a net on top of her head; she had started the school way back when—during the Boer War, we liked to say. She no longer taught, but still visited her "gels" and read Shakespeare to us in a wavery soprano. She'd begun the smock business—everyone had to wear them over their clothes—to cut down on competition. It didn't work too well; everyone wore only the very best smocks.

On my first visit to the school with my excited mother, I shook hands with Mrs. Comfort, the principal, and Miss Bradley, the sharp-featured math teacher who terrorized us with her ironic put-downs. They stared at me as if I'd just come out of the backwoods, which in a way I had, and then taught me how to curtsy when shaking hands with a grown-up. It was a slight dip and a kick backwards of the left foot. For years, even in college, that damned left foot would jerk back as if it had a mind of its own. My mother was ecstatic—this was just what she'd wanted for me. My father was amused; I looked upon it all as a kind of game. Sure, I could pretend to be a proper New York schoolgirl, wear the right clothes, say the right thing, even learn to roller-skate like the others, but I knew that I was playing a part. I knew that it wasn't me.

We had the second floor, the parlor floor, of a town house on Seventy-sixth Street between Fifth and Madison. It was elegant, with a bay window facing the street, a marble fireplace, a large bedroom and one very small bedroom that was mine. The whole environment was completely different from everything that I was used to, but it intrigued me. I liked the quiet street, town houses with gardens and filled window boxes, and Madison Avenue shops as I walked the three blocks to school. I'd turn at Seventy-ninth and get to Hewitt's a few minutes before the bell would ring. I was in the sixth grade at the Lower School, and I'd go into the Lower School Building, looking longingly at the girls going into the Upper School. If I stayed at Hewitt's, I'd be in the Upper School the next year. I couldn't believe that I would ever get there.

I led two lives during that first semester, my life at school and my life at the theatre. *Truckline Cafe* was the first play that I was around all during rehearsals. Before that, I'd always stayed in the country when my parents were in town, or out of town, with a new play. I'd visit, of course, and loved going backstage and meeting the actors, but this was different. I was at the theatre most afternoons and evenings. I knew every line of the play, fooled around with the actors, who treated me a bit like the theatre pet. I loved sitting on the empty stage lit by a bare bulb, looking out at the dark seats, and knew that I definitely wanted to be an actress when I grew up. Acting seemed easy to me; it wasn't that different from pretending that I was a born and bred Hewitt's girl.

No one, except possibly me, was happy with *Truckline* from the beginning. The Playwrights Company, which my father had founded in 1937 with Elmer Rice, Robert Sherwood and S. N. Behrman, had produced all of his plays since then, but they shook their heads over this one. My father convinced them to coproduce with Elia Kazan and Harold

Clurman, the founders of the Group Theatre in the thirties, in order to get the play on Broadway. Kazan and Clurman believed fervently in the school of method acting. My father didn't, but he needed to get his play on. It was decided that Kazan would produce and Clurman would direct, so there was my father, sitting right in the middle of an approach to theatre that he didn't agree with. He had never joined the Group Theatre in its heyday, even though my mother had been a member for a couple of years before I was born, so they weren't too crazy about him either.

Then Clurman and Kazan cast Marlon Brando, an unknown twenty-two-year-old, in one of the lead parts. Brando was talented, charismatic, gorgeous, steeped in method acting and mumbled his lines in a way that so infuriated my mother that she insisted loudly he be fired. He wasn't, of course, and grew more amazing in the part every day. He still tended to mumble, but he was so good, so completely the character, that it didn't matter if you didn't catch every word he said. I thought that he was the most beautiful thing I'd ever seen. Not long after, the world thought so too, but this was my moment to just watch him. He did push-ups backstage before his big entrance, when he was supposed to be exhausted and dripping wet after trying to drown himself in the ocean. I'd watch, mesmerized, as he brooded, getting in character, and then wear himself out physically before collapsing onstage.

There was a gentleness to Brando, and he was sweet to me backstage, or sitting quietly in the darkened seats, but there was none of the charming seductiveness that I'd felt from Marion when I was seven. Brando treated me the way an adult treats a child who's the only child around. The whole cast did, some more playful than others. Karl Malden, who my father cast in many of his plays, was one of the playful ones. He was cast as a cop, and every night he'd shoot his gun into the wings right at me and wink with the eye that couldn't be seen. Every night I'd giggle and have to stifle my laughter behind the curtain.

Once the set was up and dress rehearsals started, I got my big moment. They decided to give me a job. After the brooding and the push-ups, Brando had to have a pail of water dumped over his head so he'd be soaked for his entrance. That was my job. I'd stand on a ladder with a pail of water and, on cue, pour it all over Brando.

I told all this to the girls in my class at Hewitt's, and they were duly impressed. I was grateful; I wanted friends so badly and I felt that they were beginning to like me.

I made one friend, Silvia, a smart, dark-haired girl who would be my partner when we needed a partner for something, but I looked longingly at the really popular girls. One of them was Jane Bird, a sophisticated sixth-grader, and I secretly dreamed of being Jane Bird's best friend. The other was Eileen de Polignac, and I couldn't even approach her in my dreams. She was an honest-to-God French princess, with pale skin, curly copper hair and a slight accent. At home I assumed her accent, annoying my parents no end, but at school I simply watched her from afar.

Truckline Cafe opened in February 1946 and only ran for thirteen days. The critics panned it as they'd never panned anything by my father before. They loved Brando, naturally—further infuriating my mother, who'd never stopped complaining about his mumbling—but they decimated the play. "Maxwell Anderson hits his low with a dreadful new play," one critic said. "Anderson writes an agony column," said another. My father was devastated, in despair; then he did one of his famous slow burns. At a peak of rage, he took out a full-page ad in the *New York Times,* calling the New York critics "the Jukes family of journalism." At the time, the Jukes family was a well-known family of morons. This didn't go over too well, but it made my father feel much better. He'd finally said out loud what he deeply believed—that only the public should judge a play.

My father always went into a period of despair, for a month or two or three, after a play flopped. Then, gradually, he'd begin thinking about the next one. The next one would be the best ever, he'd start to believe; the next one would wipe out all past failures. Since he had a flop about every other year, we were used to the cycles of hope and despair, despair and hope. Helen Hayes loved to tell this story about my father: It seems that she'd offered him a ride to the country after a play had been panned, possibly *Candle in the Wind,* in which she'd starred. They rode in silence for quite a while, my father clearly miserable. Finally, he said, "You know, Helen, that I'm depressed, but you don't know why I'm so depressed. It's not just that they didn't like my play. I looked at the paper this morning, and on the front page there was a story about a man who'd murdered his whole family. Then I turned to the review of my play, and do you know they were kinder to the murderer than to me, and all I did was write a play?"

The Simons gave a party in Sidney's studio a few days before I left the barn for Barnard. The studio was above the garage, where my mother had smoked that last cigarette and died in a negligee and mink coat. We had to walk right past the garage window, her last view, to get to the outside staircase that went up to the studio. The furniture had been pushed back against the walls, and everyone danced and drank a lot. The music was loud—I don't know what it was—but I danced with Alan, with Peter Poor, with Sidney Simon, and drank more than I should have. I was usually pretty careful because I hated the feeling of the room spinning around, but I must have forgotten to be careful.

*   *   *

It's the middle of the night, the party still going on. I can hear the music and people laughing, and I'm shivering on the wet grass in the rose garden. I don't remember walking here, stumbling here, or lying down, but I have one eye closed and one eye open, staring across the empty fishpond at a rose bush. If I keep that one eye focused, everything will stop spinning and maybe I won't throw up. It's dark, the ground cold beneath me, and I don't even have a sweater, but if I get up, or if I close that one eye, I'll throw up for sure. I keep staring at the rose bush, and after a while, it has new buds and the sun has come out. My mother is wearing her sun hat and popping Japanese beetles into her jar of kerosene. Their wings are gold and emerald green, and they're spinning round and round. I try to catch them, to save one or two, but I can't—they're spinning too fast.

"Hep, we've been looking all over," Alan says as he wakes me and helps me up. Nancy is with him, and they put a jacket around my shoulders and walk me to their car. "What were you doing, you poor thing, sleeping out here? You're so cold."

"I don't know," I mumble. "I guess I just had too much—I can't drink too much," I say, miserable and embarrassed. They're understanding and take me to the barn and get me into bed, and I sleep through most of the next day. A few days later I lock the barn door behind me and leave for Barnard.

CHAPTER TWELVE

NANCY DROVE ME to the city, double-parked in front of Barnard's green gate, near the corner of Broadway and 116th Street, and helped me carry my things up to my room on the second floor. It was a very small single room with one window that looked out onto the courtyard and the faded brick walls. Nancy insisted upon staying long enough to help me arrange my closet, my dresser, my desk, as mothers were doing for their daughters up and down the hallway. Then she kissed me good-bye and hurried back to the country before dark.

In a way I was glad that my mother wasn't there—she probably would have embarrassed me somehow, asking for special treatment, or complaining loudly about something. But, at the same time, I was missing her. This was the kind of thing a mother did, and I could hear their voices, mother voices, echoing down the corridor. Their nameless daughters were probably embarrassed too, but at least they had someone to embarrass them. I laughed silently at the thought and then closed and locked my door, locking out the mother voices and the daughters' cries, "Oh, Mom, how could you?" "Mom, I'll be *fine . . .*" "Yes, Mother, I'll call every day!"

I lay down on the narrow bed and watched the bricks darken outside my window. I knew dinner would be soon and I ought to go find Arlene, tucked away in one of these little rooms, but I didn't want to face that hallway of strangers, and I decided to give myself a few minutes before venturing out. My eyes were closing, and the bricks outside began to look a lot like the brick wall outside Miss Bradley's window. I'd never seen a place like the Bradley apartment until my parents left me there. I was still eleven, still in the sixth grade at Hewitt's, and there still wasn't a space open in the boarding department. They promised a place by fall, by seventh grade, but after the *Truckline* disaster, my parents—my father, really—had to move back to the country. He had to go back and hide and recover, so that left just me, stuck in the city with nowhere to live.

My mother reassured me that it was only for three months, that Lester would pick me up and bring me home every weekend, and she made it clear that the only alternative was Street School. So my parents made a deal with Miss Bradley, the fearsome math teacher, and left me there with her—in a dismal railroad flat at 122nd Street, off Riverside.

Miss Bradley explained the term *railroad flat* to me—the long hallway with bedrooms off to the side and one larger room at the end was kind of like a railroad car, she said. It didn't look anything like the railroad cars that I knew and loved. There were no views outside the windows, only walls and other grime-covered windows, and not a hint of sunlight. The room at the end was filled with heavy furniture and dark, stern portraits of Bradley ancestors. Old Mrs. Bradley, Miss Bradley's mother, told me about them— preachers and teachers, proud New Englanders—and I got the distinct feeling that the Bradleys had seen better days.

Every Thursday night old Mr. Bradley, bearded and dour, came for dinner and a game of bridge—I have no idea where he was the rest of the time—and I was allowed to eat with the family. Other nights I either ate in my room or in the small kitchen. It was all very strange, but I wasn't paying much attention. I was focused on my days at Hewitt's, the thrill of making friends, and on my weekends at home. The road had changed somewhat. Quentin and Meg had separated and sold the first house, Margaret's house by the waterfall, to Alan and Nancy, where they'd be forever. Little Alan was four or so when Nancy and Alan had Jamie, another golden-haired little boy, the first of the postwar babies.

Alan Jay Lerner had bought the haunted Mad Anthony Wayne house in Mount Ivy from Burgess Meredith, and Burgess had moved into a renovated barn on an adjoining acre. Marion Bell, the star of *Brigadoon* and Alan Lerner's second wife, was one of the first to complain about the ghosts, saying that they wouldn't allow any marriage in that house to last more than a year or two. Her marriage didn't last very long, nor did Alan's next marriage, to Nancy Olson; nor did his next to whoever, or even his next. It may have been the ghosts or it may have just been Alan, who was attractive, tense and bitingly funny. He was heir to the Lerner Shops and had a flamboyant and difficult mother, Edie. Alan said once, "My mother began to love me when I wrote *Brigadoon*." Edie Lerner became a friend of my mother's. I remember a vividly embarrassing moment—my mother and Edie shouting each other's names across a crowded restaurant while I cringed, trying to merge into the tile floor.

Aside from the ghosts who broke up marriages, there was the ghost that lived in the carriage house, now the guest house. According to Frederick Loewe, who used to stay in the guest house when he was working with Alan, there was a ghost, clearly a male, who would walk across the room in the middle of the night, go into the bathroom, flush the toilet and then leave. Ghosts or no, the Lerner house became a favorite spot for the roving Saturday night poker games. Once the war was over and the airplane tower was abandoned, the poker game moved from house to house—a night at our house, a night at Kurt and Lenya's, a night at the Caniffs', a night at the Lerners'. They kept a running score so no one won or lost too badly.

The Hargroves bought and moved into their expensively remodeled farmhouse, across the road from Brook House, and had Christopher, their first little boy. And I had my first sight of Marion since I was eight and he'd married and broken my heart, or whatever emotion it was that had made me throw up on the brick stairs. I was crazy about him all over again, as if nothing had intervened, not the war, not his absence, not my love of Virginia, not my new life at Miss Hewitt's. And there was something new added, something that made me twist in my bed at night, a physical yearning that was almost unbearable. I'd watch his hands, slender and lightly freckled, and envy them—his hands, his fingers—because they could touch him anywhere. I'd be with him casually, at the movies, or sitting around his house or mine, and wait for the second when his hand would brush mine or my knee would accidentally bump into his.

I was eleven and a half; it was 1946, and Marion became, once more, the center of my life—his comings and goings, his interests, his books, his cackling laugh, the songs he sang, his Adam's apple gently bobbing up and down. The big difference, from the time I was seven, was that now he needed me too. He was on top of the world when I was seven or eight; now he was verging on being a has-been, a fate worse than death in his own mind, and definitely so on South Mountain Road. He *had* to write another book; he *had* to make money in order to support his family and their lifestyle. He had to be brilliant again, and he was in an unacknowledged panic, as if his thoughts were hindered by a clogged, underground river, and he was terrified that the debris would never clear.

My unquestioning adoration was the perfect tonic, the perfect distraction, and Marion needed a lot of distraction. While Alison, pregnant again, waited at home for Marion to actually write something, he wandered the road in the black Plymouth, dropping by Nancy and Alan's late at night, Milton's studio in the middle of the night, the Poors' house—he loved Bessie's acidity—and our house at any time of night or day.

Marion called my father *patroon,* an old Dutch word for the lord of the estate, and looked upon him as the father he'd never had. It wasn't that he was reverent—Marion was never reverent, and he teased my father terribly about all his peculiar ways—but it was clear that he loved him and wanted his approval. Marion also loved my mother—her brittle charm, her quick mind—and they shared a love of words and crossword puzzles, particularly double acrostics. They'd pass them back and forth and make up their own, each more difficult than the last.

And I guess Marion loved me; at least, he enjoyed my company. When I was home he spent a lot of time with me. He formed "The Rockland County Bad Movies Club" that consisted primarily of him and me, and I saw more movies than I ever had before. We'd go to matinees in Haverstraw and see the worst things possible. Marion would laugh like mad at stuff like *Duel in the Sun,* while I would take it very seriously. Sometimes, he'd take me into the city to see things he loved, a W. C. Fields retrospective, or *Destry Rides Again.* I cried at that one, identifying with Marlene Dietrich and her unrequited love as she saved Jimmy Stewart's life and died in his arms. I fantasized that, even if I could never actually be with Marion, I might be able to take a bullet for him, save him and die as he kissed me good-bye. Marion never cried at anything. It was all in his head, as far as I could tell, even though everyone on the road whispered that he had plenty to cry about—his life was falling apart around his ears while he was taking me to B movies.

Alison and Marion never seemed to have too much in common. She was a Smith girl who'd won the *Mademoiselle* contest and was interning there during 1942, the year of *See Here, Private Hargrove* and Marion's sudden success. I think his success and charm swept her off her feet, but by now, mid-1946, his success had faded, they were tumbling into debt and Marion wasn't the least bit charming around the house. He let Alison do all the housework and baby-tending while he stared at his typewriter, finagled more loans from the Spring Valley Bank, talked about the book he was *going* to write and spent the rest of his time with me. I envied Alison her proximity to him, but not much else. He was remote and impatient with her while, with me, he was gentle, fun and infinitely patient.

He introduced me to Gilbert and Sullivan, Mark Twain, Edgar Allan Poe, James Joyce, Oscar Wilde and countless other literary and artistic experiences. My parents were grateful for that. At least my crush opened some interesting intellectual doors—better, they'd say, than a lasting crush on Brando or the local plumber. They always referred to my attachment to Marion as my crush and thought it was sweet, which I suppose it was—until it wasn't, until it was terrible.

The Mikado, Pinafore or *Iolanthe* were almost always playing on Marion's phonograph when I'd enter his house, after taking the path through the woods, crossing Lenya's bridge, crossing the road and walking up his driveway. I'd usually find him sitting in the living room, in his favorite leather chair, worn to the shape of his body, reading and listening, while the life of the house—lunchtimes, naptimes, play-times—went on around him. Sometimes, I'd sit with him and let him read to me from whatever he was reading, and some-times I'd help Alison. I'd feed Christopher or baby-sit and give Alison a break. I liked Alison, apart from Marion, and I didn't care what I was doing as long as I was near him, some-where in his orbit.

I turned twelve that August, and Steven, Alison and Marion's second child, was born sometime that summer or fall. I don't remember just when, but I know that Marion in-jured his leg when the baby was about two weeks old, and he had to stay in bed for a while. He moved into the guest room, and with books and writing materials all around him, made himself as comfortable as possible. I walked, or rode my new bicycle, to their house every day and helped out. Sometimes I took care of Christopher, but mostly I took care of Marion. There was a rocking chair beside the bed in the guest room, and I'd sit in it, pushing lightly on the floor, and read to him, or he'd read to me. We were reading *Pudd'nhead Wilson* and the scariest Poe stories. Marion loved to act them out, play-ing all the parts, and I'd shiver at his forlorn cry, "For the love of God, Fortunato!" He also liked to conduct, from his bed or his chair, all the Gilbert and Sullivan operettas, and after a year or two of listening, I knew almost all of the words and music, even the gibberish Japanese in *The Mikado*.

There was a day while Marion was still in bed that Alison had to go out for a while, and she asked me to pick up the baby if he started to cry. I hadn't held Steven yet, or any baby that small, but I assured her that I could take care of him un-til she came back.

Marion's reading aloud; afternoon sunlight is picking up dust balls on the wood floor, and I'm perfectly content, rocking slightly, listening to his voice rise and fall with the inflection of the North Carolina hills. The baby starts to cry, just unhappy grunts at first, then a full-blown shriek, and I get up, rush across the hallway and go into his room. Everything is new in this room: a new crib, a new changing table, new wallpaper—and a new baby, squirming against the crib bolsters and screaming his head off.

I put a diaper on my shoulder and pick him up, carefully supporting his head, and hold him against my shoulder. He stops screaming right away, making little sounds as he catches his breath, and I pat his back and talk to him. "It's okay, Steven, little sweetheart, it's okay." He calms down, stretching his neck against my hand, and I'm surprised at how strong he is. He seems to be seven pounds of tense, wiry muscle, and, as I hold him, I feel a swelling of love. I don't think I've ever loved anyone as much as I love this strong, tiny person. Marion calls out, "Is everything okay?" and I answer and wonder if I love this baby so much because he's part of Marion. But his first son, Christopher, is part of Marion too, and I don't love him in the same way. Steven is, for some reason, the special baby, like a special kitten out of a litter, and I know at this moment that I want a baby of my own one day—I want that more than I want anything.

I started menstruating that summer, and at first I was thrilled. I looked at the spatter of blood and knew that I was on my way to being Nancy and Alison, that I would be able to have a baby of my own some day. My mother and a couple of girls at school had told me what to expect, so I wasn't frightened; I just needed a napkin and a belt, or whatever. It happened to be a day when my mother was giving a summer party. There were road people at the house, and people from town, women wearing pale dresses and summer hats. I went downstairs, found my mother and quietly told her what I needed. She brought it up to me in the second-floor bathroom, showed me what to do and then went back downstairs.

Even though I didn't trust her, it never occurred to me that she would broadcast what I thought was my secret, but she did, wandering through the party, telling everyone that her daughter had just become a woman. I heard her from the top of the stairs, broke into a flushed sweat, turned and ran into my room. It was a couple of days before I could show my face to anyone.

Another incident still inflames my face when I think about it:

It's late August, I've just turned twelve, and we're having iced tea on the terrace outside the living room. It's a lovely, late-summer afternoon. Nasturtiums are spreading in the soil between the flagstones. The white birch provides shade, and my mother's annuals garden is in full bloom—snapdragons, phlox all crowd together. Marion and Alison are visiting, along with another couple, and I'm happy because Marion is here and he and my father are laughing over some private joke. I love it when they laugh. My father gets tears in his eyes and has to wipe his glasses. Marion croaks, his eyes becoming crescent moons, and his pale skin reddens.

There was a poker game at Alan Lerner's the night before, and the game comes up in easy conversation. Who was there? Who won? Did Lenya really bluff Alan out of a flush with a pair of aces? I haven't said anything so far, haven't been noticed, and I pipe up, "Well, all I know is that Mommy got home at seven in the morning." I think it's funny; I don't think anything's wrong with what I've said, but my mother's face contorts. It's the same kind of fury that I saw when I was three and she burned my pink stroller. She strides the three or four feet between us and slaps me hard across the face. She screams, "I told you never to say when I get home! Never!" I'm totally confused. I rush at her, wanting to hit her back, but she fights me off with tight fists. I turn and run into the house and up the stairs. I'm humiliated and indignant—she never said any such thing, and suppose she had, I was just teasing. What in the world was she so angry about? I feel that it was completely unjust—I was just kidding, for heaven's sake—and she's embarrassed me horribly in front of Marion. In a surge of righteous anger, I start slamming my bedroom door. I slam it and slam it until I'm exhausted, then lie there until the cars retreat down the driveway and the day darkens. I fall into an exhausted sleep and still don't understand. She hasn't slapped me in years. What did I do?

I awoke with a start, saw the glow of streetlights on unfamiliar walls and decided that it was time to get up, time to begin my life at Barnard. I searched for Arlene, found her in the cafeteria, and, over meat loaf and soggy beans, we planned our New York adventure. It wouldn't work out, but at that moment, I didn't know that. I tried at Barnard. I went to classes and enjoyed some of them, particularly Dr. Greet's Chaucer class. He made it fun, and we began speaking to each other in Chaucerian English. But it wasn't enough. Arlene made new friends and drifted away, while I didn't make any new friends. It was so different from North Carolina, where I'd been popular, and I didn't know what it was. Maybe it was that I didn't really care. Maybe my mother's death, my father's absence, the traumas of the previous year, had changed me somehow, made me more introverted or less interesting than I used to be. Whatever it was, I was only half there, going through motions, pretending to be a normal, nineteen-year-old college girl.

I visited my half brother Quentin and his second wife, Thelma, a few times during that first month I spent in the dormitory. Quentin, twenty-two years older than I, was an English professor at Columbia. He was Lionel Trilling's protégé, part of an elite group of Columbia intellectuals, and had always intimidated me as much as he had intimidated my parents. I remembered a day, when I was nine, when my father and I had visited Quentin. Quentin had talked for an hour or so in his scholarly way, and after we'd left, my father had turned to me, his eyes laughing, and asked, "What in the hell was he talking about?"

It seemed to me that Quentin had mellowed since then. Thelma was loving, maternal, down-to-earth and brought out Quentin's innate warmth, which he'd kept hidden behind a shield of pedantry. She had a way of interrupting an academic discourse with, "Oh, speak English, Quentin," and Quentin would laugh in the same way that my father laughed, wiping the tears off his glasses. They had an airy apartment on Morningside Drive—overlooking the park that was too dangerous to go into—and they also tried to make a home away from home for me. They invited me to dinner, introduced me to friends as their little sister, but I didn't feel like a sister. I'd never known Quentin that well. He was an adult by the time I was born, and then there was the problem of my mother. Quentin had tolerated my mother, had stayed part of the family for my father's sake, but was never more than cordial to my mother. It was obvious that he didn't much like her and still resented her for destroying *his* family twenty-five years earlier.

It struck me, leaving Quentin and Thelma's one night, walking across the campus, that all of this had happened before. I knew that it had happened, knew for years about Margaret, about the life that she and my father and the boys had lived in the house beside the waterfall, but I hadn't understood that they had gone through the pain of losing everything they had known just as I had. And they'd lost it, primarily, because of my mother. Margaret hadn't killed herself, but she'd been miserable for five years before her death, while my father had openly pursued my mother. Margaret had become ill, had told people that she knew that she would die soon, months before the sudden stroke and the car accident that had killed her.

Quentin, Alan and Terry had lost their mother to death and their father to another woman in a new house with a new baby. "My God, Terry was only twelve when I was born," I said to myself. "He was just a little boy." It hit me in the heart, for the first time, how terrible it must have been for them. I kept thinking about Terry—I'd never known him that well either. He'd always been quiet, had kept to himself, and we'd never really lived together in the same house. Poor Terry, it must have been much worse for him than for the rest of us—he'd been just a little boy. My cheeks were hot, and my eyes burned with held-back tears as I continued across the campus, heading for Barnard's green gate. All at once I saw again my father's pleading eyes—beside the car, after the funeral—as he'd said, "Please love me." I understood now that he knew that it had all happened before, that he was leaving a wrecked family behind and flying off to a new love—again.

One evening at Thelma and Quentin's, feeling comfortable with them, the three of us having coffee and an after-dinner cigarette, I brought up the subject of my mother. I had so many questions; there was so much that I didn't understand, and I hadn't really been able to talk to anyone. Quentin had known that she was Jewish when I hadn't—he'd told me so at the funeral—and I gingerly began to ask questions, about her secrets, about her mental state before she died. She'd been seeing a psychiatrist during her last months alone, and I knew that Quentin believed in psychoanalysis, so I asked if he thought she could have been helped. He answered cautiously, indicating that he thought she'd been very sick, that he'd thought she'd been sick all along, probably a manic-depressive. I was stunned. I hadn't heard this before, and I sat there, staring at him, thinking about it.

"It makes sense," I said finally. I didn't know that much about manic-depression, but I knew that it involved mood swings, irrational highs and deep lows. I saw a flash of the burning stroller, heard my mother's sparkling voice in my mind—"Max is coming home, and I'm giving a big party for him!"—then saw the fury that twisted her face that summer day on the terrace.

"But could they have helped her?" I asked again.

"Possibly," Quentin said. "I don't know—"

"Because," I interrupted, "the doctor wanted me to have her committed and I wouldn't do it. I thought it would be too awful for her—she'd be caged, she'd go crazy—but maybe she was crazy. No, no, I don't think so. She just wanted to die, that's not crazy."

"They wanted *you* to commit her?" Quentin asked slowly. "Who wanted—?"

"Oh, the doctor. One of her doctors came after she'd tried at the apartment. She'd called me in the country, and I had the super break the door down. They pumped her stomach; then I got there, and the doctor wanted me to sign a paper to have her committed."

"And where was 'our father' when all this . . ." Quentin asked, with just a hint of scorn.

"In Los Angeles. He'd gone already. I think it was December—it must have been, because I was home."

"You poor dear," Thelma said gently, filling the silence.

"But was I wrong?" I asked, pleading. "I mean, if they could have helped her?"

"No, you weren't wrong, Hep," Thelma said. "You did what you felt was right."

"But maybe it wasn't!"

"I don't think anyone could have helped her," Quentin said, and I let out an unexpected sob of relief.

"She would've hated it," I said. "She hated being trapped. She hated anyone telling her what to do."

Thelma put an arm around me, gave me a tissue, another

cigarette, and I found myself telling them about the day on the terrace, about my mother's sudden rage that I still didn't understand. Quentin chuckled, and the hint of scorn in his tone became more evident.

"She was obviously having an affair," he said, "and it was important to her that no one knew when she arrived home."

Again, I was stunned and stared at him. It took me a minute to say, "No, she wasn't. She didn't have affairs—I would've known. She didn't have anything until Jerry, I'm sure of that." Thelma and Quentin exchanged a glance, a raised eyebrow, before Quentin spoke again in his professorial voice.

"I'm quite certain, Hesper, that your mother had a good many affairs."

"No," I answered, shaking my head. "No, I'm sure she didn't." It was awkward after that. The feeling of comfort dissipated, and I left soon after, even more aware that there was really no one to talk to. Back in my dormitory room, I thought about my grandmother—her powdered face, her gushing smile—and wondered if she could answer any of my questions. She'd written to me, wanting to see me, but I'd put her off: "Maybe, one of these days. I love you." It was a lie, of course; I didn't love her, never had, but I didn't want her to know it, didn't want her to feel bad, and maybe she could give me some answers. She could tell me about my mother's childhood, more than my mother had ever been willing to tell me, but she wouldn't know about her affairs, if there'd been any.

I got into bed and pulled the covers over my head, shutting out the radios and voices that I could hear through the dormitory walls. If Quentin were right—and he wasn't— who could my mother have been having an affair with? I went around the Saturday-night poker table in my mind: not Milton; not Burgess; not Fritz Loewe; not Bunny's friend, Al

Andriola; not Alan Lerner—maybe Alan Lerner. He'd been one of the ones who'd loved her. He'd said the last time I'd seen him that he still thought about Mab every day. But he'd been married to Nancy Olson, or to somebody, and I couldn't imagine Alan and my mother together. And my parents had been happy then, or as happy as they ever were. No, Quentin was definitely wrong. Nothing had happened until Jerry. I was sure of it.

I put my spinning thoughts to sleep and awoke to a perfect fall day. It was bright and crisp, and I decided to skip my classes and wander. At Hewitt's we were chaperoned most of the time, and I'd never had the chance to just idly walk the city streets. I walked down to Seventy-ninth Street, across the park and sat on the museum steps, remembering how I used to be fascinated and frightened by the mummies in the Egyptian wing. I bought some ice cream and walked the two long blocks to Hewitt's, then stood across the street from the school and watched some of the girls, wearing smocks and carrying notebooks, amble from the school building to the steps of the boarding department, which was always called the B.D. I wondered who was in my old room on the fourth floor and if they were having as good a time as Estelle and I used to have.

Of the twelve girls who lived on the four floors of the brownstone that was the B.D., Estelle and I were the youngest during my first year there. I was twelve and Estelle was thirteen; I was in the seventh grade, Estelle the eighth, but Estelle was more responsible and well mannered than I was, and I think Mrs. Ryan, who ran the boarding department, put us together because she thought Estelle would be a good influence on me. As it turned out I influenced Estelle to loosen up, break the rules and have more fun than she was used to. She was a studious girl who played the piano beautifully and practiced at least two hours a day. I've never been able to hear the famous "Polonaise," or the "Moonlight Sonata," without seeing Estelle bent over the piano in the second-floor music room, her shoulders rounded, her straight, brown hair falling down her back. She was a scholarship student, her mother a struggling single parent, so she took the whole thing more seriously than I did. If I flunked out, no one would really care. If Estelle did, it would be a big disappointment to her mother. I sort of understood this. If we got in trouble, I took the blame, and Estelle tried, for the four and a half years that we were together, to get me to study, to stop smoking out the window, to stop sneaking out over the rooftops and, in general, to behave myself.

As I gazed across the street, the girls in smocks changed, and I saw the older girls, the ones I'd idolized—Toni Dunham, tall and athletic; Diana Wellwood, dark and beautiful; Jacqueline de Bergerac, French and enticing. I'd managed to endear myself to all of them during my first semester there, by getting my parents to invite the entire boarding department to the opening of *Joan of Lorraine*. They were terribly excited, eleven girls from thirteen to seventeen, in velvet, lace and tulle. There was a standing ovation for Ingrid Bergman, and afterwards I took them all backstage to meet her. My popularity assured, I became myself at Hewitt's, no longer playing the role of proper schoolgirl. I could do it if I wanted to, but now I was the same girl walking down the brownstone steps as I was at home walking down the driveway.

I was jolted out of the past by the crosstown bus as it backfired and pulled up to the curb. I decided to take it. I'd been standing long enough at the corner of Park and Seventy-ninth. Back at Barnard, I went up to my room, took my mother's jewelry box out of the closet and opened it. Most of her jewelry was still in the safe in Suffern, but I kept special things, special letters in the box.

The first thing that caught my eye was an old Hewitt's

report card. It had always made me laugh because I had pre-
tended to be sick so often while at Hewitt's. I'd curl up in my
bunk bed, listen to soap operas and dream of being eighteen
or nineteen, old enough for Marion to love me. The report
card said, in essence, that I was so bright, so creative, that it
was a shame that I was such a sickly child.

I riffled through some letters, some pictures, and found
the last three letters that my mother had written to me. I
knew that one of them had been about Marion. She'd been
alone, fighting despair, and yet she'd been able to express
more love and understanding than she ever had before. I
opened a letter dated February 19th, 1953.

Hesper darling,

It would be nice for you to spend the summer with
Daddy and perhaps have a job too. Though I'll miss
you and hope you'll be here a little while. What would
be best would be if all three of us could be together
out there. I wish it might happen. But Daddy doesn't
and I can't just arrive and sit on his doorstep, pleading to be let in. Though I would if I thought he'd open
the door and not slam it in my face. I can't blame him
as it was I who hurt him. Though I love him and love
you and wish we could all be together again. Any
other love is an illusion and a lie. Deep down, I've always known that.

The house is beautiful, but much too quiet and
unused. I miss newspapers and magazines littered
over the chairs, and your clothes all over the beds and
floor, and the heavy tramp of Daddy's feet coming
down the stairs, and the news every half hour on the
radio, and Kurt walking in wearing his windbreaker,
and the sound of the piano playing everything as if it
were a hymn. I miss most the sense of a home, with

its daily demands, grievances, warmth and love.

Don't let me make you sad. I love you . . . Mother

My heart hurt and my eyes blurred as I folded the letter, put it back and then found the one I'd been looking for. My college roommate's brother, whom I'd been seeing, had moved on to someone else, and I was miserable.

March 2, 1953

Hesper darling,

Your letter made me so sad. But, darling, you must get over this feeling of rejection that your relation to Marion has scarred you with. I've told you, several times, that first I and then Alan asked Marion to keep away from you. I did it after that day you and he had spent on the mountain—perhaps it was wrong of me—but you were a child and he had no right to touch you as a woman. And I appealed to him to handle the whole situation with gentleness and tact, so that it would be an imperceptible easing away from you, and not a violent wrench. But Marion insisted that the only way was to make you dislike him—and I said, "Why should she be left with dislike—why not always feel proud of having chosen you to love?" But he behaved like a stupid child, and hurt you irrevocably, I'm afraid. Unless you learn to see it truly. I'm sure—we all were—that Marion, without ever admitting it to himself, because he couldn't, was really in love with you . . .

The letter continued, but I didn't read the rest. I sat there, holding the pages, wondering if it were possible. Was my mother just trying to make me feel better, or had Marion really loved me when I was thirteen, fourteen, fifteen? And if he'd loved me then, maybe he could love me again. I was grown-up now. I even liked the way I looked these days. I was beginning to look a bit like my mother. Marion was in the city; I'd only seen him once since he'd left for Paris, when I was fifteen. Maybe I should find him, call him. He probably didn't know that I was here.

CHAPTER THIRTEEN

THERE WAS A LETTER from Marion in the bottom of the jewelry box, the only one that he'd written to me after he'd left for Europe when I was fifteen. He'd left Alison and the road first, in September of 1949, and had moved to the Hotel Schuyler in the city. The hotel was on West Forty-sixth Street, dark and dingy, with the *H* missing from the neon sign above the entrance; listless goldfish swam in a tank in the lobby. I'd spent a lot of time with him there. He'd pick me up at Hewitt's, the girls giggling because I had a handsome, grown-up beau, and we'd go to his one-bedroom apartment and read aloud to each other, or go to a movie. *Lost in the Stars* was in rehearsal at the Music Box that fall, and Marion and I would sit in the back of the the-atre and listen to my father's lyrics and Kurt Weill's music until we knew every song and every note of Weill's intricate orchestration. After the opening, on October 30th, we'd sometimes sit on the plush steps that led to the mezzanine and simply listen.

I was enthralled by *Lost in the Stars*, by the power of its message of brotherhood, by its tragic love story and, above

all, by the music. To sit beside Marion on the stairs, to love it
with him, made it all so intoxicating that I'd felt that I might
burst out of my skin, spattering the ornate ceiling with bits
of joy. Then, not long before Christmas, Marion left me too.
He told me that he had a girlfriend named Gail, who had
beautiful long legs, and he couldn't see me anymore. Then I
heard about another girlfriend named Cookie—I'd listened
in on the extension when Marion had called my father one
day—and then Marion had left for Europe.

That was the New Year's Eve that Kurt's phoenix appeared in the fire and Lenya found me crying on the third
floor. I'd left Miss Hewitt's, in despair, in the middle of the
tenth grade, and entered Nyack High School as a junior. I
was determined to get over Marion. I found a boyfriend, sort
of, and hadn't even wanted to think about Marion. The
boyfriend had majored in horticulture, had a blond forelock
that tended to fall onto his forehead and enhance his very
blue eyes, and we had absolutely nothing in common. I'd
wander the rows of seedlings in the greenhouse with him,
holding his hand and pretending that I had someone just for
me. It was just as important at Nyack High School as it had
always been on the road for a girl to have a desirable
boyfriend. I was trying hard to seduce him for the same reason—and to get over Marion's rejection—but he was skit-
tish about my virginity, so I never managed it.

I wasn't concerned about my virginity, or my reputation,
because no one had ever told me to be. I'd grown up on my
father's version of romantic love, his wistful memories of
Hallie, his belief that if you loved someone then sex was
beautiful and pure. At fifty-eight my father still believed in
Romeo and Juliet as fervently as he believed that the theatre
was the temple of democracy. And by the time I was twelve
and thirteen, I believed in Romeo and Juliet, in Our Gal Sunday and Young Widder Brown, and in Mio and Miriamne,

the young lovers my father had created in *Winterset*, the year I was born. They were Romeo and Juliet all over again in a contemporary setting, dying for each other beneath the Brooklyn Bridge. I'd memorized passages of *Winterset* . . .

> Miriamne: Why does he bleed so? Mio, if you go
> I shall go with you.
> Mio: It's better to stay alive.
> I wanted to stay alive—because of you—
> I leave you that—and what he said to me
> dying:
> I love you, and will love you after I die.
> Tomorrow, I shall still love you, as I've loved
> the stars I'll never see, and all the mornings
> that might have been yours and mine. Oh,
> Miriamne,
> You taught me this.

I'm thirteen, home from Hewitt's for the weekend. I'm in bed with only the light from the hall picking out the roses in the wall-paper. I'm longing for Marion. I've spent the day with him, doing errands in the black Plymouth, seeing a Roy Rogers movie in Haverstraw, wanting to touch him, wanting him to touch me. If I think about him long enough my body quivers deliciously. I don't touch myself because nobody has talked to me about these feelings and because Teppi's warning stays with me—You touch yourself down there and you burn in hell—and I see the body behind glass, writhing in flames just as she'd described it to me.

My father comes in to say good night to me. He sits on the edge of my bed, and I try to tell him what I'm feeling.

"I want him to rape me," I say, not knowing what the word means. What I mean is that I want Marion to grab me, to hold me, to take away this terrible ache of longing.

"No, a rape is a forced thing, Hep," my father says. "What you want is for him to love you completely, to give his soul to you, which

is the most beautiful thing in the whole world." And then he goes off into his memories of Hallie.

"When I was a boy, twelve and thirteen, I fell in love with this beautiful, ethereal girl. She was blond and pale and perfect, and I loved her from afar until that one magic day when she told me that she loved me too. I couldn't believe it. I was a bumbling, overgrown farm boy, and she loved me too. It was the most amazing thing that had ever happened to me. We held hands as we walked to school; we kissed in the straw; we promised that we would always be together, and then her parents took her away. I almost died, but I didn't. I found solace in other girls, and, after a time, Hallie was just a lost dream. I was a bumbling farm boy again, who loved music and poetry, and I went off to the university on a scholarship, and I met Margaret, who said, 'You're not just a bumbling farm boy, you're a prince.' And Margaret loved me and I became a prince for her."

I'm barely listening. I've heard all this before, many times, and I don't want to hear it right now. I don't want to hear about my father's loves—I want to talk about mine. *I want to ask him questions that I can't ask anyone else because I don't completely trust anyone else. Above all, I want him to listen to me and to answer me. But he goes on, looking out at the beacon that turns from red to white, red to white.*

"I became famous, still a prince, and then I met your mother— beautiful, dazzling, smart as a whip—and she said, 'No, you're not a prince, you're a king, because I love you, you're king of the world because I love you.'"

"But what about Marion? What can I do about it?" I ask urgently as my father pauses, still looking off.

"You wait for love," my father says, turning back to me slowly. "True love, which is the most beautiful thing in the whole world. You'll see, Hep, when it comes, you'll know it. There's no greater happiness—to love and be loved in return, to lie in the arms of your love. You'll know it one day." He kisses my forehead gently and leaves the room, leaving me full of unanswered questions,

leaving me to wonder if Marion is my true love, or if Marion is just my own Hallie. Either way, my father has left me believing, once again, that love is all that matters.

Marion's letter from Paris arrived in July 1950, ten months after he'd left South Mountain Road and six months after he'd left me. I'd read the letter quickly when it arrived, put it away and hadn't answered it. Reading the letter again, almost four years later, it invoked his voice, his dry humor, his turns of phrase, as if he were sitting in the room at Barnard with me. He wrote about an article he'd been working on, said that his French was clearly better than the Parisians', because they understood every word he said, while he didn't know what in the world they were talking about. He said that he was scared to go out in the street because they all drove like lunatics, and, of course, he'd *had* to mention at least one beautiful young woman. But the end of the letter was gentle. He asked me to give his love to my creaky old parent, and to the one who was neither, and to Lenya and all the Andersons, and then he wrote, "Oh, hell, give it to everybody; I got a heart full where this comes from."

The letter was typed except for the signature, and I ran my index finger over the letters of his name—"Marion," written straight up and down. It was a signature that I had practiced, as girls do, over and over again on notebooks and the backs of envelopes. Sometimes, I'd written "Mrs. Marion Hargrove" in his up-and-down handwriting. That was a long time ago, almost four years, and no matter how hard I'd tried to get over him, no matter how many boys I'd charmed in my effort to convince myself that I was as good as dear Gail, as he'd called her, with the beautiful long legs, or the starlet on the books of bobby pins, or dear Cookie, or dear whoever, I knew it hadn't worked. I knew I wasn't over him. The last paragraph of his letter made me sad. He'd never mentioned his heart before, full or otherwise, and obviously he'd been missing us, all of us.

It took me a while to call Marion from a Barnard pay phone. I got his number from Alison. I still saw her and their children, at times, in Nyack. Several times I stood in the hallway that was lined with phones, near Barnard's front door, holding his number between sweaty fingers, unable to put in a coin and dial. If he answered, I didn't know who he would be—would he be the gently funny Marion with soft, yellow flecks in his eyes, or would he be the cold Marion with eyes that glinted like gray steel?

When I finally managed to dial, and Marion answered, he seemed pleased to hear from me. It wasn't the gentle voice, but it wasn't the icy one either. He told me that his sister had just moved from North Carolina to Queens and asked if I'd like to go with him to visit her. It was as easy and natural as if those last four, long years had never happened. He said that he'd pick me up on Saturday, and I hung up and leaned against the wall, catching my breath and trying to believe that I was really going to see him.

I called my father collect in Los Angeles, and we talked for a minute about the movie that he was writing for money, and about Gilda and the children, who he said made him tired.

"I'm too old to answer all those insistent questions," he said, and I could see him smiling, "Why, Daddy, why, Daddy? Who, Daddy, who?" I laughed and said that he wasn't old at all, and he answered that he must be young enough, "I'm loved by a beautiful young woman. Now isn't that a bit of luck?"

"It's not luck," I answered. "You're a catch," and we both

laughed. "Speaking of love—" I began, and then told him that I'd called Marion and was going to see him. There was a silence, and I knew that the smile had left his face.

"I thought you were over that. I'd hoped—"

"Not really," I interrupted. "I tried to be."

"Don't let him hurt you again, Hep," my father said quietly. "Because there are others . . . There are always others with him."

"I know that," I answered, "but I think there was something different, something special with me. I don't know—maybe I'm just making it up."

"No, there was," my father said, "but that was a while ago—on the road, and he was married . . ." His voice trailed off, and I assured him that I'd be fine.

"Who knows? Maybe I'll think he's old and boring." We both laughed again, and then I asked if I could get some new clothes. My father told me to charge whatever I needed, then asked if I was low on money. I said that I wasn't; I just thought I could be a bit more stylish. We said we loved and missed each other, and I took a cab down to Fifth Avenue.

I bought a flattering outfit at Bonwit's, a new pair of heels, and then got my hair done at the salon where my mother and Bunny used to spend Thursday afternoons. They had everything done—hair, legs, eyebrows, eyelashes. I just got my hair cut and bought a lipstick. It was all for Saturday. I'd dreamed since I was seven of being grown-up for him, and now here it was—D-Day. I locked the door to my room and examined myself, standing on the desk chair, in front of the small mirror. I'd been losing weight by the second ever since I'd talked to him, and I thought I looked good—I could actually see cheekbones.

Staring at myself—slim and almost pretty, with my father's eyes, coloring and teeth, and my mother's nose and something about the mouth—I felt, again, a wave of triumph. It was the same feeling I'd had at my mother's funeral. She was dead, swollen and blue lipped, and I was young and alive. I didn't have to compete with her beauty anymore. Not that I'd ever competed. That was the problem. I'd thought that I couldn't compete, so I'd gone the other way. I'd worn Nancy's hand-me-downs instead of the clothes my mother bought for me. I'd go weeks without washing my hair, because I thought it looked better when it was oily. I didn't ask my mother for help, and she didn't offer it. When I was twelve, Nancy told me that I was beginning to smell and gave me some deodorant. I was both embarrassed and grateful. After a minute, standing on the chair at Barnard, I felt the same rush of guilt that I'd felt after looking victoriously at my mother in her coffin, but it passed quickly. I was nineteen; I was going to see Marion, and my mother wasn't around anymore.

Marion picked me up in the Barnard foyer, kissed my cheek and took my elbow as we headed for the subway. All the way down the steps and onto the train, he filled me in on his sister's life since I'd last seen her, five years earlier. He kept talking as the subway rattled its way to Queens, and I listened and nodded and smiled, even though I couldn't hear half of what he was saying. He looked just the same, sounded just the same, and, in my mind, I could see us in his living room on South Mountain Road, Marion reading James Joyce to me while I smiled at sentences that I didn't understand a word of. Looking up at him on the subway, it didn't matter any more now than it had then.

We'd often taken the subway when I was at Hewitt's. When I was thirteen, the D'Oyly Carte Company had come from London to New York for the first time, and Marion had taken me to most of their productions. We saw *The Mikado, Pirates, Iolanthe, Pinafore,* and we'd gone backstage to meet Martyn Green, the star, who played Koko, the Lord High

Executioner, and the Modern Major General. We saw the movie of *The Mikado* too, agreed that it wasn't nearly as good as on the stage, but I was happy to be with Marion anywhere, to sit beside him in a dark theatre and wait for the moments when his sleeve would brush mine, or he'd lean toward me and whisper something, and I'd feel the rough tweed of his jacket, his breath on my face.

I'm thirteen and a half and it's March 21st, the first day of spring. I'm home for spring vacation. It's early afternoon, and I'm walking through the woods to Marion's house. It's a perfect spring day after a rainy, snowy winter. It's sunny, but the air on my face is prickly, cold and sweet, like the spray from the ocean when I used to play beside it. With a burst of exhilaration, I throw my head back like a pony and gallop, tossing my hair from side to side as I go, into the clearing, over Lenya's bridge, up her driveway and across South Mountain Road. I slow down as I reach Marion's driveway but jump over the ruts, some still covered with a thin coating of ice.

The black Plymouth isn't in the driveway, but the front door is open as always, and I find Marion in the living room, stretched out on the sofa, hugging a mangled throw pillow to his chest, his sneakered feet resting defiantly on the opposite end of the flowered couch. Marion is so sedentary it's a road joke: never sit at the typewriter if you can find a sofa, never lie on the sofa if you can find a hammock—that sort of thing, but I'm so full of spring energy I take a wild chance.

"It's so gorgeous out there," I say. "It's the first day of spring and it really is *the first day of spring. Come on, come outside, come see!" Marion gives me a fake withering look.*

"The goddess just went to the city, dropped the wee lads at your sister-in-law's; I've had ten minutes of utter peace, and now you come in carrying on about spring. Get lost, Pollyanna, I'm in no mood—"

"Oh, come on," I say, knowing that he's teasing, seeing the

lights in his eyes and the slight smile. "Come outside with me—we can do something fun, take a drive, take a walk—"

"The goddess has the car," he interrupts, "and walking is bad for the digestion." He lights a cigarette, puts the ashtray on his chest and blows a smoke ring at me.

"We could climb Low Tor," I say, the thought just occurring to me. "Right behind the house—I'll bet you've never been up there."

"You bet right," Marion mumbles, and I talk over him.

"It's so beautiful on a day like this, and it's not a bad climb at all, not nearly as steep as getting up High Tor."

"Well, thank the Lord for small blessings," he says, not moving, but I know somehow that I've got him, that he's going to go with me.

Marion says that he'll meet me out front and, after a minute, he appears in the driveway, a coiled rope slung over his shoulder.

"What are you doing with the clothesline?" I ask, and Marion gives me another withering look.

"Clothesline, indeed. Ropes, lass, ropes for the cliffs, lass, the cliffs . . ." And his voice trails off as if he's just fallen a great distance.

"There aren't any cliffs," I answer, laughing.

"No cliffs?" Marion says, as if offended, and turns back to the house. "Who wants to climb a mountain with no cliffs?"

"Oh, come on," I say, still laughing.

"Oh, all right." Marion tosses the clothesline on the driveway and starts to follow me. "Let's go climb your sissy mountain. No cliffs, whoever heard . . ."

We find the path near the road that leads up to Low Tor and follow it, single file, through a thickness of bare trees.

"How far is it up there?" Marion asks, and I point ahead.

"Not far. We have to go over the stone wall up there, walk a little ways more and then we get to the jagged part, but that's not much, and then we're at the top. It's all flat rock there, and you can see the river and the bridge and everything."

"Hmm, tell me more, doctor," he mutters, "about this jagged part, hmm?" I laugh again, and we walk slowly for a time, going steadily upward. We reach the stone wall, and Marion goes first, placing his feet carefully. As he jumps down from the top of the wall, he holds out his hand to me. I take it and land, sinking a little on the ground beside him.

"You can follow me now," Marion says. "I'm beginning to like this mad business." He walks ahead of me but keeps hold of my hand, his arm pulling mine slightly as the path gets steeper. I look down at the ground in front of me, feeling my fingers trembling in his, afraid to look up at him. The wind hits us now, blowing down the mountainside, and Marion pulls more firmly on my hand.

"The jagged part, eh?" he says, stopping suddenly and staring up at the ledge of red rock that rises in front of us. "Jesus, I should've brought the rope—I could've hung myself. Okay, here goes—" He lets go of my hand and climbs, carefully finding footholds, holding onto the rocks above, and I follow him, placing my feet where he had placed his. He turns back, his face red and perspiring, and gives me a silly, sick grin.

"I think we've almost done it," he says, and in another minute he stands at the top and leans down, reaching out to pull me up the last few feet. "What a sight," he says softly, between panting breaths, indicating with a sweep of his hand the Hudson below, Tarrytown across the river and the George Washington Bridge in the distance.

"I told you it was beautiful."

He nods and walks a few feet to a sheltered spot with the same view, sits with his back against a rock and gestures to me.

"Ah, that feels better. Come on, get out of the wind." I join him, begin to sit beside him, but he takes my hand and guides me down so that I'm sitting between his bent knees. His chin rests on my hair, and, as I lean back against him, I smell the faint mothball-and-talcum-powder smell of his sweater. I close my eyes, try to breathe normally and focus on the blotches of color beneath my eyelids.

"*You smoking in public yet?*" *Marion asks. I shake my head, smiling, and turn for a second so that I can see his face. I feel his heartbeat and turn back as he reaches under his sweater and pulls out a flattened cigarette and a pack of matches. He puts the cigarette in his mouth, leans forward and, as he strikes the match, his hand cupped against the wind, both his arms are around me. I feel that I'm going to explode with happiness. This is what I've longed for—all the hours, days, evenings of being with him when he'd never touched me except by accident—this is what I've wanted. Marion tosses the match onto the rock, leans back, but keeps one arm around me. The blood rushes to my face, my heart dances in irregular beats, and I don't say a word.*

"*Why so quiet, Hep?*" *Marion asks as he finishes the cigarette and tosses it down toward the river.*

"*Just happy,*" *I answer.*

"*Me too,*" *Marion says. "Maybe that's why I'm usually so goddamned noisy." We're silent for a while. The afternoon is darkening and the wind picks up. I shiver but don't want to move, not ever, but Marion says that we should be getting back. I get up first, give him a hand, and we stand together on the flat rock.*

"*You've got blue lips,*" *Marion says. "Here, take my sweater." He pulls it off, puts it over my head and then holds me for what seems like a long time. He kisses the top of my head, kisses my lips once, gently, and then leads the way down the mountain, not letting go of my hand until we get to the road and the driveway. We walk separately back to the house. Alison and the boys are back, and I walk home through the woods, still wearing Marion's sweater, knowing now that he loves me too, that all those seven-year-old dreams are going to come true.*

They didn't come true. It was a resounding plummet from the top of the mountain. Marion turned cold immediately. He no longer had any time for me. He said that he was, finally, really working on a new book. They'd just found out that Alison was pregnant again, and he had to make some money—the situation was getting desperate. He stopped picking me up at Hewitt's for afternoon movies and stopped dropping by our house as often as he had before. I waited, sure that it would change, sure that he would appear one day and his eyes would, again, be soft and amused, his voice gently teasing. But it didn't happen. After two months of tears, confusion and hiding in bed, all I could do was replay the day on the mountain, over and over again.

My mother found me crying in my room one weekend afternoon and said that she'd decided to tell me that she knew about the day on the mountain, she knew what had happened.

"How?" I asked, shocked. I hadn't told anyone; it was our secret, mine and Marion's.

"Marion told me," my mother answered. "He told me the next day. He was feeling guilty and worried about you—"

If she said more, I didn't hear it. I was furious, felt completely betrayed, screamed at her that it was none of her business and ran out of the room. I couldn't stand the idea that Marion had told my mother. It wouldn't have been as bad if he'd told my father—my father had told me all about Hallie and he understood me. My father never called it a crush or "puppy love" as my mother did. But Marion had told my mother, and I felt betrayed by both of them. My mother had taken my most precious thing—my secret—away from me.

I yanked my bicycle out of the garage, raced down the driveway and up the road. I dumped the bicycle at the edge of the road and took the steep path that led to the back of Marion's house. He was sitting outside, near the low terrace wall, reading. He carefully marked his place in the book when he saw me—crying, dirt on my face, nearly hysterical.

"I thought that it meant you loved me!" I said. Marion

stared at me for a moment, his face cold and unreadable except for the flicker of pain behind his eyes. And that's when he said the words that stayed with me for years:

"It didn't mean anything. It was body chemistry, nothing more."

We went to California, to Zuma Beach, not long after that, and I spent the summer that I didn't want to remember. Marion came a couple of weeks later. I guess he was working on something, though I never saw him work, and I felt that he paraded the redheaded starlet in front of me on purpose. It was his favorite way of getting rid of me, but if that was his intention, it didn't work too well. I pined away in my room and found a new soap opera, *Nurse Nora Drake*, or maybe it was just *Nora Drake*, who was a nurse. It was on at two o'clock every afternoon. It was on sometimes when I'd watch Marion flirt with the starlet on the terrace below, and it was on when the police came to tell Rex Harrison that Carole Landis had just killed herself.

CHAPTER FOURTEEN

MARION AND I spent the afternoon and evening with his sister in Queens. It was easy and intimate. He teased us both, as he always had, told amusing stories, complete with accents and details, about his time in Europe and his struggles in New York. I laughed along with his cackle and happily watched his Adam's apple bob up and down. He wanted to know about North Carolina, and I told him about the plays I'd been in, the writing classes and about experiencing the two springs—the one in Greensboro and the one in Rockland County—that he'd told me about when I was little.

It only became uncomfortable when I talked about South Mountain Road. I reminded him of our walks when I was seven and told his sister about his poltergeist who had gorgeous long legs but wasn't too bright and got lost in our woods. Marion's face tightened, and he turned to his sister.

"Hep loves to talk about the past," he said in a way that made it clear that he didn't want me to.

We got back to Barnard about half an hour before the eleven o'clock curfew. We opened the green gate and walked to the covered porch just outside the front door. In all the nooks and corners of the dark porch young couples were holding each other, kissing and saying good night. Marion led me to an unoccupied spot, and we did the same thing. I never could have instigated it. I was too afraid of rejection, particularly his, but Marion put his arms around me, found my lips, and we kissed and kissed while our hands pressed and explored. "He's kissing me like a grown-up," I thought to myself, exulted to myself. "My God, I'm a grown-up for him!"

Marion and I didn't stop until everyone else did, until all of us Barnard girls moved reluctantly through the front door, fingers slowly letting go of our dates, and the door was locked behind us. I walked blissfully to my room. All the hurt was gone—the eight-year-old hurt, the thirteen-year-old hurt, the fifteen-year-old hurt—all of it drained away, leaving pure happiness. My twelve-year wait was over. "My mother was right," I thought. "Marion had loved me then and he loves me now." I got into bed, lit a cigarette and stayed awake. I didn't want to miss a second of my newfound joy. Sitting in the dark and smoking, I began to look ahead, to my old fantasy of marrying Marion and having a little Steven of my own.

I'd played the role for four days when I was fourteen. We'd come back from Zuma sometime in August. My mother, Bunny and Lenya decided to go to East Hampton for a few days. They needed a break, they'd said, and then they'd invited Alison to go with them. "God knows Alison needs a break," I'd heard them say to each other. And who would be the perfect baby-sitter for Marion and the children? Why Hesper, of course; she's so good with the children. Marion was no longer paying any attention to me, so I guess no one was concerned. I spent four days and four nights taking care of Marion's little boys and sleeping in Alison and Marion's huge bed. Marion slept in the guest room, remained as distant as he had all summer, and by the third night of my stay, I was tired of it all and wanted to go home.

I rode my bike through the twilight, came in through the dining room door and found my father, Kurt and Alan Lerner sitting around the dining room table. Alan Lerner looked up, a gleam in his good eye, and asked, "And how is 'Life with Father'?" I laughed and said that I missed being home. I got something to eat from the kitchen, joined them at the table and listened as they talked with my father about *Anne of the Thousand Days.* He'd been working with Rex Harrison, who was to play Henry VIII, and Bretaigne Windust, the director, during the summer at Zuma. He wasn't worried about Harrison, but he had qualms about Windust. Rehearsals were to begin in the fall, and Kurt and Alan were encouraging him to think about other directors before it was too late.

It was comfortable at home, particularly with my mother away, and I listened to their voices, to the crickets and tree frogs in the woods, and didn't really feel like going back to Marion's. It wasn't much fun to take care of babies all day and then spend an evening with Marion being as remote as possible. I was beginning to understand Alison's complaints.

Alison had left a large bowl of chocolate pudding laced with finely chopped nuts in the refrigerator for the boys and me. Marion was already in the guest room reading when I got back, and I walked through the dark house to the kitchen. The boys and I had already eaten half the bowl of chocolate pudding, and I polished off the rest by the light of the refrigerator bulb before climbing the stairs and getting into bed, still praying that Marion would come to me, still praying that he'd be, once more, the way that he'd been on the mountain. But he remained distant, and by the time Alison came back, on the fourth day, I was relieved and happy to go home.

A New York dawn was breaking, and I still hadn't slept. I'd drifted off briefly, dreamed of chocolate pudding and awakened in the throes of embarrassment. About a month before, Thelma and Quentin had asked me if I'd baby-sit for another professor and his wife. They knew that I was good with children, and their friends had a difficult little boy whom they coddled and were reluctant to leave with anybody. I did well with the little boy, read to him, put him to sleep and then went into the kitchen, where I found a whole bowl of chocolate pudding laced with finely chopped nuts, just like the one that Alison had left for us. I tried not to eat too much of it. I spooned it around the edges, ate a quarter of it, and, before I knew it, the whole thing was gone. The professor and his wife never asked me back again.

Alison, Marion, chocolate pudding, home, embarrassment—it all ran together, and, in the first, gray light, I began to get angry. Why had they let me play house for Marion *after* the day on the mountain and his response to it, even if they thought it would never happen again? Whose idea had it been—mine? theirs? If my parents had wanted me to get over Marion, why had they let me sleep at his house and pretend to be Alison? And Alison, whom they supposedly cared about, they'd betrayed by letting Marion hang around Zuma with the redheaded starlet. I'd never thought of that before. What was the matter with them? Were they just not thinking, just not paying attention?

I was getting angrier by the second. I got up and stormed around the small room. Of course they weren't paying attention. My father was consumed by a new play, and my mother was consumed by her social life and her desire to be the most beautiful woman at the beach. "It must have been hard," I thought to myself wryly, "to keep up with the Joneses when the Joneses were the Gershwins, the Shaws, the Selznicks and the Harrisons." My mother was particularly competitive with Lilli Palmer, who was married to Rex Harrison at the time. My mother and Lilli Palmer were two of a kind—small, pretty, smart, charming—but Lilli was a successful actress, a star in her own right, while my mother was just the playwright's wife.

After we returned from Zuma, the Harrisons spent a good deal of time at our house. *Anne of the Thousand Days*, due to open in December, was the focus of this new friendship, but it seemed to me that Rex and Lilli were treating our house like a country inn with maid service. Every morning, Martha fixed breakfasts to order and carried two large trays up to the third-floor guest room. Rex usually wanted kippers and eggs, which made a smelly mess in the kitchen, and, fuming, I tried to help Martha with the mess and the trays. I complained to my mother: If the Harrisons wanted that much to eat for breakfast, why couldn't they come downstairs like everybody else? She waved me away, unwilling to listen. All of her energy at that time seemed to be focused on impressing Lilli and Rex.

I didn't mind Lilli, who barely knew I existed, but I considered Rex a posturing fool. He stammered and choked on his words as if he were doing a takeoff on an English lord. If he had anything intelligent to say, he never managed to get it out. At lunch one day he tried to tell us about their tour of the catacombs. It went something like, "Ooh, the c-c-catacolms—Ooh, my, my the ca-ca-ca . . . Oh, tell them Lilli," which she then proceeded to do. One evening after dinner, I found out that I wasn't alone in my feelings about Harrison. He always wore an ascot, but this was a humid September night and he had draped his ascot on the back of the sofa. My father picked it up and folded it in half. Lenya took it and folded it again. Kurt did the same thing. It came to me, and I folded it. I passed it to Marion, who folded it once again and then dropped it in the silent butler. Conversation continued;

Rex was oblivious, and the rest of us suppressed laughter and avoided each other's eyes.

When rehearsals began for *Anne of the Thousand Days* I watched in amazement as Harrison turned into a youthful Henry VIII. His lean body gave the impression of Henry's bulk; his impaired speech became articulate and charming. On stage he was handsome, poetic and sexy. I hadn't understood the "Sexy Rexy" nickname, but once he was onstage I could see it. When I told my father how surprised and impressed I was, he nodded knowingly and winked.

"The best actors are always the stupidest," he said. "If they think too much, they're in trouble. And if they *are* intelligent, like Brando or Kazan, then they want to write or direct—acting isn't enough for them."

"Really?" I asked, thinking he might be kidding. He wasn't, and I pondered this for a while, trying to put the actors we knew into one category or another. I was pretty sure that I could spot a phony a mile away, but it was hard, at fourteen, to know who was smart and who wasn't. And my father had further confused the issue by telling me many times that talent had nothing to do with intelligence. Quentin, for instance, was much more intelligent than we were, but we had the talent.

"Yeah, yeah," I muttered to myself, still pacing the room at Barnard. "The homely, bumbling ones with the talent—thanks, Daddy." Church bells were ringing somewhere, the campus below was stirring, and I was still angry. I dressed quickly and went out for coffee, wondering if Marion's removal of so much hurt the night before had unleashed all this anger. I didn't see the connection, and the mood kept building as I walked down Broadway. I found a Whelan's with a counter and sat on a stool in the far corner and ordered coffee, feeling invisible. I could see everyone coming in and out, everyone passing on the street, but they couldn't see me.

A brittle woman with an unhappy little boy were at the other end of the counter. She was talking nonstop, chiding him about this, about that and roughly wiping the crumbs off his face. I wanted to yell at her to stop, just as I'd yelled at my mother so many times to shut up, to leave me alone. It had been easy to be angry at my mother, to sustain the anger, because most of the time I found her so irritating. She'd charge around the house like a toy top out of control, criticizing anyone who crossed her path—until guests showed up, and then she'd be her charming self, all smiles and chitchat. It wasn't until her last year, when she'd become vulnerable and thoughtful, that I'd stopped being angry. It wasn't until she'd been alone and her weight had dropped to ninety pounds, just from grief, and her small hand, the nails bitten to the quick, had clutched at mine that I'd stopped being angry.

It was much harder to be angry at my father. While I was growing up I couldn't sustain the emotion for more than a minute or two. Once, when he'd kicked Toby in frustration over something, I'd remained furious for a couple of days, but that was about it. His presence was so large, so warm, even humble, and his eyes were so sad, even when he was relatively happy, that I couldn't stay angry at him for long. I'd look into his sad eyes, so hopeful, so needing my love, and I'd melt and say, "Of course I love you, Daddy. Of course I can take all that sadness away—me, your evening star, the love of your late life, your mirror image in the form of a girl. Of course I can be true and honest and adoring. You will always have me."

I was calming down, sitting at the lunch counter. The brittle mother had left, replaced by a couple of eager students, arguing the contributions of Eliot and Pound. "Everything's all right now," I said to myself. "Marion wants me, and Daddy seems happy with Gilda. I can stop being angry at what they did or didn't do. I can go forward now the way Lenya wanted me to, even though my mother's dead and our home isn't there anymore. I can go on—I can be happy too." I left the lunch counter and started to walk back to Barnard, determined to go forward even though my thoughts kept drifting back to the past.

The street signs said BROADWAY but this wasn't the Broadway I'd always known. This was upper Broadway, so different from the theatre district with its blinking lights and Shubert Alley, which seemed paved with old-world charm. *Anne of the Thousand Days* had opened on Broadway on December 8, 1948, after a couple of months of rehearsals and hilarious out-of-town tryouts. The hilarity was probably the result of financial hysteria, but I remember my father laughing so hard that tears streamed down his face. We were backstage, in Philadelphia, right after a performance. Jo Mielziner had designed an expensive revolving stage that eliminated the need for set changes. A scene would end, the stage would rotate and then stop so that the right set faced the audience. It was a good idea, but the thing didn't work too well, often stopping where it wasn't supposed to. The actors got dizzy, opened wrong doors, and the night that my father laughed so hard, Rex Harrison, in full costume, had opened a door to the stage and found himself out in the street next to the theatre. Another actor, trying frantically to get onstage, had burst into Joyce Redman's dressing room.

The Playwrights Company and Leland Hayward produced the play, and there were lots of agonizing late-night sessions in hotel suites before Mielziner's revolving stage was scrapped, replaced by minimal sets, and before Windust, the director, was fired. It was one of those legendary out-of-town nightmares that, amazingly, led to a success. The New York reviews were raves—for the play, for Harrison and for

Joyce Redman, the English actress who played Anne Boleyn and was often referred to, because of her Elizabethan bodice, as the "high-breasted Miss Redman."

I was even more involved with *Anne of the Thousand Days* than I'd been with *Joan of Lorraine* and *Truckline Cafe*, partly because I was back at Hewitt's in the city, trying once again to let go of Marion, and partly because I'd become fascinated by the Elizabethan period. My father had stacks of books on the Tudors and the Stuarts in the cabin and in his room on the third floor, and I pored over them until I was as familiar with the world of Henry and his wives, with Elizabeth and Mary, as I was with the world of South Mountain Road. I knew all the castles, the battles, the intrigues, the lovers almost as well as my father did. He told me that he didn't have to go to England or Scotland or anywhere to do research. He'd just read a few books and then see it all in his head— hear their voices as he lay on his cot in the cabin and then begin to put it down.

I'm twelve or thirteen, and there's company at the house. It's a weekend and my mother has managed to lure Valentina, the designer, to the country. She's come in a limousine with her husband, who everyone says is Garbo's lover, and my mother is beside herself. Except for the time when my mother glimpsed Garbo in an adjoining dressing room, she knows that this is as close as she's going to get to her. Lenya, Bunny and Bessie are here (Kurt, Milton and Henry are working, so they say), as well as some other people from town. Drinks are being served on the terrace, and my mother has told me to run to the cabin and get my father—everyone's dying to see him.

I walk to the cabin, happy to escape and savor the afternoon sunlight that's barely penetrating the leaves. I hear the brook as I get close to the cabin and smell the dampness—the rain machine is on. The cabin door is cracked, and I tap on it and walk in, my eyes adjusting to the dim light. The shades are down, and my father is reading by the light of a small lamp. He looks up and smiles.

"Hi, Hep. What's up?"

"Mother wants you. Valentina's there, and everyone's dying to see you," I say, rolling my eyes.

"Oh," my father says, letting out a great sigh. He marks his place in the book, sits up and slips his feet into his moccasins. "I'd much rather stay here and talk to Socrates."

"Socrates?" I ask, and he indicates the book.

"Or Shakespeare," he adds, "or Keats or Kipling," and he gestures at the pile beside the cot. "Wouldn't you? I find them so much more fun to talk to than Valentina or Bunny or—" He breaks off and shrugs, laughter in his eyes, and I laugh too and coax him home where I fix his ritual old-fashioned. It's hardly a drink at all—two sugar cubes soaked in bitters, lots of orange slices, cherries and half a shot of bourbon.

Walking slowly back to Barnard, I kept thinking about Henry VIII and my father. I felt that my father had put a lot of himself into Henry, more than he usually did. Henry, in his prime, was musical, poetic and athletic, just as my father had been in his teens and in his twenties—he'd even played football in college. Henry was a romantic like my father, idealized whoever he loved at the time, but, unlike my father, Henry was bawdy and full of lust. Or maybe my father was too, but this was the first time that he'd allowed a romantic hero to be blatantly raunchy. There's a line in the first act of *Anne* that shocked me when I'd heard it at fourteen: "Next to the haunch of a virgin there's nothing like a haunch of venison." My father had told me, for as long as I could remember, that sex and love together were beautiful and pure. He'd never mentioned that there were sexual appetites that had nothing to do with love.

Of course, no one else had either. After the mountain

episode, I didn't confide in my mother at all, and since I didn't feel that I could talk to Bunny, Lenya or Nancy about sex, I'd stumbled along, still believing in the spiritual union of sex and love—until I read *Morning, Winter and Night*. I'd even read the edited version, the sexiest parts taken out. The first version, according to Bill Sloane, my father's publisher, was unprintable. My father had begun writing *Morning, Winter and Night*, his only novel, during the winter of 1949 and had finished it in the summer of 1950. It was autobiographical, the first truly autobiographical thing he'd ever written, and he'd published it under a pseudonym, John Nairne Michaelson, so that the critics wouldn't attack it with their usual fury. My father was sure that they were just waiting to ambush him, and this book would have been a perfect target—explicit sex between eleven- and twelve-year-olds by the lofty Maxwell Anderson.

Morning, Winter and Night was the Hallie story, but with a whole new twist. It was set at the turn of the century at his grandmother's farm, and it was all very familiar to me until we got to Madie. He'd adored Hallie, as he'd told me—ethereal, blond little Hallie—until her parents had taken her away for the winter, determined to separate her from her awestruck twelve-year-old boyfriend. The boy, Jamie in the book (my father's full name was James Maxwell), was in despair until he met Madie. Madie was the opposite of Hallie—dark, vixenish and sexually active. They had a passionate, violent love affair in the woods after Madie hit him across the face with her whip. It was pure sex, with all the filth and desire that excited and disgusted him at the same time. Hallie came back, rejected him when she heard about Madie, then, after he almost died of shame and pneumonia, offered herself to him, saying that he could have had her all along. He found that he couldn't perform with the saintly Hallie and, ultimately, didn't understand a thing.

I didn't understand it either until I lay on my bed at Barnard and began to see that Hallie had been the "good one," Madie the "bad one," that Margaret had been the "good one," my mother the "bad one." I had been his pure little girl, so what was Gilda? Obviously, she was another pure one, sweet and girlish, with two young children. So where did that leave me? Still his little girl, I decided—his special child. I thought about my father's version of Henry VIII and Anne again. Henry had adored Anne until he'd moved heaven and earth to win her, then he'd begun to lose interest. When Anne committed adultery, or Henry believed she had, he'd had her executed. My father had adored my mother, even when she drove him crazy, until she committed adultery. Anne had lost her head; my mother had lost her life.

In *High Tor*, my favorite play, there were two women, one earthbound, one made of air. In the first production my mother had played Judith, the earthbound one who wanted Van Dorn, the hero, to get down off his mountain, marry her and lead an ordinary life. It seemed a fitting role for my mother, but she was replaced before the New York opening. It was her last acting job. I'd been told that she wasn't very good, but the main reason was that my father didn't want her to work. He wanted her all to himself, to type his plays, to criticize his pages, to run his house and his life. The other woman in *High Tor* was Lise, the beautiful Dutch ghost who'd been waiting for two hundred years for her lost ship to sail back up the Hudson and take her home. Of course, Van Dorn fell in love with Lise, who was as pure and idealized as only a spirit could be.

"The two women again," I thought to myself, "the dark, sexy one and the sprite." Lise was Hallie all over again. I went through some of the other plays in my mind, the ones I was most familiar with, and came up with a few more saints and sinners. The women were all one or the other, although sometimes the sainted ones fell and became sinners. No wonder my father hadn't been able to forgive my mother. She'd told him, during those last months, that she would crawl on her hands and knees to him if only he would forgive her. He'd answered, "I rot a bit every time I look at you."

I'd wanted him to forgive her. I didn't see why he couldn't. I'd accepted Lenya's view that fidelity wasn't the most important thing in a marriage. If you are best friends, helpmates, soul mates, why is a sexual liaison so important? I'd been torn apart—I'd wanted my father to recover and be happy, but, at the same time, I'd felt that if you really loved someone you could forgive them. Gazing out my window at Barnard, my brain reeling, I knew that it was more complicated than that. Partly I'd wanted my father to forgive my mother, partly I'd wanted my mother to suffer some consequences and partly I'd wanted my father all to myself. At odd moments I'd feel the sensation that I had while standing beside my father at my mother's funeral—the sense of triumph, the feeling that I'd won after a long battle—and felt terrible shame. And I remembered a line from *Morning, Winter and Night* that had startled me when I'd read it. The Westerner, the old man looking back at his boyhood at the end of the book, had said, "This horrible secret, this thing that bites into your mind and makes you flush with shame in the darkness when you are old." I wanted to know my father's horrible secret, or secrets, but I was sure that I never would.

I wondered what William Lincoln Anderson, my father's father, the red-bearded fire-and-brimstone preacher, would have said. My father had, supposedly, left all that behind, but it must have stayed with him the way the smell of honeysuckle and the road rules had stayed with me. The Reverend Anderson and his teachings had left a puritanical imprint even though my father hadn't wanted to listen. My father still believed that a man should be on the side of the angels and that a woman should be true to him, no matter what. I never met my father's parents because his mother, Perimella, who was called Premma, had died a week after I was born. They'd thought of calling me Premmalie—little Premma—but had decided against it. I was glad; I'd had enough trouble with Hesper, which was often Hester, Esther or the wreck of the *Hesperus*. I didn't know William Lincoln Anderson either, which my father had told me was no great loss, because right after his wife's death, after eight children and God knows how many years together, he'd run off to Florida with a rich widow and had died eighteen months later.

It was still Sunday afternoon in the city—more church bells, and, below me, girls returning from the weekend away. I didn't want to see anyone; I didn't want to do anything. I wanted to talk to my father. I wanted to hear his voice. I wanted to know that I still had my place in his heart.

Gilda answered the phone, her voice light and sweet.

"Hi," I said. "It's Hesper. Is Daddy there?"

"Yes, dear," Gilda said, "but, oh, he's reading to the children. Let me just see . . ." And she was gone; murmuring through a covered mouthpiece.

"Hi, Hep," my father said, after a minute.

"Hi, Daddy. What were you reading?"

"Just *Tom Sawyer*," my father answered, knowing that it wasn't one of my favorites. I was relieved. For a second I saw him at the end of my bed at home reading, "The owl and the pussycat went to sea, in a beautiful, pea-green boat." Or I heard him recite, "There was a little boy, and a naughty boy was he. He ran away to Scotland, the people for to see."

"Are you up to the cave part?" I asked.

"Not quite. Almost," my father said.

"That's the best part," I said, and there was a pause before I asked, "so is everything okay?"

"Yes," my father answered. "Terrible work. They want me to do the Jesus story again, for Christ's sake."

"For Christ's sake it would be," I said, and we both laughed.

"And my stomach still keeps me up at night," he added. "But Gilda takes good care of me and makes me happy."

"That's good. Is the hernia acting up again?"

"Oh, I suppose," my father said as if the subject were too boring to go into. "And you? How was your time with Marion?"

"Nice," I answered, "really nice."

"That's too bad," my father said.

"I still love him, Daddy—I do."

"Love makes fools of the best of us," my father said quietly, then quickly changed the subject. "Have you been to the country? Seen the boys?"

"Yeah, I go most weekends. Everybody's fine." I heard commotion in the background, the children screeching and Gilda's voice saying reverently that Max was on the phone. It reminded me of Elmer Rice's wife hushing everyone as she said, "Quiet, Elmer's thinking."

"I'd better say good night," my father said. "The troops are getting restless."

"Okay. Talk to you soon. Love you!" We hung up, and I left the phone and the hallway, thinking that he'd said, "Love you too," but I wasn't sure. Laurel and Craig had been clamoring for his attention, and I hadn't been able to hear him clearly. I went back to my room, to my narrow sanctuary, pulled the covers over my head and relived Marion's kisses before finally falling asleep.

It was a relatively happy autumn. I saw Marion again, two or three times, and we kissed at the end of each date, but I didn't see him nearly as much as I wanted to. He never invited me to his apartment, somewhere in the East Twenties, which I thought was strange since I'd spent so much time at the dismal Hotel Schuyler when I was fifteen. But I took what I could get—whatever he offered—and kept myself busy. I didn't get involved with life at Barnard. I made acquaintances, not friends, and only a couple of the classes interested me. I went to the country almost every weekend and stayed, as usual, with Nancy and Alan, Lenya or Bunny and Milton. I didn't have a car, but it was easy to get rides. Someone was always driving out on a Friday, and someone was always driving in on a Sunday. Alan was my best bet for a ride out; he was the stage manager of *Picnic*, and I'd meet him backstage before midnight and get a ride to the country. Barnard was just a jog off the West Side Highway, so it was simple for whoever was driving in to drop me off.

Social life on the road kept changing. The Simon house, my old house, became a center of activity for children and grown-ups alike. There were five children, and Sidney tended to be an extrovert, joining the poker games and the parties. Burgess Meredith and his young wife, Kaja, began hosting the Saturday-night poker games, and Bill Mauldin was everywhere. The Caniff house was still a gathering place, but Lenya and George were in town a lot, working on *Threepenny*. Besides, George said that he couldn't sleep with the brook in his ear—he said it was worse than the rumble of buses, cabs and subways.

The Spring Valley airport, which I hadn't even known existed, became popular when Bill Mauldin and Kaja Meredith took up flying. They took lessons in two-seater propeller planes—Cessnas, I think—and I liked to go to the airport and watch. Flying intrigued me. After I'd spent a month or so watching, Bill began to insist that I take lessons too. I took a trial lesson and loved it. I loved takeoff, the surge of power that lifted you off the ground, and I loved being up there. I felt so free when I was, above everything, looking down on the little airport and the tiny town of Spring Valley. Coming down was the part that I didn't like. I'd worry about landing for half an hour before I actually had to do it, and I'd breathe a great sigh of relief once we were down.

The other problem was that I had no sense of direction whatsoever. I was fine as long as I could see the ground, the square fields below and the edge of the Hudson, but turn me around, without a landmark, and I was lost. Bill and Kaja, way ahead of me, were studying navigation, learning to fly on instruments when there was no visibility. I found this really daunting. Numbers and equations tended to make me go blank. I'd see Miss Bradley's beady eyes, her thin lips, ready to pounce, ready to make me feel really stupid, and any logic that I possessed flew out of my head. I got as far as soloing. I managed to fly alone from the Spring Valley airport to La Guardia, land and fly back again. It was exhilarating and frightening—descending over the water to hit the runway at just the right spot, taking off and landing again. Afterwards I had no idea how I'd done it. It was my last flight. Navigation was the next step, and I decided against it.

It wasn't just fear that stopped me. Flying lessons were expensive; my father was supporting me, and I was aware that, since 1950, he'd worried a lot about money and taken screenwriting jobs that he didn't want. The "Jesus story" that he'd mentioned was a draft of *The Robe*, a job that he hated.

The big financial problem that increasingly weighed him down was the old tax debt of a hundred thousand dollars that had resulted from the movie sale of *The Eve of St. Mark*. By early 1950 the IRS ruled that the movie sale was taxable as income, not as a capital gain, and my father owed them the hundred thousand dollars that, of course, my parents had spent already.

The interest kept compounding, the debt kept growing, and my parents didn't change any of their ways. My father had finally agreed, in 1951, that my mother could go to work because she'd argued that she could bring in some additional money, but her earnings as an editor were a drop in the bucket compared to what was going out. After my mother's death, my father didn't do any better. I'd grown up watching him reach into his pockets and hand out hundred-dollar bills. He was still doing it, still supporting friends and relatives, and now supporting Gilda and her children.

I had no sense about money either. It almost never crossed my mind. As a recipient of those hundred-dollar bills, and anything else I wanted, why would it? No one ever suggested that I actually earn anything. I worked hard in summer stock, but that was just fun. The only good thing about me in respect to money was that, in reaction to my mother's love of things, I didn't care about them. I bought some books, some clothes and that was about it. But I was aware, in 1953, that my father was feeling burdened, and flying lessons were a luxury that I didn't need. So was the dormitory. I broached the subject sometime in December; it seemed to me that my father was paying good money for me to stay in a tiny room and eat inedible food.

"I could get an apartment near school," I said during one of my collect calls from the hallway, "and you could stay there when you come to New York. You wouldn't have to pay for the dorm or a hotel."

"It's a thought," my father said. "I might have to come east soon."

"For Christmas?" I asked hopefully.

"No. No, I'll have to be here for Christmas. For work and possibly to get myself checked out. My stomach's still bothering me, and my heart's been acting up."

"Oh, Daddy, no."

"Well, don't worry about it, sweet. It's just annoying, and I want to find out what's going on. So, yes, start looking, and if you see a place that looks interesting, let me know. Not too expensive though."

"I know," I said. "I'll start looking—it's exciting—and take care of yourself, okay? I love you."

This time I was certain that he said, "I love you too." I walked over to Broadway to buy a paper, to look at the ads, and my stomach clamped with fear. I'd always been afraid that he would die. He was an "old father," forty-six when I was born, fifty-six when I was ten, and I remembered all the times, growing up, that I'd looked at his smile and thought, "Someday I'll never see that smile," and all the times that I'd looked at his hands on the piano keys, when he'd played "Greensleeves" as if he were playing an organ, and thought that one day I wouldn't see those age-spotted hands that I loved more than all the world.

I shook off my fears. My father had just had his sixty-fifth birthday; he could live another twenty years at least. I could be forty or forty-five by the time he died, which seemed really old to me. I talked myself out of the dread that had gripped me, bought a Sunday *Times* and took it back to my room. As I looked through the ads for the Columbia area, I began to get excited. I began to daydream about the freedom I would have—I could come and go as I pleased, have my own phone, invite Marion to *my* place, and we wouldn't have to say good night on the porch at Barnard. I could make a home away from home for my father, even though I knew nothing about making a home, and he would be mine again, just the two of us. I circled ads happily, spinning dreams that part of me knew could never be.

CHAPTER FIFTEEN

CHRISTMAS WAS SPENT at Alan and Nancy's. It was the first Christmas without my parents and without our house. I'd found an apartment, inexpensive and dreary, but I couldn't move into it until the beginning of January, so I was grateful to be able to camp out on the road—at Alan's, at Lenya's, at Bunny's. Christmas had always been my favorite time on South Mountain Road. For a couple of weeks everyone came together, exchanged presents, sang carols, forgot their various feuds. Our lovingness had nothing to do with Christ, or his birthday, or religion at all. It was just a time when everyone joined hands, as we did in the circle every New Year's Eve. Bill Sloane and his family went to the small, steepled church in Mount Ivy, and Martha took Little Terry to a church in West Nyack, but that was about it. No one went to temple as far as I knew, and I never even heard of Chanukah until I was in college.

Still a secret Catholic, I took my pink rosary with the little dead Christ everywhere and put it under my pillow every night, but nobody knew this. I'd lost Teppi's catechism somewhere along the way, but I still prayed to the image of Jesus in his sky-blue robe. When I was ten and eleven and the Playwrights Company was at 630 Fifth Avenue, across the street from Saint Patrick's Cathedral, my parents used to let me go downstairs alone—thirty flights in the elevator—and I'd sneak across the street and into Saint Patrick's. I'd kneel, but I didn't know how to cross myself and felt awkward as I stared up at the vast ceilings and the stained-glass windows. I found the altar to Saint Joan, and after watching people light candles to the saints, I decided that it was all right to light a candle to Joan of Arc. My father was writing about her and loved her, and I loved her too, so I lit candles to her and prayed, and no one ever knew this either.

When I was fifteen, my father accepted an award from the National Conference of Christians and Jews. He made a speech, he told me, with both pride and amusement, in which he pleaded for the acceptance of atheists as well as Christians and Jews, Muslims and whomever. None of us really believed his avowals of atheism. In his plays, one of the main themes was the struggle between faith and the lack of it, or the struggle to reclaim a bit of faith after the loss of it. It was a personal struggle that he didn't talk about, only wrote about. Both *Winterset* and *Lost in the Stars* end with the dim hope that there is some purpose in it all, that life on earth is more than being "lost on this rock that goes around the sun without meaning."

He never went near a church, said religion was an opiate and named our Christmas angel Aimee Semple McPherson. Every year he placed her at the top of the tree, her silver wings and platinum hair gleaming in the reflected light, and wryly wished her well—and a Merry Christmas and a Happy New Year.

Bunny's tree—Milton didn't have much to do with it— was always blue lights and silver tinsel. Lenya and Kurt exchanged presents with everyone but weren't elaborate about

Christmas. Once Lenya married George that all changed. George loved the holidays. Over the years he had collected antique toys and decorations, and they were all displayed during the twelve days of Christmas. He opened up the second-floor front room, closed off since Kurt lay there in his coffin, and festooned it with branches, balls, holly, a laden tree and mistletoe. Everyone said that it was lovely to see the living room again, but some whispered that George had replaced Kurt with faggot kitsch. But then they muttered that it was good to see Lenya laugh, and, queer or not, George had pushed her back onstage and given her a reason to live.

Our tree had always been in the corner of the dining room. It was also covered with antique ornaments and tinsel, with Aimee at the top. My mother had worked hard at Christmas. She bought and wrapped for weeks on end. She wrapped everything in her study on the second floor, keeping it all secret, and her study became a mass of paper, bows, tissue and tape. She'd let me help her at times, hiding all my presents first, and I'd hold my finger on a taut ribbon while she used both hands to make a bow. She did this with as much concentration as she applied to everything—her brow furrowed, smoke drifting upward from the cigarette in the holder clenched in her mouth—unable to talk because talk was distracting.

She also worked hard on Christmas dinner. Martha did most of the cooking, but my mother did all the planning, ordering, fussing, table setting, flower arranging, and she usually cooked one exotic dessert. Crêpes suzette was my favorite because I loved to watch the flames shoot up, blue and silver, in the chafing dish. Except for the year of the disastrous suckling pig on a spit, the dinners were successful, and the whole family—all of my father's immediate family— seemed to have a good time. The Caniffs came to our house every year, and Bunny told me, after my mother's death, that she'd told my mother once that she'd felt funny about coming: "After all, everyone else is Max's family." With a strained look, my mother had answered, "That's why I want you here."

When I opened my eyes in the guest room at Alan and Nancy's, early on Christmas morning, I looked out the two paned windows to see a rare, magical Christmas morning. About six inches of wet snow had fallen since midnight, and the branches of the pine trees were bowed low and heavy with the snow that was still falling. Growing up, I'd always wanted it to snow at Christmas, and every so often it had. I'd kept a clear image in my head of one Christmas Eve—snow was falling on the woods as I sat by my window and forced my eyes to stay open so I wouldn't miss Santa Claus when he came. I waited and waited, sure that his sleigh would appear over the white treetops and skim over the smothered gardens.

I smiled to myself in the cozy bed in the guest room, thinking that I'd probably believed in Santa Claus much longer than most children do. I tended to believe everything anyone told me and didn't have any little friends around to set me straight. Sandra, my one friend, who lived back in the woods with old Mary Hyphen-Clarke, was just as naïve as I was. Alan and Nancy's three boys were downstairs, opening the stockings that we'd hung the night before, and I was sure that they'd known for years who had filled them. I smelled coffee and the fire that Alan had laid the night before and got myself out of bed. I knew that Nancy had filled a stocking for me too. My usual one, the one that I'd hung at home since I was three, was either packed away in storage with the rest of our decorations, or may even have been tossed out.

We unwrapped presents; the boys took turns playing the new hockey game and Alan made a big breakfast as he did every Sunday morning. It was comfortable and fun, and I didn't think that I missed my parents or Martha or our house. The snowplow came through, plowing the road and leaving impassable drifts beside the driveways, so we went out with shovels, clearing the drifts and making paths. Sidney Simon came down the driveway from their house in our old Jeep with the plow attached to the front. Sidney was about forty, but he was a city boy, and this morning he looked like a kid with his first toy truck. He zigged and zagged and waved and called out that we should all come up later. Alan called back, two gloved hands cupped around his mouth, that we'd be there if Sidney and the Jeep weren't in the pond by then.

After an early Christmas dinner—less elaborate but just as good as my mother's—Nancy, Alan, the boys and I walked up the driveway to the Simon house. As we rounded the curve in the driveway, it still looked like my house to me— white and snow covered against the woods and the gray sky. The snow was letting up, and clumps of snow were sliding off the bent branches of the apple trees, the birches and the dogwoods. It wasn't until we entered through the dining room door that it struck me, once again, how different everything was. Children of all sizes were tearing through the house; cookies, drinks, toys and wrapping paper covered every surface, including the floor.

In the living room I sat near the fire and began seeing ghosts. Behind the children running up and down the brick stairs, Margaret's ghost, as I'd imagined it as a child, flickered against the wall. In the far corner of the room where the chess table used to be, I saw the smoke, the cards, Bunny's blond hair, Lenya's carrottop, my mother's dark curls. And behind the card players I saw the open casket, only one dark curl visible above the gleaming wood. On the other side of the room, Kurt sat at our baby grand, playing "September Song" and singing, "Ven I vas a young man courting ze girls . . ." In front of the fireplace, its copper hood gleaming with heat, my father sat on his haunches and splashed kerosene on the red-hot logs, sending flames soaring and waking Toby, stretched out on the Oriental rug.

I made small talk with a few people around me who weren't seeing ghosts, laughed at nothing, played with the children and left by myself. The snow had stopped, and moonlight fell across the drifts and the untouched lawns as I walked back to Alan and Nancy's. I stood at the bridge, looked down at the black water, the snow-covered rocks, and wiped away tears that slipped from my eyes and took me by surprise. I thought I was feeling good. "I *am* feeling good," I told myself, as I crossed the bridge, "and it's going to be a wonderful new year."

My father had told me to take whatever furniture I needed out of storage, and I watched the movers as they carried my mother's bed, dresser and "Ginger Rogers" dressing table into the bedroom of my new apartment. I gave the dressing table that name because it was such a forties piece—curly maple with a semicircle mirror. The bedroom furniture looked out of place in the dark bedroom, and the living room furniture that I'd taken—the Carroll French sofa and two chairs, the rug, a table—looked even more out of place against the green walls. I knew nothing about New York apartments, so when I chose one on the first floor that had green walls and barred windows, I had no idea that it was going to look and feel like a green cave.

It had a wallpapered foyer that led into a small kitchen straight ahead, and to the left, a good-sized living room, bathroom and bedroom, all painted a deep green. Past the kitchen there was another small room, where I put a daybed and a desk. The apartment would have been fine except for its darkness and its greenness. I hadn't known that I could ask the landlord to repaint, and I hadn't realized that sunlight never penetrated a first-floor apartment. The building was on the corner of Ninety-seventh Street and West End Avenue, and the building on the opposite side of Ninety-seventh managed to block out all light. I had to go out to the avenue to find out if it was raining or if the sun was shining. I thought my father might like it; even though he didn't like the city, the apartment was as dreary as his cabin in the woods. All we needed was a rain machine.

I was excited when he told me in early January that he was going to come stay with me in New York for a few days. He had a meeting at the Playwrights Company, a meeting with his lawyer and accountant, and an appointment with a New York doctor. He'd had a hernia operation in 1950, but his condition was bothering him again, and he was concerned about his heart. He took Seconal to sleep and kept nitroglycerin handy in case he needed it. I was frightened when he told me all this, but he looked wonderful when I met him at the airport—as large and warm and healthy as he'd always looked. I couldn't wait to show him the apartment, where I'd tried hard to make a home away from home, but I could tell when we first walked in that he was somewhat appalled. He covered his reaction and was a good sport about the whole thing, insisting that he stay in the small room off the kitchen and leave me the bedroom. I worried that he didn't want to sleep in my mother's bed—the one that they'd slept in together, and where she'd lain wet and naked after a suicide attempt—and I worried that the furniture from our house would upset him, but after his initial reaction he didn't seem to notice.

The first night that he was there we sat on the sofa from home, in front of the marble-topped coffee table that had cracked during the move, and he talked about Gilda, about how young and sweet she was, about his belief that she'd saved his life. He knew that I still felt that he could have forgiven my mother and, once again, he said, "I had to save myself. You understand that, don't you, Hep?" His eyes were pleading, and I nodded—yes, I understood, even if I didn't quite. He talked about the new play that he was working on, about Elizabeth I in her old age. He was hoping to interest the Lunts, who had starred in *Elizabeth the Queen* in the thirties before I was born.

"No one's interested in verse plays anymore," he said with a tired shrug. "But who knows? It gives me a bit of hope."

"They might be," I said. "With the Lunts?"

"All Broadway wants," he answered, "is big musicals, plotless ramblings or pointless trash." Heroes and big themes were out of fashion, he said, and so was he. I tried to reassure him, telling him that he could still have a hit—it was all so unpredictable. He gave me another weary smile and said that he would keep trying—he had no choice. And he would keep writing stupid movies for stupid people—at least it paid our rent.

He left sweet little notes for me during his brief stay. "I'm very excited about my new blood test and I've gone to get it. I love you, Daddy." "You're still sleeping. I've left a check on the table and a little something under your pillow," where I'd find a ten- or twenty-dollar bill. It was obvious that he was concerned about money—a ten or a twenty instead of the old hundred that he used to peel off a wad. The day that he came back from his appointment with Howard Reinheimer, his lawyer-accountant, who was advising him about his increasing tax problems, my father told me that he'd given a third of the royalties of several of his plays to my mother. She'd been a great help to him, he'd said—listening to his pages, editing and typing. Because my mother had left everything to me, that meant that her share of royalties would automatically come to me. Since he was supporting me and needed the money, would I consider turning over my mother's share to him? I agreed without question. My father had always taken care of me, and I was sure that he always would. I went to Reinheimer's office, signed the necessary papers and didn't give it another thought.

We saw Alan and Terry at Quentin and Thelma's apartment while my father was in town, but he didn't go to the country. He wasn't ready to face South Mountain Road yet, he said—maybe in the near future when he could bring Gilda and the road had forgotten. Once he had had his meetings and the doctor had told him that there was no immediate danger, my father booked a flight back to Los Angeles. I went with him to the Waldorf, where he'd arranged for a limousine to take him to the airport, and, after hugs and blowing kisses to the departing car, I found myself in the same corner drugstore where, in November of 1952, my parents had said their last, tense good-byes. It wasn't intentional; I wanted a cup of coffee and a bite to eat, and it wasn't until I sat on the red-vinyl stool and ordered that I realized that this was where we'd been—my mother, Lenya and I—after my father had left for the last time. My mother had sobbed at the counter, and, as usual, Lenya and I had felt that she was being overly dramatic. Embarrassed, I'd led my mother outside, and Lenya had gone for the car.

"You don't understand anything!" my mother had cried again and again, and she'd been right—I hadn't understood a thing. The romantic beliefs that I'd grown up with didn't leave room for conflicting emotions, didn't leave room for the turmoil of loving two people at the same time, or needing them in different ways. As far as I was concerned, you either loved someone, as I had loved Marion, or you didn't.

"But Jerry loves you and you love him," I'd said to my mother. "So why can't you be happy? If Marion loved me like that I'd be so happy."

Tears streaming from her swollen eyes, she'd looked at me as if I were an idiot. "You don't understand anything," she'd screamed again. "Just get away from me—leave me alone!"

It had been impossible to comfort her, I thought, as I made my way back to the green apartment. We'd all tried—Lenya, Bunny, Bessie, her friend Maggie Perry—but she'd sob and hit out at us with small, balled-up fists and say that all she wanted was to die.

"I'm so sorry, Mommy," I whispered to no one as I unlocked the apartment door. As I entered the silent rooms I realized that I hadn't called her mommy in years. I got undressed, curled up in her bed and tried to remember when I'd switched from mommy to mother. It was probably when I went to Hewitt's. I remembered when I was seven, running to her with a little glass bird that I'd bought for her at the Street School rummage sale. "Look, Mommy, look what I got for you!" I'd said, and she'd looked so happy as she'd taken the little bird in both her hands. I got out of bed, went to her dressing table and found the glass bird, which I'd kept. I held it, rubbing its wings, trying to remember what she'd looked like when she'd been happy.

I pictured her at different moments—laughing at one of my father's quiet jokes, winning a poker hand, cocking her head and smiling as she arranged a vase of flowers. There was always an edge to her happiness, a tenseness that didn't allow a full laugh or a soft smile. She knew this about herself. She'd said as much in one of the letters she'd written to me at college. I replaced the glass bird and reached into the bottom of my jewelry box, which had been hers, where I kept her letters. As I opened one and then another, I thought about the difference between her spoken voice and her written voice. Her spoken voice was as tense as her smile; her written voice was gentle and beautiful. I'd found it hard, at times, to put the two together. Would she have ever spoken those gentle words? And if she had, would they have come out the same way, or would they have been lost in the brittleness of her voice?

I found the letter I was looking for. I'd treasured it because she'd said things in it that I felt she never would have said in person, and because she'd given me a rare compliment.

December 3rd, 1952

Hesper darling,

That was the most unsatisfactory good-bye at the station on Sunday—a hasty peck and you were off and I couldn't even follow you with my eyes because I was so busy maneuvering the car through the post-holiday traffic. I presume you met your friend and that all is well. You're in the midst of rehearsals so I don't expect to hear from you until some time next week.

There were so many things I wanted to say—but couldn't. And maybe never shall. I seem to have a curious reticence where you're concerned. I never know whether it's because I'm afraid of hurting you or afraid of being hurt. As a result both seem to happen and we hurt each other without meaning to.

You looked radiantly lovely, darling—alive, glowing, all round in your personality, without the sharp edges that most people have. I sit back and envy you, thinking that's how I should like to be—that's how I shall make myself become. But it's not easy for me, who am so different. All edges. Always hanging on desperately to fight the hysteria within. Even when I seem most sure of myself on the surface. Perhaps that's why I have sudden gusts of extroversion—to combat the deep gloom within myself. And in the last months it's reached a climax. And it has made me and you and everyone around very uncomfortable. I'm sorry, darling. I only hope you'll bear with me a little longer. Some peace will come eventually. I'm certain.

I'll know about my advertising agency job in a few days. They have to be convinced I'm worth all that money 52 weeks a year. I have no real urge to work, but it would be better than this endless brooding over past sins and failures. I'd rather cook and wax furniture and kneel on my haunches in the garden. A belated choice, isn't it?

Tonight I am going with Al Andriola to see the French company do *Hamlet*. I'll be home over the weekend, though the house will seem empty without you and Daddy. I'm looking forward to Christmas. It will even be nice to get annoyed with you over the cyclone in your room.

No word from Daddy. I presume he's all right.

I love you, darling. And be good in the play.

Mother

Dover Hotel
687 Lexington Ave.
ELdorado 5-0100

The letter had been written just days after that last good-bye to my father when her sobs had so embarrassed me. The job she'd anticipated hadn't come through, and she'd given up her two rooms in the dreary Dover Hotel. She'd moved back to the country and into a steady decline until her death in March. I folded the letter and replaced it, murmuring again, "I'm so sorry, Mommy. I'm so sorry."

I was still trying to remember when she'd been happy. I glanced at the dates on her other letters, beginning in the fall of 1951 when I'd gone away to college. It seemed to me that she'd been happy and excited when she'd first gone to work.

I reread letters that I hadn't read since her death, and I found clippings that she'd sent me and I'd forgotten. One was a picture of her, looking lovely, in an ad for Blue Bonnet margarine: "Mrs. Maxwell Anderson puts on Blue Bonnet margarine for F.N.E.—Flavor, Nutrition, Economy!" I realized, gazing at her photograph in the familiar blue bonnet, that they must have needed money pretty badly for her to do that. The Caniffs' Willie had said angrily, after my mother died, that she would never again buy Blue Bonnet margarine. I couldn't quite make the connection. What had Blue Bonnet to do with her death? But Willie was adamant, and I didn't question her. I took most of Willie's statements with large grains of salt. Willie had been just as adamant in her belief that Martha had hastened my mother's death by doing voodoo on her with a witch doctor in West Nyack. And then there was Willie's speech to me about my mother's deathbed secret, the secret that Willie could never tell. I put as much faith in that as I did in the idea of Martha sticking pins in a Mab doll.

I found another clipping, this from *Time* magazine, May 5, 1952, and another photograph of my mother, with the caption "Editor Anderson." That must have pleased her, I thought, reading the article, to be recognized for herself instead of as the playwright's wife. The *Celanese Theatre* had just won the Peabody Award, "For productions of American plays which are done with 'fidelity, intelligence, and scrupulous regard for the intentions of the playwright.' " The article continued, "In its first year on TV, *Celanese* has put on more grown-up drama than almost any of its rivals . . . As in all TV drama, the scripts have to be boiled down to less than one hour. The job is given to adapters who work under the supervision of Script Editor Mab Anderson, in private life the wife of playwright Maxwell Anderson. But scripts are shown to the original authors before going on the air, and no deletions, changes or shifts of emphasis may be made without the playwright's consent. Says Editor Anderson: 'I would never change a play basically, its intention or meaning.' "

I reread her letter in which the clipping was enclosed.

May 2nd

Hesper darling,

I had planned to spend a quiet evening writing letters, but now it's eleven o'clock and this is my first one—and the others will be postponed indefinitely, as always. Daddy and I had dinner in the apartment, and then I washed dishes and straightened things here and there—for beyond a certain point, mess and confusion are a jangle to my nervous system. Then I lay down to rest and Daddy read aloud Mary Shelley's letter to a friend describing Shelley's last days and the discovery of his death. A beautiful and frightening letter, written to this one friend but with a knowledge that she could never say it twice, and so it was a document for the world, which indeed it has become. Then Daddy read Shelley's letter to Keats and various others—and I found myself listening more to the sound of his voice than to the words. You know how shy and mumbling he is when he reads his own work—but this he read with great beauty and clarity and emotion. I began to reflect how one takes other people's qualities for granted—the way one ceases to observe the color of the eyes or clothes or characteristics of any sort that have been established by memory—and suddenly one sees them all fresh again, as if for the first time. And that got me thinking of you, and I looked at your photographs in the apartment, and I could almost hear your voice too. You became very near and very dear. And in front of me is a bill from Peck & Peck and that reminded me of you at the studio on your last visit home. And writing to you now I feel I could never be really angry with you again—though of course I shall, a thousand times over the years—but it's all petty and inconsequential, and can't possibly affect any basic relationship.

Yesterday was the Peabody Award lunch. I'm enclosing a piece in "Time" with a horrid picture of me. If I thought I looked like that I'd feel worse than you do about your looks. Fortunately I don't know what I look like. Photographs capture one in repose—so they can't tell the truth. It makes me feel better to think so, at any rate.

I stopped reading, for the moment, and stared at the photograph she was referring to. She didn't look the least bit "horrid." She looked like a very pretty woman getting older. I suddenly saw her, standing naked, in front of the full-length mirror in the downstairs bathroom. The door was ajar, and I'd walked in unexpectedly. She was examining the tiny lines on the back of her thighs, the purplish veins running up her legs, her thin, sagging arms, her flattened breasts. And she was crying.

I pushed the image away and took the packet of gray-blue envelopes back to her bed. I turned on her bedside lamp and continued to search for a time when she'd been happy. I'd been away so much of those last two years, 1951 and 1952, that I'd missed many of the changes. I was trying to piece it together. I glanced again at the date on the last letter I'd read—May 2nd, 1952. She'd been deeply involved with Jerry Stagg at that time, and my father had just returned from working in Los Angeles with Rouben Mamoulian on a musical that never got off the ground. She spoke so warmly of my father in that letter, but it was only two months later, the beginning of July, when all hell broke loose. My father had picked up the phone at home and heard my mother speaking softly on the extension, saying, "Oh, darling," or something like that, and then he'd heard Jerry's voice answering her. He'd known immediately who it was. Jerry and my mother had been working together for nearly a year; Jerry and his wife, Maxine, had come to the country for weekends. "Max and Maxine," I said to myself, a wry afterthought, "the betrayed couple."

My father had slammed down the phone, stormed into my mother's room and confronted her. When she admitted the affair, he'd called her a whore and a slut and a bitch. When she'd tried to explain that she'd felt lonely and unloved, he'd shouted that she'd made a complete fool out of him—cuckolded him—and called her more names. She then tried to say that an affair couldn't compare with married love, that Lenya had affairs, that Bunny had affairs. That was as far as she got. My father turned, left the house and drove recklessly down the road to the Caniffs'. He ran up the outside stairs, found Milton at his drawing board and asked if it was true.

That was as much as I knew about that awful day. I wasn't home, and Milton would never tell me, or anyone, what he'd said to my father or what my father had said to him. I arrived home a few days later, after a carefree vacation at Myrtle Beach with some college friends, to utter devastation. My mother cried and pleaded with my father for understanding and forgiveness. My father lay on his bed on the third floor, day and night, with a damp, white handkerchief covering his eyes. He didn't eat. He barely spoke. He told me, when I tried to comfort him, that my mother had humiliated him, lied to him, destroyed him.

I'd been as shocked as he had been. I'd spent time with my mother and Jerry during Christmas and spring vacations. I'd liked Jerry—he was fun. And being my naïve self, the thought of anybody having an affair with anybody had never entered my mind. I'd liked visiting my mother at the studio, seeing her in action, seeing all that excess energy being put to good use. She was proud of the work she was doing, proud of the money she was making, and I was happy for her. But was *she* happy? I thought so, but I was seventeen and much more involved with my own happiness, or lack of it, than with anyone else's. My moods swung wildly between hating college and loving it, between being crazy about some boy and not being able to stand him. My parents, and home, were where I looked for support and encouragement. It didn't occur to me to worry about *them*. They were old and settled. That was my thinking, anyway, until it all blew up, until I was forced to see them as confused, fallible grown-ups, acting even more adolescent than I was.

"Can I do something for you, Daddy?" I'd ask, "Can I get you anything?" He'd shake his head slightly, without removing the white handkerchief, and I'd stand at the foot of his bed trying to think of a way to comfort him. Sometimes he'd say again that he was nothing more than a great fool, a cuckold, that my mother had totally destroyed him. I tried to reassure him: "No one thinks of you that way, Daddy. We all love you, admire you, just like we always have." But it didn't do any good. I couldn't help him, couldn't get him to smile or take the handkerchief off his face.

My mother was even harder to reach. I'd find her in the garden, jamming a spade into the soil, tears and sweat running down her face.

"Daddy's just really hurt," I'd say. "He'll get over it, I'm sure he will. He just feels—"

"He has no right to burden you with his feelings," my mother would spit back angrily. "You're a child. He has no right to pour out his self-pity to you."

"I'm not a child. I'm almost eighteen, Mother. I *can* understand. If you'd just talk to me, tell me why it all happened—"

"No, you *can't* understand, darling. You think you can but you can't."

"Won't you just talk to me about it?"

"No. This is our problem, mine and Daddy's. I don't want to burden you with it. I want you to—to just live your life. Now please leave me alone, darling. I have to finish this." And she'd continue her attack on the soil, her invisible wall firmly in place.

"And just what life am I supposed to live right now?" I'd answer angrily. "My summer job fell through, remember? The one your friend Jerry was supposed to set up? So what am I supposed to do, hang around here and change Daddy's handkerchief and watch you cry?" I'd storm away, really more hurt than angry that she wouldn't let me help, that she insisted on thinking of me as a child who still needed protecting.

In the kitchen, Martha would bang things around and go into one of her tirades about "that woman." She was freer now to say out loud every disparaging thing about my mother she could think of: "That woman never had it so good and she went and threw it all away because some hotshot wanted her. I told Mr. Anderson, I told him, you let that woman get all dolled up and go into town, get some job, some apartment, and she's gonna go foolin' around. I knew what she was up to long before he picked up that telephone. And she's still carrying on with that Jerry, with all her tears and all—" She'd shake her head, drops of sweat bouncing on the kitchen counter, and I'd leave the house by the back door before she could catch her breath and continue.

It was a hot July, and I'd wander down the driveway and dive into the pond, loving the feel of the dark, cold water just above the rocky bottom. I'd visit with Nancy and the children, play games with them, then walk up to Lenya's, where I'd hear that both my parents were being foolish: "Max with his cuckold business—no one has been cuckold since the Queen Victoria time. And Mabbie with her opera—she is Aïda and Isolde all at the same time. Come, Hep, I give you some strudel."

At the Caniffs' no one talked about what was happening. They'd just say that they were sure my parents would work things out. They'd give me dinner, we'd watch *Kukla* or play cards, or I'd sit in the studio with Milton and read or watch television while he worked on his strip. Then it would be time to go home.

There was a thunderstorm one night, taking the edge off the heat, and the lightning reminded me of the times that I'd walked with my father during storms, holding his hand as lightning flashed around us, and feeling so safe. I didn't feel safe anymore as I drove back from the Caniffs' through the rain, thunder and streaks of light against the mountain. I parked in front of the garage, crossed the driveway to the house, which was dark as usual, but I could hear my parents fighting, shouting at each other. It was something about Jerry—did she think she loved him? I made out my father's voice. Was she still sleeping with him, fucking him? Something like that. I stole up the stairs, not wanting them to know that I'd overheard.

I got into bed, and after a while the yelling stopped. I lay on my back, Teppi's pink rosary clasped in my hands, praying that everything would go back to the way it was—my old prayer, that everything would be the same, that nothing would ever change. I heard my father's footsteps on the stairs and called to him, "Daddy? Daddy, are you all right?"

He comes into my room, haggard and sallow, his shirt and pants hanging loosely. He sits on the edge of my bed, his head bowed, his hands clasped between his knees. He doesn't say anything until we hear the dining room door slam, the car start up with a roar and then tear down the driveway.

"She's gone to see Jerry," he says quietly.

"I don't think so," I say. "She loves you, Daddy."

He shakes his head and begins the story I've heard so many times: "When I was a boy, just twelve, staying on my grandmother's farm, I fell in love with this beautiful little girl named Hallie. She had blond ringlets, robin's-egg blue eyes and a smile that could shame the heavens. I never dreamed that Hallie could love me, a clumsy farm boy, but as if a miracle had taken place, she told me that she did. I felt like a prince, as if the frog had really been kissed by the princess, until the day her parents took her away. They agreed with me—I wasn't worthy of their princess—and they took her away and I nearly died of grief."

"I know," I murmur, only half listening. I know this story so well.

"I was a frog again," he goes on, "less than a frog. But then I went off to college and met Margaret. She was beautiful and smart, and I fell in love with her. And, miracle of miracles, she loved me too, and I became a king with Margaret. We had children, the queen and I, but then it began to go sour. I found others and she found others and I wasn't a king anymore. Then I met your mother—young, dazzling and beautiful—and she loved me and told me that I was even more than a king. She made me feel like an emperor, even a god, because she was so beautiful and she loved me."

"I know," I murmur again.

"But then she betrayed me," he says, "and now I'm even worse than a frog. I'm a dwarf, crippled and ugly, and a laughingstock."

"No, Daddy," I say, startled by this new ending to the story. "You're not." But he doesn't hear me.

"And now," he says, standing up, "I'm going to go down to your mother's room and look in her stocking bag and see if she took her diaphragm with her when she tore out of here. Did she take it with her to her lover, who she says isn't her lover anymore?" He tries to smile, tries to make light of what he's doing as he adds, "Do you want to go hunt with me? Do you want to sleuth with me?"

"No, Daddy," I say, after a moment, appalled. "No, I don't want to go with you." He shrugs slightly, kisses my forehead and leaves the room. I listen to his footsteps going down the brick stairs. I can't believe that he can stoop so low. I can't believe that my father, who's been famous, even revered, who's won a Pulitzer Prize, would go search for my mother's diaphragm in her stocking bag. I feel so sad for him, so ashamed, so disillusioned, and I know that my prayer hasn't been answered.

CHAPTER SIXTEEN

AFTER TWO or three weeks my father took the white handkerchief off his face, rose from his bed on the third floor and began, obsessively, to search for answers. He questioned everyone—Lenya, Bunny, Alan, George, Bessie, Martha—and then moved on to those in town. He questioned Alex Segal, *Celanese Theatre*'s director, Maggie Perry, Lilli Palmer, other acquaintances in the city, and Gilda Oakleaf, the young woman who worked as a production assistant on *Celanese Theatre*. He asked intimate questions; he *had* to know how long he'd been lied to, how long he'd been made a fool of. He *had* to know who knew and who didn't, and he pressed for every detail. He even asked me, but I didn't know very much. I told him that my mother and Jerry had taken me to dinner a couple of times after I'd visited the studio. I told him that I'd liked Jerry and my mother had seemed to be happy. That was all I knew.

"Yes, she'd seemed to be happy," I told myself, in the middle of the night as I lay in my green bedroom. "For a brief time, before that shattering phone call, before my father called her a whore and said he rotted a bit every time he looked at her."

His insistent questioning had lessened after he'd gone to see Gilda. She was living at the time with Maxine and Jerry Stagg, in an extra room of their town house. Maxine was a large, strange woman with a small, high voice and she and Gilda were old friends. When Gilda's marriage broke up, leaving her with two small children to support, Jerry had offered her a job on *Celanese Theatre*, and Maxine had offered her a place to live until she could get on her feet. Gilda had accepted, leaving her children with her mother in Providence temporarily and moving in with the Staggs.

My father had noticed Gilda before he began to bombard her with questions about my mother's and Jerry's affair, but I don't think he fell in love with her until he went, shattered, to her house and she listened to him rant and held out a gentle hand. There she was, just his type, small and dark, with an understanding smile and sympathetic eyes, even though one did wander off toward the wall. My father was sixty-three and Gilda was thirty-eight. He told me later that he'd more than noticed Gilda the first time he'd seen her. He'd watched the live performance of *Winterset* from the *Celanese Theatre* control booth, and Gilda, a production assistant, kept running in and out. When they were introduced he'd held her hand and said, "*You* should be playing Miriamne." Miriamne . . . my father's Juliet, his Hallie, the virginal girl-child that was my father's ideal.

"He was ripe," I said to myself. "My mother had crashed off her pedestal, such as it was, and here was this sweet, girlish woman ready to heal the wounds, ready to take her place."

My mother was fond of Gilda. She'd wanted to help her with her lonely struggle in whatever way she could. She'd invited her to the country, given her clothes, gifts for her children. She'd written to me about a weekend when Gilda had visited. I searched again through the pile of gray-blue envelopes but couldn't find the date I was looking for. I finally found the letter, without the envelope or the date, but it was clear that it was written at the end of May 1952.

Hesper darling,

This is your last week of school for the year, and I'm so glad it all turned out well and that you've been happy there. Not all the time, perhaps, but in the main. And that you've made good friends and had fun.

For me this has been a difficult year—successful—but not really well adjusted. Perhaps I'm too old to break the pattern of so many years of my life. Not break it, precisely, but alter and fit new experiences into it. Of course your going off to college would have changed it even if I'd remained stationary. Or your growing up would have changed it. Nothing is basically different—we'll be there when you get home, happy to see you and have you with us—but with a knowledge that it's all temporary, for soon it won't be just your going off to college, but marriage, and a home of your own, and an empty nest for Daddy and me. Yesterday, I was showing Gilda your photograph album—the years of growth—and it's not possible so much time has passed since those first baby pictures. The only comfort is you've grown so beautifully with so much grace of mind and spirit. And these have been *good* years. We're all very fortunate, aren't we?

Saturday I brought Gilda and her two children out for the weekend. We went for a long walk on the other side of the waterfall, dogs, children and all—it's my favorite part of Rockland County. The pink lady slippers are blooming profusely, wild azalea in bud, the dogwood still clinging, though Sunday's rain must have washed it all away. A terrific down-pour all day yesterday, and it was hard to keep the children amused indoors. Then I drove them all back to Conn.—got lost and it took hours, and I was feeling quite ill. So today I'm in bed, just pampering myself really. And a day in bed seems like a vacation. I have one more script to cut and my work for this season is over. It would be nice to have a real vacation—but where? Daddy's still struggling with his musical and wouldn't go anywhere anyway—so I guess I'll get what rest I can right at home.

No baby at the Mauldins' yet—but soon. Saw Alan and the boys yesterday—more beautiful than ever, all of them. Little Terry is a new person since I gave him the dog. He's so gentle and loving, not only with the dog but with all of us.

Said something funny to Daddy—at least Gilda laughed. He was sitting with his usual faraway expression and I said, "Are you thinking? Because I don't think it's very nice of people to think in public."

I stopped reading, crumpled the letter and threw it across the room. I was furious. It all sounded so cozy—Mommy, Daddy and Gilda. And they were all lying. My mother was sleeping with Jerry. Gilda knew my mother was sleeping with Jerry. My father was staring off into space, probably dreaming of Gilda, and Gilda was being my mother's friend while she was making walleyed doe eyes at my father. I hated all of them at that moment. I got out of bed, lit a cigarette, paced the ugly room and told all of them to go to hell. My voice echoed from the empty bedroom to the empty living room and back again.

"And that's another thing," I said out loud to my mother. "You said home would always be there—over and over you said it would always be my home. You said it in these damn letters. Well, guess *what?*" I shouted, and was answered by another echo. I scooped up the crumpled letter, flattened it out and slammed the whole pile back in the jewelry box.

I finally slept but was jolted awake by my own hoarse scream.

I'm playing dress-up with Virginia on the third floor. I never go up there by myself because it's where Margaret's trunk is kept, the one with all her letters and, at times, her ashes. But I'm fine up here with Virginia. We're pulling costumes out of the costume trunk and trying them on and giggling. I'm wearing the long, fringed scarf that my mother wore, long before I was born, for an illustrated story in a magazine. I love the picture—she's wearing just the gypsy scarf and batting her eyes at a handsome man with a mustache who's calling her a little witch. It says that right below the illustration. I'm imitating my mother's look, draping the scarf and batting my eyes for Virginia. Suddenly the door to the closet opens, the one with Margaret's trunk, and my mother and Margaret walk out together. But they're both ghosts, wispy and menacing. They come toward me, arms outstretched . . .

My scream was more like a gurgle, but it woke me. I was damp, cold and shivering. I pulled the covers up over my head, huddled under them and went right back to sleep.

After classes the next day I looked for my mother's album, which I'd taken out of storage. The apartment was a mess. I didn't really know how to clean. I'd learned whatever I knew by osmosis, by hanging around Martha, Teppi and the various cleaning people. And I had no inner discipline—none had ever been instilled. I laughed to myself about the fact that I was the only person I knew who could leave anything half done. I could clean half a bathroom, read half a book, write half a letter with no compunction to finish. So I searched through the mess and the unpacked boxes and finally found the album. My mother had put it together a couple of years before. There was also one for me and one for my father.

I opened my mother's album and there was the first baby picture, my mother sitting between her parents. It was the only photograph of her father. Then there was the picture of my mother and her sister as little girls, the one where they had bows in their hair. Then there was nothing. That must have been the orphanage years. I didn't suppose they took too many family portraits in orphanages. Again, I wished I knew more. I wished I'd asked more questions, wished that I'd probed more deeply when my mother had changed the subject, saying she didn't want to talk about it, didn't want to remember.

The next photographs were of my mother as a teenager, beginning to turn into a beauty. There were her early modeling pictures, wearing almost nothing—it was the twenties after all—and then one shot of her with the musclemen who couldn't lift her. She'd told me about that; she'd toured the country in an act where the strongest men had tried to lift her but couldn't get her off the ground. It was a trick of breathing, she'd told me, but wouldn't show me how to do it. Then there were the acting pictures, mostly proofs, in which she looked her most beautiful, and the magazine illustrations that she'd posed for. I found the one with the gypsy scarf. The story was called "White Light Winnie," and my mother was Winnie, fiery and seductive in every pose.

There were a few snapshots of my mother and Charles Maynard, her first husband, and then several photographs of my mother and father before I was born. My favorites were the ones of them beside the Pacific, my mother playing with her whippets—she had four at one time—and playing and laughing with my father. In one snapshot they're pretending to box—my large, muscular father—and my tiny mother. "Yes, she looked happy then too," I thought, and wondered if these pictures were taken before or after Margaret's death.

Just as Gilda had visited while my mother and father were still together, my mother had visited my father and Margaret before Margaret's death. My mother had climbed down the ravine and gone under the waterfall with my father, trying to impress him, she'd told me. She'd laughed and said that it had been freezing cold, and once he'd sworn his love for her, she'd never done it again.

I moved on to the first photographs of my parents after they were married and to my first baby pictures. There was one of my father holding me, as an infant, outside the first house (his and Margaret's house), and one of Martha holding me, but none of my mother and me until I was nine months old. My parents had left me with the Scottish nurse for my first three months and then gone to California for the next six, so we didn't all move in together—and I didn't really know them—until our house was finished when I was nine months old. There was a gap in the photographs, though not nearly as long or as drastic, similar to the gap in my mother's album. I knew that nine months with nurses didn't compare with years in an orphanage, but still I felt that I must have missed a lot and wondered if I would have had an easier time with my mother if we'd seen more of each other during that first year.

I turned the album's black pages, with names and dates written in white ink beneath the pictures, through the photographs of the next eighteen years. My mother hadn't aged well. Her beauty, which had been startling during her twenties, had begun to fade in her thirties. By her forties she was still a pretty woman, but there was nothing startling about it. Her skin became grayer and more freckled, and her violet eyes became a bit watery. By her late forties, just before she died, she weighed eighty-five pounds. Her hair was pepper and salt, and her face was lined with grief.

I closed the album and held my forehead against the grainy, black leather. I could see her, during that last summer—thin, haggard and frantic. In August of 1952, when she realized that my father had fallen in love with Gilda, had switched his entire allegiance to her, my mother had become desperate. My father called Gilda every evening. He wrote to her every day and sent love poems that were romantic and full of longing, the kind of poems that he'd sent to my mother when he was still with Margaret. My mother knew that she'd lost him, but she did everything she could to hold on. Her first, botched suicide attempt was on a hot, mid-August evening, not long after my eighteenth birthday.

It's almost midnight. I've been asleep for about an hour, and something wakes me. I heard running water in my dream and, still half asleep, stumble toward the upstairs bathroom. In the hallway, at the top of the brick stairs, I see a light on downstairs and hear noises in my mother's room. I go downstairs cautiously. Her bedroom door is ajar, and a light is on in her room. I push open her door, move inside her room and see her, lying naked and dripping wet on top of her sheets. Her eyes are closed, and I think she's dead. She's very white. My father sits on the other side of the bed, his feet on the floor, his face in his hands.

I rush to my mother, feel her face and neck and scream at my father to do something. He doesn't answer; he doesn't move. My mother moans slightly and turns her head from left to right. I pick up the phone beside the bed and call our local doctor, Doctor Blatt, in Haverstraw. He says to make coffee, spoon it into my mother's mouth and, once she's conscious, to walk her back and forth across the bedroom. He'll be here in ten minutes. I cover my mother's wet body, run to the kitchen, make a cup of coffee and carry it back to the bedroom. I sit beside her, spoon the coffee into her mouth and watch most of it slide down the folds in her neck and onto her breasts. But she's coming around, muttering and pushing the spoon away. My father still hasn't moved. I put the coffee down, get a robe from the bathroom and try to get my mother into it. She flails her arms, pushing me away.

"Help me, Daddy! Jesus, help me!" He doesn't seem to hear me. He sits paralyzed on the other side of the bed, his face in his hands, his shirt soaked from lifting my mother out of the tub. I give up on the robe and hoist my mother off the bed. I walk her back and forth on the cork floor, the way I've seen people walk drunks, my arm under her armpit, her arm slung over my shoulder, my hand clutching hers. She's naked, wet and slippery, but she's walking, not just dragging her feet, and we keep this up until Dr. Blatt arrives. He tells me that she'll be all right, that I did a good job and to go up to bed now. My father blinks once, turns his head slowly and looks at the small, bald doctor, who's taken over.

"Do you know what she took, Max?" the doctor asks, and my father gestures toward the bathroom.

"Some pills. I don't know," my father says. "She was under the water. I pulled her out."

I lifted my head from the album, the bedroom scene still vivid in my mind. My father's face, as he'd sat there—in shock, he'd said afterward—had also been haggard and full of pain. A day or so later, after my mother had recovered, he'd shown me a poem that he'd sent to Gilda in which he'd written that he had died, *was* dead, at the time that she'd found him and brought him back to life. All he wanted was to be with her. His words were much more poetic than that, but that was the gist of it. But right after the first suicide attempt my mother started seeing a psychiatrist in the city, who conferred with my father and told him that my mother wasn't strong enough yet for him to leave her. My father should give it some time. So he stayed, or his body did—it was clear that the rest of him was elsewhere.

Near the end of August my father went to see Gilda in Providence for a few days and they went out on the Sound in her brother's boat. He told me that they cooked fresh lobster in the galley and ate it in cups of melted butter. They slept on deck and took long walks on the beach. Gilda's children liked him, he said, and he wanted me to meet them. He'd had a perfect time, and when he came back, he'd felt even more trapped than he had before.

In early September my father arranged a time for me to meet Gilda and her children. I drove into the city with him—he had a meeting at the Playwrights Company—and we all met for lunch at the Mayan Room, a restaurant on the first floor of the building. My father and I were the first to arrive, and I waited, more curious than anything else, for my father's new family. They came toward us—Gilda, small and gentle in a full-skirted dress; Laurel, a beauty at eleven, eyeing me with curiosity similar to my own, and Craig, cute, bright and pressing for attention.

I thought the lunch went well. I was as ingratiating as possible, feeling that I needed to be accepted by them. The writing was on the wall—this *would* be my father's new family, and I would have to be a part of it. If not, I might lose my father, and I could never let that happen. Besides, I really did want my father to be happy. I hated watching his misery, and if this would make him happy, then he should have it. I wanted my mother to be happy too, and I couldn't see why she couldn't be happy with Jerry and let my father be happy with Gilda. It was that naïve thinking that caused the huge row between my mother and me at the breakfast table a few days later. We were arguing, once again, about the fact that she wouldn't talk to me. She'd sob, attempt suicide, but refuse to talk to me about it. In the midst of her silence I blurted out that my father had taken me to meet Gilda and the children. My mother flew into a rage.

"Behind my back," she'd screamed, "getting you on his side, pouring out his poor, goddamned soul to you, taking you to meet his new love. God, he's disgusting! He's shameless—he makes me sick!"

Again I made the mistake of saying what I had been thinking: "Then why don't you just forget it? Jerry loves you—be with him, let Daddy be with Gilda, and I'll be with all of you." Once more she'd looked at me as if I'd lost my mind and rushed, in tears, from the room.

"You don't understand, you don't understand." She'd said it over and over again. I still didn't. I put her album back in the box, wondering if I would ever understand. Maybe when I grew older, as she'd said, maybe when I'd suffered as she had. But I *had* suffered, I told myself, and it had never occurred to me to die. Then I wondered again if she had really wanted to die. During the seven attempts she had always called someone, or found some way to be discovered. That was one reason we—Lenya, Bunny and I—became so impatient with her. We'd stopped taking her threats and her attempts seriously. But the last time had been different; she'd made sure that no one would look for her. That time she had meant to die.

I'd missed some of the suicide attempts. I'd been visiting somewhere or was back at school. I'd missed the second one, not that I'd minded missing it. It had been only pills, and my father had found her in time. My mother was still seeing the psychiatrist, who was still telling my father that my mother's mental state was too precarious for him to leave. He was still trapped, but Gilda was nearby. That changed when Gilda told him that she couldn't stay in the middle of this mess, that she couldn't feel responsible for my mother's life or death and that she was moving—fleeing—to Los Angeles with her children.

My father was inconsolable. His poems were wretchedly forlorn. It was at that point, sometime in September, that I went back to college for my sophomore year. I threw myself into whatever I was doing—acting, writing, dating, escaping—and didn't come home until Thanksgiving. I knew that my mother had spent most of October in the city while my father stayed in the country, but they had done that before, and I didn't look upon it as a real separation. But then the news came. My father wrote to me at the end of October to say that he was planning to leave my mother and move to Los Angeles right after my vacation. I assumed that the psychiatrist had told him that my mother was well enough now to handle it. I wrote back on October 29th.

> Dearest Daddy,
>
> Your letter came just a little while ago, and, some-
> how, I knew what it would say even before I opened it.
> Matters just couldn't go on the way they had been, so
> I think a final decision of some sort ought to happen.
> I hope Mother is all right now and that you aren't too
> lonely. I keep wanting to run right home and brighten
> everything up a bit but I don't believe that either of
> you would really want me to do that. But I miss you
> terribly, and love you so much . . .

We had the usual Thanksgiving dinner, the last one, with my brothers and their wives and children and the Caniffs sitting around our round dining room table. Then, on that Sunday, Lenya, my mother and I drove my father into the city, said good-bye at the drugstore, and my father flew to Los Angeles, to Gilda, leaving my mother sobbing at the counter, embarrassing Lenya and me. We took my mother home, played cards with her for a couple of hours, gave her a sleeping pill and tucked her into bed. The next morning my mother drove me into the city, through the first, light snow, and I took a train back to North Carolina.

When Marion called at the apartment a few days later, and I found the nerve to invite him to dinner, I put everything away—the albums, the nightmares, the circling thoughts and questions. I simply let myself be excited. I unpacked and cleaned as best I could and planned a perfect dinner. I went to the country for the weekend before the dinner, partly to quiet my expectations and partly because Bunny had called to tell me that Toby wasn't doing too well.

Toby was as happy and wriggling as usual when he saw me, but he was thin, and his eyes were clouded. When we played ball, he tired quickly and seemed to just want to lie at my feet, his head on my shoe, or stretch out next to me on the carpet. I stayed with him during the Saturday-night poker game, kibitzing from the floor and thinking about the cast changes in the game that had gone on for so many years. Sidney Simon had replaced my mother at the green, felt-covered table; Lenya was here without Kurt. I was reminded of "The Ten Little Indians." The game could go on for another fifty years, gradually losing players—and then there was one, and then there were none.

I got a ride into town the next day with Bill Mauldin, Alan and Nancy. About halfway we stopped at a restaurant they liked, and I told them that I was expecting Marion for dinner that night. Alan was not pleased, mumbled something about "the bastard," and Nancy told me not to let Marion get away with anything.

"If you really want the guy," Bill said, jumping in, "stand him up."

"Stand him up? Oh, my God, I couldn't!"

"It'll work," Bill insisted. "Go to a movie, go anywhere—let him ring the bell, flowers in hand, no little Hesper, and he'll come running back—trust me."

"I couldn't," I said, shaking my head and laughing.

"Then don't come crying to Uncle Bill," he answered, grinning and licking the paper of a cigarette he'd just rolled.

I replayed that conversation in my mind many times later, but that afternoon, as I shopped for groceries on Broadway, I couldn't imagine not seeing Marion if he wanted to see me. I'd loved him for so long, and he knew it—I couldn't start playing games at this point. I bought a dinner that I thought I knew how to cook—steak, baking potatoes, salad, wine. I'd learned to cook the same way I'd learned to clean, by osmosis, by hanging around Martha's kitchen.

Marion arrived, without flowers, but I'd bought some yellow roses and put them in a vase on the coffee table. I'd set two places with my mother's silver and lit two candles in her silver candlesticks. We chatted about nothing and drank some wine while the potatoes cooked and I fixed a salad. I seasoned the steak and put it under the broiler, the way I'd seen Martha do it, but when I served it the meat was so tough we could barely chew it. I was embarrassed, but then we laughed about it. We realized that, while I'd cooked it properly, I'd never actually bought a piece of meat before—my mother had made a list every morning and ordered from Eberling's Grocery in New City—so I hadn't realized that there was steak, and then there was good steak.

We had dessert, smoked cigarettes, and then Marion reached for me, his hand sliding along the back of the sofa and then pulling me to him. We kissed and held each other, as we'd done on the porch at Barnard, and slowly began to undress each other. My heart was racing, and I had a flash of Dr. Blatt—the same round, bald Dr. Blatt who had told me to spoon coffee into my mother's mouth—sitting on the edge of my bed when I was twelve, taking my temperature and my pulse. Marion had walked into my sickroom, just to say hello, and Dr. Blatt had become alarmed by my pulse rate. I started to laugh in the middle of a kiss.

"What? What's so funny?" Marion asked, backing away slightly. I told him about my image of Dr. Blatt and my pounding heart, and he laughed with me before pulling my sweater over my head. I was twelve, thirteen, fifteen again, longing for him to touch me, but now his hands were touching me everywhere, and I was touching him in return. We moved into the bedroom, losing the rest of our clothes, and into my bed. Marion made love to me, and although I was sexually inexperienced and didn't really know what to do, I responded with the pent-up longing of all those years. Afterwards he lay on top of me and I held him and smelled him and felt that I'd finally eclipsed the joy that I'd felt that day on the mountain when I was thirteen.

We stayed that way for a while. He dozed off while I savored his closeness, and then, partially dressed, we went back into the living room, looking for the cigarettes and the rest of the wine. Marion sat cross-legged on one end of the sofa, in his shorts and a turtleneck sweater, and we talked with more intimacy than we ever had. We talked about the day on the mountain. I told him that it had been the happiest day of my life.

"Did you know I went to a shrink about that?" Marion asked.

"You did? Why?"

"Guilt. I wanted to know if I'd done—done any damage to you."

"Really?" I asked. "So what'd he say?"

"He said not to worry about it."

"That's a relief," I said mockingly. "You only broke my

goddamned heart." He was smiling at me, the yellow flecks dancing in his eyes. "Do you remember, on the beach with your starlet, when you told me I had very beautiful toes?"

"Ah, the dear," he said as if he'd forgotten her.

"Well, you have very skinny, white legs."

"Why, thank you kindly," he said with a slight bow. "I wonder whatever happened to her."

"I was so jealous of her," I said.

"I was just escaping from Alison. I couldn't stand the sight of her at that point."

"But you had another baby?"

"It wasn't my idea," Marion answered, stubbing out a cigarette and lighting another one. "I guess the goddess thought she could save our marriage. Remember that song I used to sing to her, drove her totally crazy?"

"Oh, yeah," I said, laughing. "It was really mean. 'I gotta gal—' "

"I gotta gal," Marion sang, picking it up, "six feet tall, sleeps in the kitchen with her feet in the hall. Has anybody seen my gal?"

We both laughed, and then I said quietly, "And I remember the one you used to sing to me."

"She's just a particular friend of mi—ne," Marion sang, his voice gentle.

He left in the middle of the night, saying he would call soon, we'd see each other soon, and I went to sleep, hugging the sheets, wrapped in his scent, delirious with happiness. My euphoria lasted for almost three days. Marion called me in the afternoon of the third day. I'd picked up the wall phone in the foyer next to the kitchen and, at the sound of his voice, sank into the straight-backed chair I'd placed beneath the phone. My voice was warm, his was cold. He said that he'd called to let me know that he was about to marry Robin Roosevelt and move with her to Los Angeles. I was shocked, momentarily blinded by red splotches in front of my eyes, and blurted out the same words that I'd said at fourteen: "But I thought—I thought it meant that you loved me," I said.

"You seduced me," Marion answered.

"No . . . no. Who is Robin? You didn't tell me—"

"A lovely lady I've been seeing, recently divorced from Curtis Roosevelt."

"Who's that?"

"FDR's grandson," Marion said with an edge, as if I should know. "And she has a beautiful three-year-old little girl."

"Oh."

"And you'll be happy to know," Marion added, "Robin's a damn sight prettier than you are. Good-bye, Hep." And he hung up.

I sat there, in the straight-backed chair, letting it grow dark, not feeling anything. I didn't feel anything for the next two days. On the third day I walked up to Broadway for milk and cigarettes and, at the newsstand by the subway, I saw Marion's picture on the front page of the *Daily News*. It was a picture of Marion and Robin outside the courthouse, with a caption that said something like, PRIVATE HARGROVE TAKES A BRIDE. I bought the paper, went back to the apartment and stared at the picture. Like the picture of my mother on the front page of the *Daily News* after her death, the photograph was grainy black and white, but Robin wasn't dead. I wished she were. I wished she was dead rather than, in essence, killing me. And I stared at the photograph to see if she was really prettier than me. I couldn't tell.

Why had he said that? I asked myself. Why had he felt the need to go for the jugular? He knew that I'd hurt all my life because I wasn't nearly as pretty as my mother. Why be cruel and rub that in? Was it the old "make her hate me thing," like his cold insistence that it was body chemistry, nothing more? Why come close and then be cruel, over and over again?

I wrote him a long letter, saying the obvious, that I'd always loved him, that I'd grown up for him, that he was my only dream, and why, when the dream seemed so close to reality, did he have to smash it? At the end of the letter I reminded him that he owed me twenty dollars. He'd borrowed it one night when we'd gone out. It wasn't that I cared about the twenty dollars; it was any excuse to stay in touch with him. Maybe he'd return it before he left forever, or maybe he'd return it and not leave. The twenty dollars was my one glimmer of hope.

In the midst of this, my brother Alan called to say that he and Bunny had taken Toby to the vet, and the vet had said that Toby was riddled with cancer. He said that Toby was in a lot of pain, that he'd arranged to take him back on Monday to put him to sleep, so if I wanted to see him I should come to the country over the weekend. I went to the Caniffs' on Saturday and spent the afternoon with Toby. He knew that I'd come to say good-bye. I held him, in his bed in the kitchen, and looked into his sweet, brown eyes, and he licked the tears that ran down my face.

I noticed, at some point, that the paper with Marion's picture on the front was on the kitchen table.

"I guess your boyfriend decided to marry money," Willie scoffed when she saw me looking at the photograph.

"What?" That thought had not occurred to me.

"Well, I guess a Roosevelt, any Roosevelt's, got more money than he has," Willie answered.

"But she was just married to a Roosevelt," I said.

"And you don't think they pay through the nose?" Willie asked.

"I don't know," I said, and went back to Toby in his

wicker basket. I thought about Alan taking him to the vet to put him to sleep. I thought about Alan calling me to tell me my mother was dead. It was always Alan that took care of these things, and I remembered the day that Alan had saved Toby when he'd fallen through the ice on the pond. Alan had crawled on his stomach to Toby, who'd been trapped, breaking the ice around him as he'd tried to scramble out, and Alan had calmed him, reached out with a long stick, and Toby had grabbed it in his mouth and been pulled to safety.

I managed to say my last good-bye to Toby without sobbing, but by the time I got back to my apartment, I couldn't stop. I sobbed for everything—for my mother, my father, my home, Marion, my dog. I knew that it was a cliché, like a scene in a book or a movie, to release so much pent-up grief because my dog was dying, but I did it anyway—I couldn't help it. I cried for three weeks. I mourned everything that I'd only begun to mourn before.

I got out of bed and stopped crying for one day. Marion sent my letter back with a note saying that he didn't want its contents to embarrass me at some point in the future. He enclosed a check for twenty dollars. I got dressed and went to his bank at Twenty-third and Lexington to cash it. I hung around the bank, just hoping for a glimpse of him, but he didn't show up—he'd probably left town by then.

I didn't ask for help. I called Alan and Quentin to see if I could come to visit, but when they seemed to have plans I didn't push it. I wrote to my father but didn't tell him all of it. I stopped going to classes, stopped going out at all, and, by the end of the third week, Quentin showed up at my door. He called my father and said, "I think Hesper's having a breakdown."

My father was very concerned but he didn't know what to do. "Find her a good doctor," my father said. Quentin, who'd been in analysis, called around and got an appointment with Dr. George Gero, who I was to see the next day. I was glad to have someone to talk to, but I didn't think I was having a breakdown. I felt that I was finally beginning to grieve for all the losses. There would be more grieving to come, but Marion's final rejection and Toby's death had opened the floodgates. I pictured the pond at home in the spring when Alan would open the gate to the dam and all the twigs, dead leaves and debris would begin to pour over the dam into the waterfall.

CHAPTER SEVENTEEN

URING THE three weeks that I cried and stayed in bed, I woke up every morning with a stabbing pain just below the navel. It was the pain of loss, of rejection, of being kicked in the stomach. It was the same pain that had resulted in my throwing up on the brick stairs when I was eight and overheard Alison and Marion's early-morning lovemaking. It was a familiar pain, and I'd wait it out. I'd stay in a fetal position until I felt that I was able to turn without a sudden, torturous jab to the same injured place.

After Quentin's visit I had to wait out the pain each morning before I could sit up, put my feet on the floor and make it into the shower. I had to get up. I had a daily appointment with Dr. Gero.

Dr. Gero was middle-aged, portly and charming. He had a heavy Hungarian accent, from his country of birth, tinged with Viennese from his time of studying with Freud. He lived and worked in a brownstone on Ninety-third between Park and Lexington, a street that was referred to as "analysts' row." He had a dark, lithe wife and a chubby nine-year-old daughter, whom I caught glimpses of dashing up and down the stairs between the bottom floor and the third-floor living quarters. His office, or consulting room, was the second-floor parlor with the usual bay window and high ceilings. A mahogany desk was in front of the windows. On the other side of the room was the couch and his armchair behind it. I went four times a week for fifty-minute sessions, waiting for my appointments in a vestibule off the large second-floor hallway. Dr. Gero's bills were sent to my father—another expense that my father couldn't afford—along with little notes on my progress. I knew about the notes because my father mentioned them in his letters.

March 20, '54

Dear Hesper,

Sometimes it seems that the way to live is to plan on the worst that could happen and take it when it comes. I'm certainly sorry about this Marion business. In a way, I am. Glad in another way because it means the end of an epoch or an episode or a mirage.

I'm writing away at that play. Haven't heard from the Lunts since I told them the subject. But somebody else may do it.

It's too bad about Toby. Dogs don't live long enough lives to associate with humans.

You do have three hopeful things going on. Work with Machez, progress with Dr. Gero, and a sensible desire to get thin. Keep that diet within bounds though. I'm hoping to see you in a play sometime soon.

I love you . . . Daddy

He was referring to Herbert Machez, a friend of Lenya's, who was a director and gave acting classes. I joined one of his classes after officially dropping out of Barnard—it was something to do besides trekking across town to Dr. Gero's. The diet was something else to do. I'd gained some weight during the weeks that I'd stayed in bed and lived on food that I could get delivered, mainly Chinese and deli sandwiches. There wasn't anything that I really wanted to do. There wasn't anything I wanted, except to go back in time a year or two—before my father left, before my mother died, before Marion's reappearance and cruel disappearance.

From the start, Dr. Gero decided that all I needed was a husband and children of my own. He wasn't the kind of Freudian who never said anything; he said quite a lot. After about a month on his couch he made it clear that he liked me, even loved me, and from then on the one thing I wanted was to get upstairs in his house. I transferred quickly; he was the new daddy and, if he really loved me, he'd take me upstairs to live with his wife and daughter. Of course, he couldn't do any such thing—transference was part of the process, he explained—and I was supposed to work through my daddy-love stuff until I was free of it. I was much too impatient for that. I watched his wife and daughter run up to the third floor, where I imagined loving snuggling, the kind I used to experience when I'd climb into my parents' bed after a nightmare and curl up beside my father's large, warm body. That was what I wanted. Nothing less would do.

But Dr. Gero insisted on being a proper, although loquacious, Freudian. He insisted that, somewhere inside me, there was penis envy and all sorts of Electral/Oedipal goings-on. I knew that he was right about the Electra business, but I didn't want to just talk about it, endlessly go over dreams and memories. I was too devastated, too lonely, and if Dr. Gero wouldn't take me upstairs to the intimacy of the third floor, then I'd find it elsewhere. Did I think that out loud? I don't think so. It was just that the next thing I knew Sidney Simon fell into my lap.

It was at a party at Kaja and Burgess Meredith's. It was the first South Mountain Road party at which I was really accepted as a grown-up. I'd been to other road parties, but I'd always left or been taken home before the real drinking and fooling around got started. There was one exception, a party at Alan and Nancy's when I was thirteen. I'd looked for Marion, couldn't find him and was told by somebody that he'd taken another man's wife up to an empty bedroom where they were probably screwing. I'd been shocked and hurt and walked home.

But at this party, at the Merediths', I was part of it. I was nineteen and no one seemed to think twice about the fact that I was watching grown men urinate in the fireplace, grab other men's wives in inappropriate places and drink until they were nearly senseless. I'd come to the party with Alan and Nancy, but they'd left by midnight, and Sidney had said he'd drive me back. He'd been flirting and touching even before they left, taking me completely by surprise. Sidney was married to Joan, and they lived in my house with their five children. Sidney was handsome—pale skin, black hair, dark eyes—and he was tall with a barrel chest and lots of boyish charm. I didn't think he'd ever noticed me, but there we were, sprawled on pillows on the floor, his head in my lap, looking up at me with deep, flirtatious eyes.

We left the party, and with barely a word spoken, walked down the Merediths' driveway toward Alan Lerner's pool and tennis court. There was a sauna next to the pool, which was a distance from the house—old Mad Anthony Wayne's place—and we entered the cold sauna and closed the door. I wondered, for a moment, if Mad Anthony was up to his old, marriage-wrecking tricks.

Sidney was a slow, gentle lover, something I hadn't experienced before, and we spent a couple of hours on the sauna's wide, wooden bench. I didn't love Sidney and he didn't love me. We almost never talked, but he was sweet and fun, and I loved his body. I finally wanted something again. I wanted his touch and his warmth next to me, and if he lived in my house and was married to Joan, all the better. I couldn't get upstairs in Dr. Gero's house and replace his wife or his daughter. I couldn't take Marion away from Alison or the starlet, whom he barely remembered, or Robin. I couldn't take my father away from Hallie or Margaret or my mother or Gilda. But I could have a bit of Sidney all to myself. I didn't want more than that; I didn't want Joan to know. He was a delicious secret.

Sidney was a painter and sculptor, and he taught an art class in the city on Wednesday evenings. He would usually call after his class and come by my apartment where we would spend a couple of hours in bed—making love, laughing, smoking. I think one of the reasons we didn't talk too much was that Sidney was more visual than verbal, something I appreciated after Marion, who thought words were God. The other thing that limited conversation was that Sidney, in his early forties, was already partially deaf. I thought that he might have just been tuning out five very young children, but he was as deaf on West End Avenue as he had been on the road. And he was deaf in his studio above the garage the couple of times I crept up the outside stairs. He was waiting for me but surprised by the sight of me.

It was midnight, the house was dark as I turned the curve in the driveway and passed the bushes my mother had planted—laurel, rhododendron, forsythia that was a faint yellow in the moonlight. My mother had died on the first day of spring the year before, and here was another spring. Her bulbs were sprouting green folds, the willows were turning a light green, but no one had wrapped her roses in burlap for the winter. I saw their exposed stalks and the empty fishpond as I walked through the white birches to the garage. I passed the garage, where my mother had died, without looking in the window, and I didn't glance toward the bloody stump behind the garage where Lester had killed the chickens and my mother had burned my wicker stroller. I ran up the stairs to the studio, which once had been Martha's apartment, found Sidney in the dark and we made quiet, fearful love on his single bed beneath the upstairs window.

I didn't stay long. I tiptoed down the stairs and past the dark garage window that seemed like a black hole, a void that could suck me in if I looked at it. It wasn't until I was in front of the garage, heading for the cover of the birches, that I stopped. I suddenly saw in my mind an image of our black Packard at night, its motor running in the garage, and me at about three, being carried to the car by Martha.

I'm half asleep, still in my pajamas, rubbing my eyes and blinking against the overhead light in the garage. Mommy is throwing suitcases in the car. She's angry, and Daddy isn't anywhere around. Martha puts me in the backseat with a pillow and blanket, and Mommy starts the car and backs out of the garage.

We're in Florida with my grandmother, who's fat and smells funny and pinches me. Mommy cries a lot. She says she's left Daddy and she's never going back. I miss Daddy; I want to go home.

We're on a houseboat in Florida, and I like it. I like the water all around and the birds. Then we go to St. Augustine and there are cobbled streets. A horse and wagon go by, filled with bright, red geraniums. I love the horse and wagon. We go back to the houseboat, and Daddy's there. He's come to find us, to take us home. I run to him and he picks me up and holds me and, for the first time since we left, I'm safe and happy. I didn't even know how scared I was until I feel his arms around me.

The memories were piecemeal, and I tried to connect them as I stood in the driveway, staring at the garage. I didn't know why my mother had left with me in the middle of the night. I didn't know how we got to Florida. I didn't know whose houseboat we'd stayed on, or why we'd gone to St. Augustine. The memories were images with nothing in between, no explanations, no practicalities. This was something else that I'd have to ask my grandmother about, if I ever worked up the nerve to ask her anything at all.

I backed toward the concealment of the birches, still staring at the garage and its black window. I wondered what my mother had been feeling, lying on the front seat of the car, her head on a pillow she'd brought from the house, smoking a last cigarette. Willie had told me that my mother had been very calm that evening. She'd told Willie to go home, that she was fine. She probably was fine, I thought, and anxious to leave us, anxious to leave the pain behind. I knew a bit more about pain this spring than I had the spring before. I knew that when the morning pain hit, sleep helped, oblivion helped. Maybe she'd just wanted to sleep for a long time—until it was over.

Dr. Gero said that suicide was an angry gesture, like homicide or any other killing, but I wasn't sure. I knew that part of my mother had been angry—that note that said that Daddy would never write another play and I would never finish college—but there were other notes, asking forgiveness, and beautiful letters. I felt that she'd died of pain rather than anger. She'd never let me see the worst of the pain. Like the time that she'd called me in the country from the apartment, saying she'd taken an overdose, and I'd called the super, and an ambulance, and raced into town. When I got there, she'd cried, "Don't let her see me like this! She can't see me like this!" They'd pumped her stomach, or whatever they did, and I'd sat in the living room with the doctor who wanted me to sign her commitment papers. I didn't go into the bedroom to see her—she didn't want me to—and I wouldn't sign the papers; she would have hated it too much.

But she'd thought I didn't need her. That was what was killing me, shivering in the birches. I'd gone to my roommate's during the February break because it was so hard at home, with my father gone and my mother wanting to die, and she'd thought that I didn't need her anymore, that I only needed my father. She'd been partly right but, "Oh, God, Mommy," I whispered to the black window, "I needed you, I wish you hadn't died—I'm so sorry, Mommy."

Dr. Gero was nonjudgmental about my affair with Sidney, but he was clearly irritated that I felt the need to do it rather than just talk about it. I argued that Sidney was good for me. He was showing me that sex and kindness could go together. I assumed that there were other young women, but it didn't matter. He never hurt me and I never hurt him. We never even said good-bye; we sort of sweetly drifted apart before the summer.

I kept seeing Sidney and seeing Dr. Gero and going to acting classes during April and May. Herbert Machez decided that I was really talented on the day that I couldn't stop crying. It was an exercise; I was up on the small stage, and Machez told me to think of something sad and to cry. At that moment in time, nothing could have been easier. I didn't even have to think of anything. I just started to cry—and cried and cried, and sobbed, and sobbed some more until they had to practically carry me off the stage.

In early June, I went back to Los Angeles with my brothers Alan and Terry. My father was to have an operation to find out why his heart was bothering him so much, and we felt that we had to be there. I stayed in Gilda's apartment, which my father had moved into earlier in the year. It was a nondescript, two-bedroom apartment in Park La Brea, not far from the tar pits. Gilda had moved a few antiques into it, giving a bit of character to the off-white walls, the sliding windows, the parquet floors, but it was still the most ordinary place we'd ever lived in. My green cave in New York seemed to have a certain charm compared to this apartment, even though this one was flooded with golden California sunlight every afternoon. My father still hated the constant sunlight, the blazing blue sky, but he was too much in love and too grateful to Gilda for rescuing his ego to complain that much.

Gilda and my father slept in Gilda's four-poster bed in their bedroom. Laurel and Craig had twin beds in the second bedroom. I slept on the sofa in the living room. It didn't even pull out; it was the kind of sofa that you turned into a bed by piling the back pillows on the floor and tossing a blanket and pillow on it. Alan and Terry were only in Los Angeles for a few days while my father was recuperating, and I'm not sure where they stayed. But we all had dinner together. Gilda made large pots of spaghetti in the narrow kitchen, and we ate at the dining table that was against the wall in the living room.

It turned out that my father's heart was fine, but that part of his stomach had moved up through his torn diaphragm and was pressing against his heart. The doctors at Cedars of Lebanon performed a first operation, alleviating the problem, but told my father that he'd have to have another operation—a bigger one—in a few months in order to cure it.

My father was under an oxygen tent and very weak when Alan, Terry and I went into his room after the first surgery. My father opened his eyes, looked up at us, anxious at his bedside, and smiled.

"Anyone seen the morning papers? Any news?" he asked. We laughed, said nothing dramatic had happened in the last twenty-four hours, and my father nodded and went back to sleep. I loved him so much at that moment and thought how brave he was. He didn't ask for sympathy; he didn't ask for anything for himself. He simply wanted to know what was going on in the world during his brief absence.

Alan and Terry went back east as soon as my father left the hospital, and I stayed on, sleeping on the sofa. My father wanted me to stay, and he wanted me there for his wedding. It was a very small, spur-of-the-moment ceremony in the living room at Park La Brea. On the morning before the wedding I walked with Laurel and Craig to the nearest boulevard to buy presents—trinkets really—for my father and Gilda. We wanted them to be happy, but even more we wanted them to love us, to remember that we existed when they looked into each other's eyes.

Some sort of minister presided, and my father and Gilda looked deeply into each other's eyes—Mio and Miriamne at sixty-five and forty—during the familiar ceremony that always made me cry, even on a soap opera: "Will you take this woman? I will." I liked that so much better than "*Do* you take this woman?" I knew that it was the ceremony I would have, if I ever got married, and I wondered what kind of ceremony my parents had had. They had never mentioned it. I stood beside Laurel and Craig and Gilda's sister, Hilda, and twisted my mother's wedding ring on my little finger, the ring that she never wore, and suddenly I was crying for her. I was all that was left of her, and it was important that I stand here in her place while my father married Gilda. It was important that she not be forgotten—all the years, all the Christmases, all the spring flowers and the summer roses. I wanted to cry out that someone had to remember, but I just twisted the ring and cried for her.

My father and Gilda didn't have a honeymoon. Their lives went on as usual, except that now they were married. Gilda was now Mrs. Maxwell Anderson as my mother had been and Margaret before her. It didn't seem right to me that someone should take someone else's name, thereby wiping out the one before her and the one before that. But that's how it was done. I was nineteen and desperately wanted a name of my own. Not Hesper Anderson—that was a nothing, like Anne Poor, a talented daughter and an old maid—what the hell was that? The road rules rang loud and clear. I had to be loved; I had to end up as Mrs. Somebody.

I began to seduce anyone I thought halfway appropriate. At least, they had to have potential. If they were struggling at the time, they could become successful eventually, and I could go along for the ride and take lots of credit, like Bunny loving Milton at fifteen, like Lenya loving Kurt when he was just a poor music student. I began by seducing a fellow student at the Pasadena Playhouse. My father had convinced me that I could study acting in Los Angeles as well as in New York, and I had enrolled in the summer program there. My first seduction was an intense, darkly Jewish young man who reminded me of Sidney. He decided that he was crazy about me, and I liked him all right. I didn't really like having sex with him, but I got to sleep in his bed in a tiny one-room apartment in Pasadena. That was the main thing I wanted. I could sleep in his bed, with warm arms around me, instead of driving back to Park La Brea and sleeping on the sofa while my father and Gilda held each other in the four-poster.

My second seduction was a beautiful blond young man— an actor and a friend of seduction number one. He was so beautiful that, obviously, if he loved me, I would be beautiful too. That was what it was all about—to be beautiful in some-one else's mirror; to be loved, which proved to me that I wasn't a nothing. It didn't matter who they were, these boys, as long as they wanted me, as long as they, for an instant, wiped out Marion's rejection and the loss of my father to his new love.

My third seduction was the clincher. Seduction number one was sending me bad poetry about his heartbreak after I left his bed. Seduction number two was so beautiful that I think he could only love himself. Seduction number three was engaged to another woman, a beautiful heiress, and, of course, that was the one I had to have. When number three finally chose his heiress, I curled up on Gilda's sofa in despair.

My father and Gilda had not been happy with me that summer, and for good reason. My father worried when I came in late or stayed in Pasadena. He worried about the young men in my life and my highs and lows of infatuation. He tried to talk to me as we had always talked, but he had very little time. He was writing a new play and he had a new wife and two new children who were constantly wanting "Daddy." For the previous nineteen years no one but me had called him Daddy. Gilda said, at some point, that they had been so good to me, and I had been so impossible. I'm sure they tried to be good to me—Gilda made lots of pots of spaghetti—and I know that I was impossible. I didn't have a room or any of my things, and I wanted to go home, so at the beginning of August I did go home to my green cave.

Not long after I got back to New York, Herbert Machez asked me to join his summer-stock company in Lake Hopatcong. I drove my Sunbeam, which a friend had driven east for me, and spent two weeks at the summer theatre. I played a couple of different parts, seduced the married set designer, who for a week I believed I was in love with, and then quit. I went back to the apartment, so dank and hot in the summer that it smelled vaguely of mildew, like my father's cabin in the woods. I'd decided that I didn't want to be an actress. It was easy for me, but I didn't want to work at it. I didn't have the drive. I didn't want it the way I wanted to marry somebody and have his babies. Acting was still an in-between step.

I decided to go back to school. That was an in-between step that everyone would approve of. Besides, my mother had written that my father would never write another play and I would never finish college. I felt that I owed it to her to get a degree, and it would give me time. I applied to NYU—if they accepted my credits, I'd have a year to go.

I filled out the forms and waited for Dr. Gero to get back from his vacation. He was in Sag Harbor, and I could call him if I was on the verge of suicide or some such, but I wasn't. I went back and forth between the city and the country, killing time, until my father's letter arrived. I opened it expectantly, as I always did, and then felt a shock, a disbelief, a hurt deeper than any I'd felt before. The ground beneath me had washed away. There was no floor, no ceiling, no past, no future as I read his words: "Dear Hesper, If you don't mend your ways, you will turn into a whore like your mother . . ." *A whore like your mother.* There was more, a lecture on virtue—I was on the edge of being a fallen woman—and I knew that I had become my mother in my father's mind. I was no longer his adored little girl—Gilda was that now, and I had become the bad one. When I had become my mother at his wedding, and gone searching for love, I had become my mother in his heart. And in his heart she was bad and she was dead.

It was dark by the time I got in my car and drove. I wanted to die. It was the first time that I'd wanted to die. Before this, I'd never understood why my mother would choose death over life, but I understood it now. I drove ninety miles an hour through the fog, along the cliffs of the Palisades, along the steep curves of 9W, sure that I would crash the car somewhere, but strangely, I didn't, and I ended up at the gates of Mount Repose, the cemetery where my mother was buried beside Kurt, where plots waited for my father and Lenya. The gates were open, and I drove to the top, beneath High Tor, where I knew the graves were, but the fog was thick, the sky black above the Hudson, and I was as frightened as I had been as a little girl in Mary Clarke's cemetery. I walked the hillside but couldn't find the graves, and I was shivering with cold and fear. I knew that I didn't want to join them there, my mother and Kurt on that hill, and I ran back to my car.

I drove back down to Route 9W, turned right, drove along the Hudson until I turned onto the quarry road that cut through the mountain to South Mountain Road. I drove home and up the driveway and parked in front of the dining-room door before I remembered that this wasn't my house anymore. The house was dark; the Simons were asleep, and, after a few minutes, I restarted the car, drove past the circle of white birches, ghosts in the darkness, drove back down the driveway and down the road. I turned up the Caniffs' steep driveway, appeared at their front door, and in the middle of the night—as always—they took me in.

CHAPTER EIGHTEEN

I STAYED AT the Caniffs' for a couple of weeks. Willie and Martha fed me; Bunny took me shopping, and I slept in the guest room in Bunny's silky sheets. Sometimes, late at night, I'd sit quietly in Milton's studio while he worked at his drawing board or chatted with an insomniac neighbor who happened to drop by. I walked on the mountain, watching out for copperheads, while the dogwood berries turned orange and red. The maples began to turn too, the beginning of fall. I spent time with Alan and Nancy, Lenya and George, and I missed having Toby beside me when I walked or drove the road. I didn't tell anyone about my father's letter—I was too ashamed.

When I got back to the apartment I wrote to my grandmother and invited her to come and visit. I'd avoided her since my mother's death, but now that I was alone, or felt since my father's letter that I was alone, I had the improbable thought that she might be able to replace my mother in some way. At least she might be able to answer some questions. It didn't work. Anna Klein was thrilled to be with me in the green apartment, to dress up and go out to dinner with me, to go to the theatre with me, but she was just as pigeon-breasted, powdery and self-centered as she'd always been. Every night she asked me to brush out her waist-length silver hair that was wound in braids around her head during the day. I sat behind her and brushed and brushed. She never asked if she could do anything for me. So if she wasn't able to replace my mother in any way, she gave me more of an idea of what my mother had come from. First this mother, then her father's death, then an orphanage, then this mother again, wanting from her for the rest of her life.

When I finally asked my grandmother why my mother had never told me that we were Jewish, she didn't seem to know any more than I did. "Because of the war," she'd said, "and she wanted to protect you." Then she went into a reverie about how she and my mother sang Yiddish songs together when they were alone in the car, and about my mother making her promise never to mention it. I couldn't quite picture it. Maybe, I thought, but it didn't sound like my mother to me, not like the mother I'd known anyway.

After my grandmother left, I spent three weeks in the library, reading everything I could find on the Holocaust. I read translated transcripts detailing the Nazi war crimes. I read the testimony and the diaries of concentration camp survivors. I became horribly familiar with Auschwitz, Bergen-Belsen and the Warsaw Ghetto. I didn't think about what I was doing. I just *had* to know. A lot of it was guilt. I'd grown up on South Mountain Road without a real clue of what was going on in the world, of what that war was all about that had glued my father to the radio every hour on the hour, and that had frightened my mother away from her own identity. And part of it, like inviting my grandmother to visit, was an attempt to find my mother, to try to understand.

* * *

In early October, my father called to tell me that he and Gilda and the children were moving back east. He acted as if nothing had happened, as if everything were the same between us, but I knew that it wasn't. He said that there were two reasons for the change—a second hernia operation, which he would undergo at New York Hospital, and a new play, *The Bad Seed*. He said that it was a potboiler, that he'd done it for the money it might bring, but it was a damn good potboiler.

They rented a house in Stony Point, about ten miles from South Mountain Road, but they only went to the road once. I joined them at Alan and Nancy's for the one weekend that they were there, hoping to entice them back, I suppose, but it was a strained and awkward two days, and they never went back again. They wanted to build their own life together, away from the road—totally understandable—but it left the rest of us out. I visited them in Stony Point, but it wasn't that different from Park La Brea—a new family, new children— and I didn't really fit in. They tried; Gilda cooked, and my father was gentle with me, but it was so clear that it wasn't my home.

After the move back to the East Coast, my father took a great deal out of storage. I had taken some things when I'd moved into the apartment, the boys had taken some, and there was a certain amount of confusion. In the midst of it, I received my mother's strongbox. It was a small steel box that contained her papers, and there was a note on the top of it: "Please destroy in the case of my death." No one had paid any attention; just as they had ignored her note that asked for cremation, they had ignored this note.

It took me a while to open the box. I put it on a shelf in my closet, glanced at it, wondered about it, but put off opening it. When I finally did, alone in the apartment, the first thing I noticed were documents and notarized letters. I saw

my mother's first marriage certificate—to Charles Maynard—and their divorce decree, but I didn't see a second
marriage certificate, recording her marriage to my father,
and in that instant I knew that they had never been legally
married. I wasn't surprised. I must have known it, in that
way children have of knowing secrets that no one thinks
they know. No wonder I'd never heard about a wedding or
seen photographs of my mother as a bride. There were all
those albums, pictures of my parents together before they
were married, or said they were, and pictures of them after,
but no wedding pictures. I must have known.

I looked quickly at the notarized letters. They were all
from 1943 and '44, the time that my father was in England
and North Africa during the war. He had wanted my mother
to join him in London, but clearly she had needed to prove
her citizenship. She had been born in Montreal, but her father, Benjamin Higger, had been an American citizen, making her a citizen. There were depositions and letters from
her mother and various relatives, Higgers that I had never
heard of. Why did she need all this? It must have been because, without a marriage certificate, proving that she was
married to an American citizen, she was considered an alien
and was unable to get a passport.

It started to make sense. I remembered her ranting about
government red tape when I was eight, but I didn't understand why she had worn a wedding band for a time—the one
that was now on my little finger—and then put it in her jewelry box and never taken it out again. I began to read the letters in the strongbox, and I was shocked to find all of my
mother's last letters to my father. There were also letters to
my father from Martha during that last year. They were all
mixed up with my letters to my mother, letters to her from
friends and family members, clippings and the citizenship papers. Had my father just stuck these letters in here after my

mother's death, and, by mistake, they had come to me? I wasn't about to ask him, and I wasn't about to give them back—I was too curious.

The letters to my father were all on my mother's blue-gray stationery, and the dates were from mid-December 1952 to March 1953, the time of her death. I didn't read them in order; I read the last ones first, and my curiosity quickly changed to heartbreak. She expressed her despair to my father in a way that she never had to me. She'd kept up a semblance of a front in her letters to me, and during our conversations, but these bits of blue-gray paper held pure despair. She pleaded for him to find a way to divorce her so that no one would ever know that they had never married. She vacillated between love and hurt, compassion and indignation, and I could picture my mother as she wrote, smoke circling through her curls, her once-violet eyes staring at the beams in the empty living room and at the bare, winter trees outside.

February 6th

Dear Max,

Perhaps it's with deliberate intent that in each succeeding letter you destroy yourself in my eyes. You never mean to hurt—you envelop yourself in a cloak of gentle steel against which I can only break my fists and dash my head. As always—an old pattern. Turn to Max for help and where is he? Reaching in his pocket. Allaying all fears, easing all pain with a generous hand and a withdrawing heart.

When I wrote of our common-law marriage, I wasn't thinking of a property settlement. Perhaps I phrased it badly when I said, "I don't know what the common law is, but we have a home and a daughter." I was concerned only about Hesper. I'd like to protect

her emotionally. It's no light matter for a child to dis-
cover that she is illegitimate.

There is nothing I want you to do legally, but
since you're the one away from home and can therefore support a lie more successfully than I, you might
let it be known that we are getting a divorce, and later
that we are divorced. Hesper would accept it as a fact
and never question it. Or if there is any way of filing
suit for a separation or divorce without having to produce a marriage certificate, then do that.

Please, please get this clear. It's partly for my
sake—but mostly for Hesper's. Don't talk dollars and
cents to me, for you only succeed in humiliating me
when you put it on that basis alone. Have you no love
for anyone but yourself, not even for Hesper who
loves you more than anything in the world?

I am reluctant to tell you how troubled I have been
all these years by your unwillingness to ease my anxiety on this score. Once or twice I did bring it up. After you returned from England and I had found it
impossible to get a passport without presenting a
marriage license. I had written to you in desperation
and you had never answered or made any reference to
it, and I'd thought you'd say something kind when
you came home. But you never did, and when finally I
brought the subject up, you turned on me viciously. I
never could understand why, but I never recovered
from the deep hurt. If you had explained to me quietly
why it was impractical, I would have accepted it—but
you only made me feel that I was being cheap and
petty and vulgar and that my anxiety was beneath
contempt. I never spoke of it again until it became an
important issue in relation to Hesper. I remember
that night I took my wedding ring off, and I have

never worn it since. That was about ten years ago. You never noticed.

I must have loved you very much, to have stayed with you. In your book there is only one thing a wife cannot do—in mine there are many a husband can do, if one truly loves him.

Mab

The metal box was on my bed—my mother's bed, hand-carved for her years ago by Carroll French—and I lay back against the pillows and headboard and gazed at the yellowed blinds and green walls of the apartment bedroom in a kind of pained stupor. I had learned too much too quickly. I could barely take it in, yet at the same time, my mind was filling with questions, more questions than answers. *Why* had my father not wanted to marry my mother? Why had he written such loving, lonely letters to her during the war and then turned on her "viciously" when he'd come home? What were the practical reasons that she mentioned? Was it that everyone thought they were married and if they got married now it would complicate things?

In the midst of my whirling questions, I realized that this was the secret that Willie had promised my mother not to tell on the night that my mother died. It was to protect me, Willie had said, and I suddenly understood that was part of it. But I didn't think it was all of it. My mother knew me well enough to know that I didn't care that much about image or propriety. Even now, reading the letter, I didn't know why she'd thought I'd be so upset. Being illegitimate seemed rather romantic to me, like Edmund and Heathcliff. But then I realized that so much of my mother's life was about im-age—her image as a beauty, as a hostess, as Mrs. Maxwell Anderson. And the big one, being Mrs. Maxwell Anderson, had been a lie. Her beauty was going; without the name she was no longer a hostess, and the name was a lie. Her whole identity was a lie. She was a Jew who wasn't Jewish and a wife who wasn't a wife.

"Oh, my God," I whispered to myself, as people do when they're hit by truth and can't think straight. "Oh, my God," I said as I shifted my gaze, sat up and reached for another letter.

February 18th

Max dear,

I've been getting all the income tax papers together and I can't find the bank statements and cancelled checks from September on. Do you remember where you put them? Or did you give them to Alan?

I stopped my labors long enough to write to Hesper and say how nice it will be for her to be with you this summer. If I weren't so certain you'd close the door in my face I'd come too. I can't think of anything that would make me happier than for the three of us to be together. It's not what you want, I know. But I'd clean and scrub and cook and do the laundry and type—anything—just for us to be together in the same house. You don't have to answer this—I know what you'll say, and it's better left unsaid.

Here the winter has been mild. The snowdrops have been in bloom, the tulips and hyacinths are several inches high, and soon the magnolia will be in bloom. From outdoors comes a whish of wind, but indoors it's so unbearably still. And I miss the clutter of newspapers and magazines on the furniture, and the news on the radio every half hour, and the tramp of your just coming down the stairs and the fire in the fireplace and your stomach rumbling. I miss the violence of political disagreements and people dropping in, and Kurt in his fur cap and wind-breaker and all the turbulence and peace that go to make a home.

What a stupid, restless, rebelliant, defiant fool I have been! And what a heavy weight my belated wisdom is to me, since there is no one but you I want to lavish it on. Anything else I may say is out of hurt, and a lie. I have and want no other love.

Mab

Don't, don't say anything to hurt me. Better leave this unanswered. But I had to write it.

In going through the files I found old letters of yours, and Valentine poems, and everything after is nightmarishly unreal, and you are the Max you used to be to me, and I the Mab I used to be to you. So I say good-night, my darling, as if all were peace between us.

It was night in the apartment, and I couldn't stand any more. I was drinking coffee, smoking and crying. I reached for a couple of Martha's letters, as a diversion, and then was appalled. They were barely literate and vile. I knew that she couldn't stand my mother—I'd heard it all my life—but I didn't know that she was capable of this. She'd apparently been spying for my father, or pretending to spy and lying to him. I hoped to God he hadn't asked her to.

January 22, 53

Dear Mr. Anderson,

All is quiet in the house today. The "lady of the house" went to town yesterday which was Tuesday. Jerry called her Monday about five thirty, I listen, glad I did. Jerry was feeling good from the time she was in last week. Both of them stilled felt the *glow*, Ha, ha.

Mab wants me out of here because I am in her way since she will be living here all the time. She do not care about no one. But she do not kick me anymore, she goes around not speaking. I really do not care. Every time she goes to town one of *those things* go too, you know what I mean. She is having a fine time this week.

Take care of yourself. Love,

Martha

February, '53

Dear Mr. Anderson,

Please do not be fooled by those letters. This woman can really take care of herself. I can not believe that she means any one of you men any good because she is playing one against the other. Each time you except her sweet letter that is a blow below your belt and she is calling you *sucker.* I told you before she would fix Jerry so she plays both of you for suckers. She feeds you sweet letters, her trap is set and her sweet letters are leading you right in with your eyes wide open. My love and all good wishes for you,

Martha

I crumpled the letters, wanting to wring Martha's neck at that moment. I didn't care if it was true or not true—how terrible for my mother to be alone in that house with a woman who hated her and spied on her. I remembered Willie's claim that Martha had gone to a witch doctor in West Nyack who had stuck pins in a Mab doll. I wouldn't have put it past her. Martha probably brought my mother breakfast trays with arsenic in the orange juice. Whatever loyal love I'd felt for Martha left me as I read those letters.

There were more, but I couldn't deal with them. I turned again to my mother's letters.

February 17th, '53

Dear Max,

Your letter mailed on the 10th arrived today. I'm very relieved to know that it is possible to get a formal divorce. Since you are out west, perhaps it would be simpler and less expensive for you to manage than for me, if and when you want it and can afford it. I'll do anything you decide, and sign any papers you send me.

My divorce from Charles was final the 5th of December, 1933, and Hesper was born in August, 1934. It's true that I hadn't wanted to marry when I married Charles, but that was the fashionable attitude in the early twenties and I had long outgrown it when I met you. There were many times when we were away from New York—driving to Florida, for instance, and particularly through Baltimore, where marriage was immediate, when I hoped you would say, "Let's stop here and get married," but you never did and I couldn't bring myself to ask it. I did feel badly about it, and I always gave myself the reasons you stated in your letter, and my emotional reaction wasn't really acute until that time you returned from England. Why didn't you say it simply and affectionately then? It would have made such an enormous difference to me, and there wouldn't have been that deep and festering wound.

There've been so many unnecessary hurts, and now it's too late, and I dread any new bitterness between us. Why, oh why, did you keep Margaret's death mask and ashes in our house all these years? I found

them when I was looking for books in your cabin, and
it was irrational, perhaps, but I was thrown into deep
despair. Perhaps you had some compulsion to keep
them near you, and you're a strange and complex person, and I loved you so deeply, but there have been so
many things I couldn't reconcile with your love for
me. I wish I were wiser and gentler and had not been
"a bitch and a termagant wife." I wish I could start
over with all the bitterness gone from my heart and
yours. Why does one arrive at everything too late?

You must go your own way to find what happiness
you can. I'll go mine, but there's nothing I want.
Peace within myself, perhaps, instead of this hollow
despair.

There was more but I stopped reading, seeing a flash of
Margaret's death mask, which I'd completely forgotten about.
I was nine or ten, in the cabin, and I'd come across it, or my
father had shown it to me. It *was* a mask, with flat, closed eyelids and a plaster outline of Margaret's full lips that looked so
much like Quentin's. It was so strange, I thought, that I'd remembered the urn but not the mask. Maybe it had been too
frightening.

I went back to my mother's letter . . .

Max, Max, where did we get lost? We started
with such riches of love. I remember your saying to
me as we were driving to Spring Valley one day, "I
have a new wife and a new house and a new baby, and
now I shall write great plays." Why did we allow
guilts and fears and anxieties to corrode our love?
And still it remained strong—until with one wrench I
tore it loose. Not meaning to, not knowing how ut-
terly catastrophic it would be—lying to you in the

hope that if you didn't know then maybe it could be wiped away as if it hadn't happened. And you said to me, "You must tell me the truth; it's the only basis on which we can start again." And so I did, believing you, and wanting so much to start again. And then there was no way to reach you ever again. And so I tried to run from you when the only thing I really wanted was to run toward you. But you didn't want me and kept driving me away.

I dreamed the other night that you bent over me and kissed me very gently on the lips, and I woke feeling clean and happy, and for a whole day the tight lines around my mouth were gone and something in me that had been cold and shriveled became alive and glowing again. But when I called you you hung up on me, and that was the reality, and how should I bear it?

I'll call about the house tomorrow—and either sell or rent it, whichever is more advantageous. Though it will be hard to leave it now and face being in a rootless place alone with myself. Isn't there some way I can live in it cheaply, by doing all the work myself and closing off the upstairs rooms? But I'll do what you wish about it. You're not coming back—I know that now—and Hesper will spend the summer with you— and yet it's the only thread I have to cling to—and nothing will be left of our life together but Hesper, and she's so much more yours than mine. Good fortune to you, wherever you choose to be.

Love, Mab.

6:30 A.M. . . . . I just woke from a terrible nightmare. I was being put to death, and it was going on interminably, and I begged for something quick, and finally a man came with a phial of poison and assured me it would take only ten minutes. And I was trying once more to reach you, and you said, "You think you are Diogenes bringing light," and I said, "Oh, darling, in my last hour of life, can't I make you understand— can't I make you believe me?" But you just stood there, calmly telling me your plans for the future. And I said, "I want you to marry again. I want you to be happy. Only try, try to believe me." But you paid no attention, and I turned hopelessly to take the poison. Then I awoke and now I can't go back to sleep. The days and nights are longer than they used to be.

I couldn't handle any more. I carefully refolded the letter and put it back in the strongbox. "I should have been there— I should have gone home," I kept repeating to myself. If only she had said some of this to me—she said it so beautifully— but I knew that she could only express herself this way on paper, and she'd kept up a front for me. I suddenly needed to talk to someone who would understand. I knew that Lenya was in the city, and even though it was late when I called, she said to come right over.

I took a cab to her Second Avenue apartment, and she met me at the door with a vodka on the rocks. She told me that it was buffalo-grass vodka, and I saw the green stalk in the bottle when she put it on the coffee table in the living room. We sat on the sofa, cigarettes and ashtray between us, and looked out over the city lights and the East River. Lenya was a star again. The revival of *The Threepenny Opera* at the Theatre de Lys, with Lenya as Jenny, was a big success, but Lenya was just the same—as real, funny and unpretentious as ever. I told her about the strongbox and my mother's letters.

"Did you know that they were never married?" I asked.

"What does it matter anymore?" Lenya said gently.

"It doesn't matter. But it mattered a lot to her. Did she ever tell you why—or did he?—why he'd never married her?"

Lenya shook her head, "No, not why. Mabbie was very afraid people find out. I told her to say they were married on a ship, by the ship's captain, and there are no records."

I laughed, and it felt wonderful to laugh after all those tears. "But she didn't say why?" I asked again.

"No," Lenya said. "Here, have more vodka."

"Sure," I said, and Lenya poured it, and we talked about other things for a few minutes, mainly her current success.

"It is all for Kurt," Lenya said, "for his music." And I knew that was true.

"Did you know about the death mask and Margaret's ashes?" I asked, bringing the subject back to my mother.

"They were in the cabin," Lenya said. "Mab was having fits when she finds them."

"Yes, she wrote about that in one of her last letters. She said it sent her into despair."

"She was in despair a lot," Lenya said, with a look.

"I know."

"And there was nothing you could do."

"I know—I guess."

We were quiet for a while before I asked again about Margaret's ashes. Why did my father keep them, and what happened to them?

"You don't know?" Lenya asked, her eyebrows raised.

"No," I answered.

"You really don't know?"

"No."

"Your father buried Margaret's ashes on top of your mother's coffin."

"What?"

"He put the urn on top of your mother's casket. I was there when they bury them, after the ground thaws."

"In the same grave?" I stammered, shocked. Lenya nodded. "Oh, my God. Lenya, my God, what was he thinking? How could he do such a thing?"

Lenya smiled slightly, a mischievous light in her eyes, and shrugged that familiar European shrug.

"Oh, Hep," she said, "one woman, another woman— what's the difference?"

"You mean like the mask?" I asked, starting to laugh again. "The Margaret mask, the Mab mask, the Gilda mask? They're all interchangeable?"

"Like in a play in his mind," Lenya said, and I reached for her and she held me while we both laughed and cried and then laughed again.

I never asked my father why he hadn't married my mother, or why he put Margaret's ashes in my mother's grave. I meant to, but he died suddenly of a stroke five years later, in February 1959. I'd spent those five years regaining his love. I'd married in 1955, making Dr. Gero happy, and making my father happy—I was a good girl again, pure again in a white dress, even purer in maternity clothes. My father died right after my second son was born. He came to the hospital to see the baby, and the last time I saw him was when the elevator doors closed in the hallway of Lying-in Hospital. He was smiling at me, that warm, wonderful smile that I can still see whenever I think of him.

Almost all of them are up on Mount Repose now—Margaret and my mother, Lenya and Kurt, Henry and Bessie, Bunny and Milton—and I can picture them, loving and feuding and having all-night poker games. My father isn't there.

Gilda buried half of his ashes beneath the beech tree at their home in Connecticut and the other half in the Anderson cemetery in Geneva, Pennsylvania. But I like to think that my father joins them at times, for a hand of Red Dog, or to bring Kurt a new lyric. My father would chat with everyone beneath his mountain, while Kurt pulled a new melody out of the stars.

The bride in 1955.

INDEX